Managing Built Heritage

Managing Built Heritage

The Role of Cultural Values and Significance

SECOND EDITION

Stephen Bond
Heritage Places
UK

Derek Worthing
Uppsala University
Sweden

WILEY Blackwell

This edition first published 2016
© 2016 Stephen Bond and Derek Worthing
First Edition published in 2008

Registered Office
John Wiley & Sons Ltd, The Atrium, Southern Gate, Chichester, West Sussex, PO19 8SQ,
United Kingdom

For details of our global editorial offices, for customer services and for information about how to
apply for permission to reuse the copyright material in this book please see our website at
www.wiley.com.

The right of the author to be identified as the author of this work has been asserted in accordance
with the Copyright, Designs and Patents Act 1988.

Wiley also publishes its books in a variety of electronic formats. Some content that appears in
print may not be available in electronic books.

Designations used by companies to distinguish their products are often claimed as trademarks.
All brand names and product names used in this book are trade names, service marks,
trademarks or registered trademarks of their respective owners. The publisher is not associated
with any product or vendor mentioned in this book.

Limit of Liability/Disclaimer of Warranty: While the publisher and author have used their best
efforts in preparing this book, they make no representations or warranties with respect to the
accuracy or completeness of the contents of this book and specifically disclaim any implied
warranties of merchantability or fitness for a particular purpose. It is sold on the understanding
that the publisher is not engaged in rendering professional services and neither the publisher nor
the author shall be liable for damages arising herefrom. If professional advice or other expert
assistance is required, the services of a competent professional should be sought.

Library of Congress Cataloging-in-Publication Data

Bond, Stephen, 1955- author.
  Managing built heritage : the role of cultural values and significance / Stephen Bond and Derek
Worthing. – Second Edition.
     pages cm
  Includes bibliographical references and index.
  ISBN 978-1-118-29875-6 (pbk.)
  1. Historic buildings–Conservation and restoration.   2. Historic sites – Management.
3. Historic buildings – Management.   4. Cultural property – Management.   I. Worthing,
Derek, author.   II. Title.
  TH3401.W675 2015
  363.6′9–dc23

                                                                                        2015024769

A catalogue record for this book is available from the British Library.

Cover image: Copenhagen © Derek Worthing.

Set in 10/12.5pt Sabon by Aptara Inc., New Delhi, India
Printed and bound in Malaysia by Vivar Printing Sdn Bhd

1 2016

Contents

About the Authors

Stephen Bond runs the UK-based consultancy, Heritage Places, providing advice on the historic environment to national and local government, management and institutional clients, and charitable trusts. In the 1990s, he undertook a seven-year secondment to Historic Royal Palaces, initially as its Surveyor of the Fabric, and subsequently as Director of the Tower Environs Scheme – a major regeneration scheme focused on the urban setting of the Tower of London. Today he works throughout the UK and on international projects, most recently providing heritage input into area-wide plans and capacity building programmes in Africa, Asia and Europe. He was involved with the Master's Programme in Conservation of the Historic Environment at the College of Estate Management for more than 20 years, lectures widely on heritage matters, and holds an honorary doctorate from De Montfort University.

Derek Worthing has a professional background as an academic and a Chartered Building Surveyor. Until recently he was Head of the School of Land and Property Management at the University of the West of England, Bristol, where he was also co-director of the Centre for the Study of Sustainable Buildings in the Faculty of the Built Environment. He has carried out consultancy work in relation to the built cultural heritage for a number of national UK heritage organisations and has published research papers in relation to conservation plans and the maintenance and repair of listed buildings. He now works as a consultant and as a Visiting Professor at Uppsala University in Sweden where he has carried out research on the sustainable management of built cultural heritage as well as work on conservation plans for the Swedish Heritage Board.

Chapter 1

Introduction

In recent years, increasing focus has been placed upon the identification of heritage values that are enshrined in our built environment and in cultural landscapes. This is based on the notion that all buildings and spaces, whatever their age and however modest, make some form of contribution or have value to society.

This book is primarily concerned with how heritage is managed in order to protect and enhance it. Although it focuses on built heritage, we believe the principles and processes that we discuss are applicable to many aspects of cultural heritage. The book brings together our experience of research, consultancy and practice over a number of years, and integrates this with current thinking on approaches to the management of built heritage. It inevitably, and deliberately, does this within the context of a discussion of the benefits and the value of conserving heritage. In our view, this remains a much-needed publication. More than seven years after the first edition, surprisingly little has been written and published on the practical application of heritage values and its importance to the management of heritage assets. This is disconcerting, given that the need to assess significance and use it to manage change is being 'written in' to heritage policy in an increasing number of countries around the world.

This book is chiefly about the important role that effective management plays in protecting and enhancing the historic environment. It concerns itself with what has now become known in some quarters as 'values-based management', but which we have referred to generally as 'significance-based management'. Essentially the book is concerned with the need to identify and assess what is important about a heritage asset, and with devising management strategies, processes and actions that focus on the need to protect and enhance those values.

The collection of values associated with a heritage asset is generally referred to as its 'significance'. The idea of significance has been around for some time, but it was perhaps clearly articulated for the first time, and more importantly

---

Managing Built Heritage: The Role of Cultural Values and Significance, Second Edition.
Stephen Bond and Derek Worthing.
© 2016 Stephen Bond and Derek Worthing. Published 2016 by John Wiley & Sons, Ltd.

linked specifically to the management of a heritage asset by the original Burra Charter, dating from 1979 (Australia ICOMOS, 1979). The idea was developed in several later versions of the charter, with the latest (at the time of writing), being the 2013 edition (Australia ICOMOS, 2013). Building from that, modern conservation planning says that, by understanding the particular significance that a heritage asset holds for society, informed and better management decisions can be taken that will respect and potentially enhance that significance.

The basic premise behind this 'significance-based management' approach, then, is that in order to manage and protect a heritage asset, one has first of all to be able to identify and articulate why it is important and which of its different elements contribute to its importance – and how they do so. That is, we are concerned with determining why a heritage asset is valuable and what embodies and represents those values. This may seem like a simple and rather obvious concept – that you cannot protect something unless:

- You understand why it is important; and
- You know what it is about it that contributes to that importance.

Yet, until recent years, this was not an explicit approach. However, if we accept that as English Heritage (2008) observe: 'Change in the historic environment is inevitable, whether caused by natural processes, through use, or by people responding to social, economic and technological advances', then the key challenge in conservation is essentially about managing change to an asset while protecting, and hopefully enhancing, its significance. In order to meet this challenge, it is vitally important that heritage values are clearly identified and assessed.

If heritage values and their interrelationships can be identified and fully comprehended, this knowledge can then be used to assist in taking management decisions now and in the future that will strengthen and enhance the benefits that accrue to society from that asset. The sense is that there needs to be an understanding of the significance of an asset to be able to articulate and justify its designation, but it can also be, and in fact should be, both a focus and driver for managing the asset.

The concern addressed in this book is the need to develop an approach that guides management planning so as to optimise the benefits that can be gained from an asset without diminishing its value and potential for the future.

In this sense, the management process for a heritage asset is not dissimilar to approaches in other organisational arenas, which effectively ask a series of questions, such as:

- Where do we want to be?
- What have we got now?
- How do we get to where we want to be?
- How are we doing?

In recontextualising this, we can suggest that a coherent approach to the management of heritage assets, whether a single asset, a complex site, an area or indeed a town, will involve:

- Identification and measurement of heritage values;
- Identification of the attributes or elements of the asset that embody and represent those values – so that it is clear what needs to be protected and hopefully enhanced;
- Identification of any factors that may adversely affect heritage values now and in the (measurable) future. That is, in what way are the values vulnerable and what are the processes and situations that may lead to an erosion and loss of those values? Therefore what are the actions that need to be put in place in order to avoid or nullify those threats – or at least mitigate them?
- Identification of opportunities to protect and enhance significance, including by proactively seeking out opportunities for positive changes;
- Identification of 'where are we now?' in relation to matters such as the condition and use of the asset;
- The development of a management strategy and process that link the assessment of heritage values to the operational needs and activities of the asset and to the objectives of the organisation that owns or occupies it (and which integrates built cultural management planning into the general built asset planning on 'mixed' estates). Such a management approach must focus actions, processes and priorities on the protection of built cultural heritage values, i.e. be primarily concerned with the implementation of management practices that maximise protection and enhancement of heritage values;
- The development of evaluation and review processes that address issues of 'how are we doing?' while also considering the continuing validity of (heritage) objectives.

Note

This second edition of the book reflects new international guidance concerning heritage values and significance, as well as developments in national heritage policy in the UK since the first edition was published in 2008. The first edition put considerable focus on the preparation and use of conservation plans in the management of heritage assets. While much of that content has been retained and updated, in this new edition we have felt it appropriate to lay greater emphasis on the process of assessing significance (which, after all, lies at the heart of conservation plan preparation, too) and the use of assessments of significance as a 'plug-in' front end to a wider range of conservation management documents and tools.

Shortly after the completion of the text for this second edition, English Heritage, England's national advisory body for heritage and conservation of the historic environment, was split in two. A new charitable body, retaining the name English Heritage, has taken on responsibility for running the nation's National

Heritage Collection of historic sites and monuments. The current organisation's wider duties and responsibilities as the UK Government's independent expert advisory service for England's historic environment has been handed over to a new body known as Historic England. This edition of the book retains the name English Heritage where this relates to the published work of the unified single organisation of that name.

References

Australia ICOMOS (1979) *The Burra Charter: The Australia ICOMOS Charter for Places of Cultural Significance*. Burwood, VIC, Australia, Australia ICOMOS Inc.

Australia ICOMOS (2013) *The Burra Charter: The Australia ICOMOS Charter for Places of Cultural Significance*. Burwood, VIC, Australia, Australia ICOMOS Inc.

English Heritage (2008) *Conservation Principles, Policies and Guidance for the Sustainable Management of the Historic Environment (Second Stage Consultation)*. London, English Heritage.

Chapter 2

Heritage Assets: Their Nature and Management Implications

Introduction

The premise running through this book is that management decisions about the care and use of an asset will only prove to be sustainable in the long term if they have been shaped by a coherent understanding of its wider significance to society and the ways in which that significance has, is, or could yet be, compromised by change, misuse or neglect. Planning and management decisions built from any other platform are likely to result in the heritage interest and cultural value of the asset being diminished in some way. A significance-based approach to management can be applied to any kind of cultural heritage or built asset. It is just as appropriate to use an evaluation of significance and vulnerability as a means of developing conservation management policies and consequent strategies for action for an historic area – for instance, the core of a town like Delft or a city such as Baalbek – as it is for a relatively simple historic monument such as Nelson's Column or the Taj Mahal. Indeed, a consideration of significance can be made at sub-regional or even regional levels, permitting this approach to heritage management to be fed beneficially into regional and national planning processes.

Some explanation needs perhaps to be given at this juncture about the use of the word 'asset'. Over recent decades, and particularly since we have begun to consider the nature and role of significance, our appreciation of what is encompassed within the term 'heritage' has expanded markedly. Terms such as 'monument', 'building', 'site' or 'place' are no longer sufficiently inclusive. Strangely, there are few options in the English language that are suitably all-embracing: arguably the only alternatives to 'asset' are 'resource' or 'property' and both these have insuperably specific connotations that rule them out. Asset is the best word that we have to describe and include the breadth of our heritage and it has the advantage of meaning something of value.

Managing Built Heritage: The Role of Cultural Values and Significance, Second Edition.
Stephen Bond and Derek Worthing.
© 2016 Stephen Bond and Derek Worthing. Published 2016 by John Wiley & Sons, Ltd.

This book aims to consider the notion of significance as it relates to the management of built heritage, internationally, yet all the while providing a specific focus on the situation within the United Kingdom. That presents us with difficulties when we seek to define terms, since these inevitably vary from place to place: indeed, in the UK alone, there are at all times potentially four different sets of heritage legislation and policy that might need to be considered (that is, for each of the four countries that make up the UK). Unashamedly, therefore, in order to move forward, we must make choices. In this book, any reference to heritage assets should be understood to imply buildings, monuments, archaeological deposits, sites, places, areas or historic urban or rural landscapes that, through some meaningful heritage interest, have a degree of significance warranting consideration in the development planning process. This accords closely with, for instance, the definition of heritage assets enshrined in the current national heritage policy of England.

Heritage assets take many diverse forms. This chapter looks at the range of typical heritage asset types and examines in outline the management implications of each. For each asset type, we seek to define:

- Typical values that we might ascribe to such assets today;
- Who or what is likely to be responsible for managing use and change in and around the asset;
- The level at which management policy and action need to be implemented to be effective in the sustainable care of the asset and its value to society.

Some introductory thoughts about heritage assets

Viewed from a heritage perspective, built and other assets in the environment are either heritage assets or they are ordinary assets. As the UK Government's *Planning Practice Guidance: Conserving and Enhancing the Historic Environment* observes, 'A substantial majority [of assets] have little or no heritage significance and thus do not constitute heritage assets. Only a minority have enough heritage interest for their significance to be a material consideration in the planning process' (DCLG, 2014).

Although age sometimes represents a criterion for being designated a heritage asset, in itself, simply being old, being part of an ensemble or area that is, as an assemblage, recognisable as a heritage asset, having a history of use, bearing a similarity to components in the locality that are heritage assets, or conversely being physically distinctive within its setting or wider context do not *per se* transform an ordinary built asset into a heritage asset. Adopting and building from the definition of 'heritage' set out in Historic England's *Conservation Principles* (English Heritage 2008) (that is, 'all inherited resources which people value for reasons beyond mere utility'), heritage assets can be distinguished from other components of the environment by the meaning for society that a heritage asset holds over and above its functional utility. So, to be regarded as a heritage asset, an asset must have some meaningful archaeological, architectural, artistic, historical, social or other heritage interest that gives it a value to society that transcends its functional utility. Therein lies the fundamental difference between heritage assets and ordinary assets; they stand apart from ordinary assets because of their significance – the summation of all aspects of their heritage interest.

Sometimes heritage assets are protected for the heritage interest that they hold for society; often they are not, having been overlooked, misunderstood or simply because they fall outside the relevant national or local criteria set for being classified and safeguarded. The absence of national or local classification/protection should never be taken as implying that the value of such heritage assets can be simply and safely ignored in the development planning process. As government guidance in England notes:

> *Some non-designated assets, such as buildings of good local character or sites of archaeological interest, are of heritage significance but not at a level that would pass the threshold for national designation. Such assets can, singularly and collectively, make an important, positive contribution to the environment. The desirability of conserving them and the contribution their setting may make to their significance is a material consideration, but individually less of a priority than for designated assets or their equivalents.*
>
> (English Heritage, 2012)

The foregoing is important also for connecting heritage assets (whether designated/classified or not) with a 'setting'. It is a fundamental principle, internationally, that all heritage assets within the built environment have a setting and that the setting constitutes an integral part of the assets' historical and cultural significance. The concept of setting is seen to encompass both tangible and intangible attributes, so that the protection of a setting may not be just a matter of physical protection. As guidance from Historic Scotland (Historic Scotland, 2010) explains:

> *Monuments, buildings, gardens and settlements were not constructed in isolation. They were often deliberately positioned with reference to the surrounding topography, resources, landscape and other monuments or buildings. These relationships will often have changed through the life of a historic asset or place.*
>
> *The setting of [a heritage] asset can incorporate a range of factors, not all of which will apply to every case. These include:*
>
> - *Current landscape or townscape context;*
> - *Visual envelope, incorporating views to, from and across the asset;*
> - *Key vistas, framed by rows of trees, buildings or natural features that give an asset or place a context, whether intentional or not;*
> - *The prominence of the [asset] in views throughout the surrounding area;*
> - *Character of the surrounding landscape;*
> - *General and specific views including foregrounds and backdrops;*
> - *Relationships between both built and natural features;*

- *Aesthetic qualities;*
- *Other non-visual factors such as historical, artistic, literary, linguistic, or scenic associations, intellectual relationships (e.g. to a theory, plan or design), or sensory factors;*
- *A 'Sense of Place': the overall effect formed by the above factors.*

In 2015, Historic England issued new guidance on settings, replacing somewhat more detailed guidance published by English Heritage in 2011. Among other things, this advises that:

> *While setting can be mapped in the context of an individual [planning] application or proposal, it does not have a fixed boundary and cannot be definitively and permanently described for all time as a spatially bounded area or as lying within a set distance of a heritage asset because what comprises a heritage asset's setting may change as the asset and its surroundings evolve or as the asset becomes better understood or due to the varying impacts of different proposals; for instance, new understanding of the relationship between neighbouring heritage assets may extend what might previously have been understood to comprise setting.*
>
> (Historic England, 2015)

As the earlier English Heritage guidance made clear:

> *Construction of a distant but high building; development generating noise, odour, vibration or dust over a wide area; or new understanding of the relationship between neighbouring heritage assets may all extend what might previously have been understood to comprise setting ... While many day-to-day cases will be concerned with the immediate setting of an asset, development within the extended setting may also affect significance, particularly where it is large-scale, prominent or intrusive.*
>
> (English Heritage, 2011)

Thus, in considering heritage assets, it is important to understand not just the physical fabric of the asset itself, but also the nature of its wider context, when it was designed and created/built, and how its setting has changed over time. That appreciation may well be of critical importance in attaining a balanced objective assessment of the asset's significance.

Heritage assets and their management implications

Buried archaeology

Buried archaeology, by its very nature, is culturally precious. Physical intervention or investigation leads to its compromise or destruction. As an asset, it is unusual in that, under normal circumstances, its nature and extent cannot be fully comprehended and frequently can only be guessed at. This can make its management and care in the ground complex or problematic.

Buried archaeology consists of the surviving remains of earlier cultures and their environmental contexts. As a result, such deposits may be valued today for a wide range of reasons, including educational, artistic, social or religious significance. Extracting the complete range of cultural values from archaeological remains is a time-consuming and ultimately destructive process and, accordingly, is increasingly regarded with caution.

In the United Kingdom, the legal arrangements for the ownership of property (including land) mean that, in principle, buried archaeology may be the property and hence the management responsibility of individuals, property-owning organisations, local or central government, or the Crown. This remains the case whether or not its existence is known or recognised, and irrespective of any statutory protection that has been given to the asset through its designation as a scheduled monument.

Archaeological remains are vulnerable to both inadvertent and deliberate damage. This may, at least in part, be associated with a failure to understand sufficiently the value of the asset. When the presence of buried archaeology is known or foreseeable, appropriate care to safeguard its value comprehensively necessitates active management to prevent any disturbance or intervention whatsoever. This sets an onerous level at which effective management needs to take place to safeguard the integrity and possibly unknown significance of the buried asset. When this is unavoidable, a watching brief should be kept of development works, and time and funding allowed for investigation and recording of data, as necessary.

Archaeological sites and monuments

In general terms, archaeological sites and monuments consist of a combination of buried archaeology and above-ground structures or, depending upon circumstance, of foundations and superstructure alone. Many such sites and monuments will be protected by legislation, while others will be without protection despite their cultural value. Internationally, a growing number of archaeological sites are inscribed as being World Heritage Sites due to their 'outstanding universal value'.

Inevitably, 'archaeological sites and monuments' covers a wide group of assets, running from the simple burial mound or barrow through multi-building and multi-phase sites such as Fountains Abbey in the UK to complex ruined cities such as Kandahar in Afghanistan or Byblos in Lebanon.

As with buried archaeological deposits, a wide range of cultural values may be ascribed to these assets, ranging from architectural, historical and archaeological values through social, cultural and religious to symbolic and economic values. Numerous archaeological sites and monuments are open to the public and contribute to the local economy through cultural tourism or spin-off enterprises.

In some situations, archaeological sites and monuments are managed actively and positively for their cultural value, but elsewhere their care is of marginal

(a)

(b)

Figure 2.1   Ephesus is a well-known archaeological site in Turkey (a, b). The library of Celsus is shown in (c).

(c)

Figure 2.1   *(Continued)*

interest to, or indeed may be seen as problematic for, the core activities of the owner/manager. Typical examples of the latter are where prehistoric burial places occupy valuable farm land in private ownership, or where a commemorative monument (such as a garden structure, obelisk or mausoleum) once formed an integral part of an estate that has now been split up or put to a very different use.

In order to prevent harm or compromise to its significance, active management of an archaeological site or monument is likely to involve protection and preservation of its historic fabric (including its remaining buried archaeology) and, frequently, of its immediate setting or environmental context. A typical example of this focus is the management of cultural tourism at archaeological sites in ways that attempt to limit wear and tear and/or degradation resulting from large numbers of visitors, their requirements for facilities (toilets, orientation and signage, shops and restaurants), and the impact of their transport (pollution, vibration and car parking).

Individual historic structures and buildings

Undoubtedly, this category of historic property is the broadest and the most common. This makes generalised comment regarding management practice difficult. Conceivably, almost anywhere in the world, individual historic structures and buildings may variously be owned by individuals, a multitude of different types of organisations, institutions and companies, or by local or central government. Undoubtedly, the majority of individual historic structures are not fully appreciated for their heritage value, but are considered simply as a built envelope within which activities of one kind or another take place. They are generally managed accordingly.

In the UK, individual historic structures and buildings deemed worthy of protection are designated statutorily as 'listed buildings' and graded – traditionally, according to perceived architectural or historic merit, close historical association with nationally important people or events, or group value within their wider setting – as being of 'exceptional' (Grade I/A depending upon country), 'more than special' (Grade II*/B) or 'special' interest (Grade II/C). A small number of historic structures and buildings are also designated for protective purposes as 'scheduled monuments'. (Note: Proposals to do away with separate categories for scheduled monuments and listed buildings are, at the time of writing, still to be enacted. The proposal to 'have a single national designation system with a single legislative base' (DCMS, 2007) reflected concerns about the logic and effectiveness of the system which remain valid.)

Given the diversity of this group of assets, it is unsurprising that a very wide range of values may be variously ascribed to them by individuals, communities and society at large, including as being of historic, architectural, technological, associational, aesthetic, archaeological, educational, recreational, economic, social, commemorative, symbolic, spiritual, or ecological importance (Figures 2.2 (a)–(c)). However, as has already been mentioned, the great majority of historic structures are valued prosaically for housing day-to-day functions (in other words, their use).

Where statutory protection exists, depending upon circumstance, it is likely to seek to safeguard the structure's surviving historic fabric (including 'fossil' archaeological evidence of previous use or change in the built fabric), plan form, external appearance, distinctive character, massing, materials, or long pertaining use. Thus, conservation management policies for individual buildings and structures tend to be focused (though not to exclusion) at this level of interest and attention. In the past, the starting point for conservation management generally – reflecting a strong cultural and philosophical bias towards the importance of the preservation of historic buildings and monuments – centred on a set of principles, including tenets such as minimum intervention, reversibility, and so forth which lay at the heart of the Venice Charter (ICOMOS, 1964). These principles have been reinforced in later international charters such as the Burra Charter (Australia ICOMOS, 2013). In the UK, there is currently perhaps less prominent reference to these principles now than in the recent past, but they are

(a)

Figure 2.2 (a)–(c)   Examples of archaeological sites that are to be found in Coventry (a), (b). The *SS Great Britain*, which is moored in the Harbour at Bristol, is a Scheduled Monument (c).

implied in or underlie various guidance documents. These principles and how they are used are discussed in Chapter 8.

Management of protected buildings and structures involves some level of interaction between the owner or occupier of the property and the statutory authority responsible for administration of the relevant legislative procedures. In the UK, some of the problems with the current arrangements include:

- Listing descriptions that do not indicate which aspects of the asset contribute to its significance, meaning that owners/occupiers do not know what it is that they are 'stewarding';

(b)

Figure 2.2   *(Continued)*

- A widespread and mistaken concept that listing is intended to 'freeze' a place in time;
- Although admittedly this has perhaps lessened in recent years, an essentially adversarial relationship between the statutory authority and the owner/occupier;
- A lack of understanding of conservation ideas and principles by many owner/occupiers, which results in, among other things, a sense that the external appearance of a building is of overarching importance (and therefore if elements deteriorate or are damaged, then as long as they are replaced with 'replicas', no loss has actually occurred).

(c)

Figure 2.2   *(Continued)*

Almost inevitably, many highly significant historic structures are left largely or entirely unprotected by national statute or are severely undervalued or misrepresented on descriptive lists of classified/designated assets. Management of unprotected assets is dictated more often than not by the short-term goals and wants of the owner or occupier, irrespective of their long-term impact or potential detriment to sustainable use.

Cultural landscapes

In devising the term 'cultural landscape' in 1925, Carl Sauer, an American cultural geographer, wrote: 'The cultural landscape is fashioned from a natural landscape by a culture group. Culture is the agent, the natural area is the medium, the cultural landscape the result.' More recently, the term has come to be highly inclusive. Another cultural geographer, Pierce Lewis, writing in 1979, observed:

> *It is proper and important to think that cultural landscapes are nearly everywhere we can see when we go outdoors ... [Saying] that certain things in certain areas are somehow more historic than other things or places ... is rather like saying that there is more geography in one place than another.*

This mirrors the more recent shift that has occurred in the conservation world – rather than in the discipline of cultural geography – where the term 'historic landscape' has been adopted to reinforce an appreciation that everything that surrounds us, whether in the town or country, is the result of ongoing cumulative change. As Peter Fowler has noted (2001, 2002):

> *By recognising cultural landscape, we have, almost for the first time, given ourselves the opportunity to recognise places that may well look ordinary but that can fill in our appreciation to become extraordinary; and an ability in some places to do that creates monuments to the faceless ones, the people who lived and died unrecorded except unconsciously and collectively by the landscape modified by their labours. The cultural landscape is a memorial to the unknown labourer.*

In this book, under the heading of cultural landscape, we include cultural routes, such as the ancient trade route, the Silk Road, which passed from the shores of the Mediterranean through Bukhara and Samarkand to Xian in Central China, and more modern aspects of heritage such as Brunel's Great Western Railway from Bristol to London.

The cultural landscape represents a manifestation of a vital interaction between mankind and the natural environment (or perhaps more accurately the pre-existing cultural environments) over time. Values that may reside in a cultural landscape are diverse. Scazzosi (2002, p. 55) reflects that:

> *Places are ... a document full of material and immaterial traces of man and nature's history. In this sense they are a vast archive, available to anyone willing and able to read it, that allows us to improve knowledge of culture, techniques, ways of life, as well as the nature, climate and vegetation of the past ... When we use the term 'landscape', we stress the relationship between the world and ourselves: a window through which we can look at the world with the eyes of our cultural tradition.*

In UNESCO's (2012) *Operational Guidelines for the Implementation of the World Heritage Convention*, cultural landscapes are sub-divided into three categories:

1 *Clearly defined landscape* – designed and created intentionally by man (embracing gardens and parklands as landscapes constructed for aesthetic reasons);
2 *Organically evolved landscape* – which results from an initial social, economic, administrative, and/or religious imperative and reflects a process of evolution in their form and component features; and
3 *Associative cultural landscapes* – which have been called 'landscapes of ideas' and are distinguished by their associations with the natural environment rather than by their evidence of material culture, which may be minimal or entirely absent.

Figure 2.3   Subak in Bali – a cultural landscape shaped by centuries of use and Hindu custom.

It has been noted that the range of natural features associated with cosmological, symbolic, sacred and culturally significant landscapes may be very broad, including mountains, caves, outcrops, coastal waters, rivers, lakes, pools, hillsides, uplands, plains, woods, groves and trees. Organically evolved landscapes fall into two categories, fossil or relic cultural landscapes. In the UK these are numerous, for example, the prehistoric landscape around Stonehenge; the industrial landscape of the Ironbridge Gorge; and the extensive surviving areas of historic landscaped elements, such as medieval ridge and furrow. Living cultural landscapes perhaps need less explanation, for they surround us everywhere – old and new gravel workings in the Thames Valley, fruit cultivation and its associated structures in the Vale of Evesham, the thatched villages of Devon and Cornwall, and so forth. It is being argued that our towns and cities are as much cultural landscapes as are designed rural landscapes, formal gardens or parkland, and that they should be interpreted and managed as such.

In a paper on social significance Byrne *et al.* (2003) refer to the Landscape of Memory as being 'the invisible component of the cultural environment which consists of the associations which both natural and "built" features of the landscape have for people'. Places like the Indonesian island of Bali are viewed as a single cultural landscape, since it reflects in a vital and deep-seated, often intangible, way the interaction between the natural landscape and Balinese Hindu culture and its unique cosmology over the last 1000 years (Figure 2.3).

Understanding the range of cultural landscapes that exist and their specific nature is fundamental to their proper management. If we want to safeguard and nurture such assets, we have to know where they are, how they are characterised and why they are culturally valuable. Cultural landscapes are to be found in

(a)

(b)

Figure 2.4 (a)–(c)   Silbury Hill in Wiltshire (a) lies in close proximity to the standing stones at Avebury (b) and (c). They are both part of the wider cultural landscape in this area that includes Stonehenge. Silbury Hill is the largest man-made mound from prehistoric Europe (at 40 metres). Its purpose is unknown. Silbury Hill was built approximately 4600 years ago at about the time that Avebury was being completed.

(c)

Figure 2.4   *(Continued)*

desert landscapes and oasis systems, in sacred mountains, in the vineyards of France and South Africa, as cultural routes such as the Silk Road, in the rice terraces of the Philippines, the canals and irrigation systems of the Fenlands and in the Netherlands, the gardens of Versailles, the Darjeeling railway as much as Brunel's Great Western Railway, and the Cedars of Lebanon. Of course, they exist for 'everyday' places as well and are stored in 'mental maps'. As Byrne *et al.* (2003) observe: 'Such mental maps have been built up over a lifetime and are more complex than any map on paper could ever be ... [Social] significance assessment is partly to do with attempting to give validity to the maps that people hold in their mind.' It is perhaps an obvious point that individuals and indeed different groups (based perhaps on class, age, ethnicity, etc.) within a particular geographical area will have varying mental maps of that same area, based on their past experience and the way that they interact with the area now. For the individual and group, that mental map is likely to change over time, for example, when they have children, they will use and experience the area in a different way. The mental maps of an individual or group will also, of course, change over time. This highlights the importance of engaging with the wider community when undertaking an assessment of significance of an area. It also raises issues regarding relative, changing and perhaps competing significance.

   Until very recently, many cultural landscapes have not been recognised as having overriding significance as a unified assemblage. As a consequence, some cultural landscapes are partially protected through the designation of individual component parts, although the landscape as an entity is unrecognised, an example of this situation is the important wider prehistoric landscape that includes both Stonehenge and numerous burial mounds in Wiltshire, England.

The universal presence of cultural landscapes means that their ownership and management patterns are often extremely complex. Some of the cultural landscapes to which reference has already been made cross modern national borders. Even the less dramatic are likely to be in multiple ownership and may extend across the boundaries of more than one planning authority. This makes the establishment or imposition of a unified beneficial management regime problematic and frequently impossible. As a consequence, caring for a valued cultural landscape often depends upon some form of designation or legislative protection. By and large, this will not necessarily result in a system of proactive day-to-day management, but it may provide a regulatory mechanism for managing large-scale physical change to such assets. Arguably, this is particularly unsatisfactory when dealing with continuing living cultural landscapes, since the inhibition of change may well destroy the essential characteristics of the landscape, in other words, its continuity of change.

As we have already noted, the values present in a cultural landscape may be diverse, including historic, archaeological, aesthetic, panoramic, scenic, educational, recreational, economic, social, commemorative, symbolic, spiritual, or ecological interest. Although the minutiae of the fabric of a cultural landscape may have, in some instances, relevance, management focus tends to need to occur at a higher level than, say, for individual historic structures and buildings, being involved with protection and care of whole rural and/or urban areas rather than single assets.

Landed estates

From the Norman Conquest onwards, large landed rural estates have been a significant feature of the landscape, society and economic well-being of the United Kingdom and, indeed, much of Europe. The aggregation of massive land holdings has been equated with power throughout much of our history. As just one example, within twenty years of the Norman Conquest, the Baron William de Mohun held 56 Manors in Somerset, 11 in Dorset and one each in Devon and Wiltshire. The family name is thus repeated in, for instance, National Trust information today for properties in Cornwall, Devon and Somerset. Equally, the Acland family of the nineteenth and twentieth centuries is often referred to in the National Trust's literature for the same area of the country. At the end of the nineteenth century, roughly 90% of rural England and Wales was tenanted: land ownership was dominated by families who generally depended upon the income from their estates for their livelihood. However, this long-standing pattern was about to change with the effects of the Industrial Revolution, taxation, agricultural depression, the First World War and subsequent sweeping social change. The 1874 return of *Owners of Land* recorded that 17% of England was occupied by large estates in excess of 3000 acres and 24% by great estates in excess of 10 000 acres. Over the twentieth century, the pattern of land holding changed dramatically. The number of land holdings over 700 acres in size increased fourfold between 1950 and 1970, yet behind this lay a fundamental change in the pattern of ownership and management responsibility. In 2010, the magazine *Country Life* reported that the top 10 landowners in the UK were:

the Forestry Commission	2,571,270 acres or a little under 975,000 hectares;
the National Trust	630,000 acres or approximately 240,000 ha;
the Defence Estates, on behalf of the Ministry of Defence	592,800 acres or 225,000 ha;
pension funds	550,000 acres or slightly over 208,000 ha;
public utilities companies	500,000 acres – 190,000 ha;
the Crown Estate	358,000 acres – roughly 135,000 ha;
the Royal Society for the Protection of Birds	321,237 acres or 122,000 ha;
the Duke of Buccleuch and Queensberry	240,000 acres or 91,000 ha;
the National Trust for Scotland	192,000 acres – approaching 73,000 ha;
the Duke of Atholl's trusts	145,700 acres or 55,200 ha.

(*Country Life*, 2010)

Scotland is an interesting case, as it has been observed that more than half of the country is owned by fewer than 500 people (a figure of 432 is often quoted) and this means that 'Scotland has one of the most concentrated patterns of private land ownership anywhere' (Cameron, 2014).

Landed rural estates have been defined (Bettey, 1993) as 'any landholding of at least 3,000 acres, subject to a single owner, whether an institution or an individual, not necessarily made up of a single compact territory, but which has been administered as a unit and where the effects of a single ownership can be recognised'. For our purposes, we may take a wider view of the landed rural estate to include smaller holdings in the ownership of individuals as well as larger estates (in foreign ownership), non-governmental organisations (NGOs) and government departments. In short, day-to-day management control and decision-making will normally be in the hands of the tenant or a professional manager, unless the holding is essentially owner-occupied. It seems readily apparent from the foregoing that the vast majority of the UK's surviving historic landed estates are managed not for their heritage, but for their economic value. This undoubtedly influences the day-to-day decisions that are made and implemented.

Arguably, historic landed rural estates can be regarded as being cultural landscapes. In their entirety, they are each an organically evolved landscape of a continuing nature. Many will also contain other distinct cultural landscapes – for instance, relict medieval ridge and furrow landscapes or significant areas of mineral or stone extraction – or they may be bisected by a significant cultural route such as a canal or railway. The whole estate may have coalesced around a mansion and its pleasure grounds and parkland, in itself a clearly defined

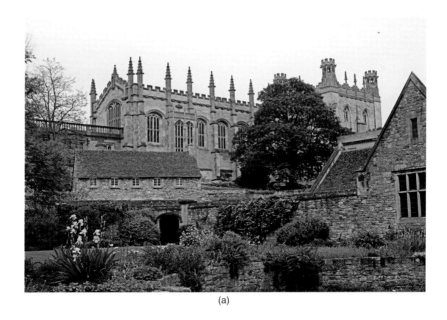

(a)

(b)

Figure 2.5 (a)–(c)   The Colleges of Oxford University are a historic urban estate. Photograph (c) courtesy of Lee Stickells.

cultural landscape. Such hierarchies of heritage assets must be recognised and understood in order that appropriate management strategies and planning can be put in place for the individual and distinct areas.

(c)

Figure 2.5 *(Continued)*

Urban estates can be contrasted distinctly with landed rural estates. Inevitably, because of their context, they tend to be significantly smaller (in terms of land area), while usually containing buildings whose total floor area far exceeds their rural counterparts. These buildings may well be subjected to considerably greater use pressures and demand a style of management that is very different from the rural estate.

Although small in area in comparison to expansive rural estates, some historic estates can dominate and dictate the character and culture of whole towns and cities. The University of Oxford and the University of Cambridge are good examples where a major part of the cultural and economic values of a modern city continues to be focused on historic estates that lie at the core (Figure 2.5). Other estates may be woven deeply into the historic grain of an urban area, while being less obvious to the uninformed visitor – the widespread ownership of property around Bloomsbury in London by the Bedford Estates in London is a typical example. Here, a substantial part of the valuable urban area separating the West End from the City of London has been owned and managed by the Duke of Bedford's estate since 1669. Undoubtedly, this has had a dramatic impact upon its development, form and significance.

The types of estates already cited are interwoven into the fabric of towns and cities, but are essentially dispersed and, to a greater or lesser degree, outward-looking. Others are more self-contained and introspective, more like walled or defended complexes: Royal Palaces, residential estates – such as the *Spaarn-dammerplantsoen* in Amsterdam which has three public housing blocks designed by Michel de Klerk (Figures 2.6 (a) and (b)), or Albany off Piccadilly in London – and governmental estates fall into this category, as do a number of listed post-war housing estates such as the Barbican in London (Figures 2.7 (a) and (b)), the Byker estate in Newcastle, and Parkhill in Sheffield.

Where historic structures predominate in these various urban estates, it may seem reasonably obvious that management should take account of their heritage interest. More problematic for the general estate manager is the situation where a largely twentieth-century portfolio of structures of little architectural significance (but, of course, potentially rich in other cultural values) contains one or a small number of protected heritage assets – typical examples might be Post Office estates, underground railways, hospital complexes, and the like. In such cases, standard prescribed management processes devised for the estates as a whole may well not act in the best interests of the individual heritage asset. Indeed, standard prescribed management processes may cause substantial harm to their significance. Conversely, adaptation of the estate-wide management arrangements and procedures to suit the needs of heritage components may render the management organisation as a whole inefficient, cumbersome or costly. This reinforces the need for management plans to work with, rather than against, the 'grain' of management organisations in order to be successful.

Due to circumstance, historic urban estates will rarely – in the UK, at least – be owned by individuals. Most will be in the ownership of institutions, trusts, central and local government, management companies, pension funds or the Crown. Management tends to be in the hands of professional managers or their agents. The implications of the foregoing are critically important. Many historic urban estates contribute substantially to the primary urban grain or character of modern towns and cities. They may also play an important part in maintaining or contributing to the economic health and sustainability of the wider area or sub-region. Despite this, many will be managed on a day-to-day basis with little regard to their heritage value, let alone their overall significance. This implies that they may well not be managed (to echo the Brundtland Report (United Nations, 1987)) to optimise their benefit to society, while safeguarding the needs and interests of future generations. Unsustainable management is surely bad management.

Historic areas and urban landscapes: towns and cities

As of 2014 there are somewhere in the region of 10,700 historic areas in cities, towns and villages around the UK that are recognised for their special character, having been designated as Conservation Areas: England – around 9500; Scotland – 628; Wales – 500; Northern Ireland – 60. There are substantially more areas of heritage interest throughout the UK that are not recognised or protected in any way. Indeed, we can regard the historic environment as involving everything around us.

Currently, there is considerable debate as to whether historic areas of settlements and conurbations, and urban landscapes more generally, should be

(a)

(b)

Figure 2.6 (a),(b)   The *Spaarndammerplantsoen* in Amsterdam is another example of a historic urban estate.

(a)

(b)

Figure 2.7 (a),(b)   The Barbican development in the City of London.

(a)

(b)

Figure 2.8 (a)–(c)   In Conservation Areas, both the buildings and the spaces between buildings are important.

regarded as being 'extreme' or ultimate forms of cultural landscape. On the one hand, just as with other cultural landscapes, historic areas and urban land-scapes have undeniably been 'fashioned from a natural landscape by a culture group' (Sauer, 1925). However, others would argue that the natural landscape contributes almost nothing to such places. In our view, this would deny that

(c)

Figure 2.8   *(Continued)*

topography and 'natural' features (for instance, rivers and undulating land) frequently play a major part in urban morphology. We believe that, as an asset type, historic areas and urban landscapes should be accepted as being a separate grouping of cultural landscapes. However, they are characterised by some quite distinct features that are not shared by other cultural landscapes and this will have an effect on how they should be managed.

By their very nature, whether protected or unprotected, historic areas usually contain numerous individual properties, frequently in separate ownership. Management responsibility is thus often split among numerous individuals or property-owning companies or institutions. In the UK, the public areas and spaces will generally be vested in and managed by a local authority. If protected as a conservation area (Figure 2.8), that same authority may hope to encourage the good management practice of the individual premises within the area. This can be encouraged either positively by providing design and care guidance, or administratively (and restrictively) by removing certain permitted development rights and by regarding the special character of the area as a material consideration during the planning process. Where historic areas are unprotected statutorily, their significance is exposed to diminution by the management decisions of individual property owners, except in so far as the normal planning process might apply some protective control.

Management of a historic area can and should take place at several levels. Gradual erosion of the quality of an area's character frequently occurs through ill-judged or careless intervention with historic fabric, especially those interventions involving changes in traditional material usage or to external elements such

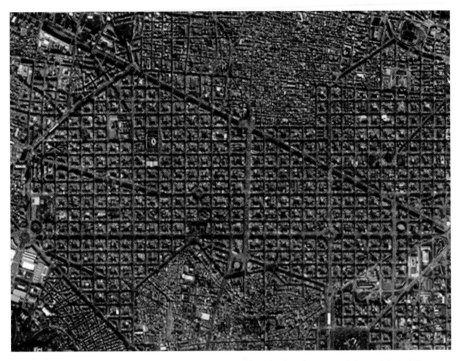

Figure 2.9   The remarkable survival of Barcelona's historic city plan. Copyright QuickBird ©
Digital Globe, 2001, distributed and by courtesy of Eurimage.

as the profile of roofs or design of windows. Damage can also be occasioned
within a short time by the accretion of modern communications equipment, such
as satellite dishes or television aerials to external elevations and chimney-stacks.
Similarly, changes to the design of, and materials used in, streetscapes can damage the special character of an area. However, historic areas also need to be managed in terms of building heights, building lines, massing, street patterns, vistas,
and so forth. The remarkable historic grid of Barcelona is an excellent example
of a situation where, if this aspect is to be retained, management needs to take
place at a strategic level far removed from cares about retention or intervention
with historic fabric (Figure 2.9).

The multi-layered value of historic areas and the need for multi-layered management have been described by Feilden and Jokilehto (1993):

> *For the pedestrian, there are many subtle qualities in streets, lanes, even
> canals and bridges, and these urban spaces combine to give visual drama
> by the sensations of compression, expansion, surprise and the careful
> location of fine architectural set pieces. Views of the principal buildings
> from various places provide reassuring reference points. Citizens who
> know the history of the place will enjoy the rich feeling of participat-
> ing in its history, and a sense of continuity and identity. Some of the key
> buildings are symbolic; without them, the place would never be the same.*

> *In an historic town, the substance and archaeological potential that embody historic values and material authenticity lie in the structures of all buildings and in the infrastructures. Often a large part of urban fabric may consist of simple buildings without special artistic qualities, anonymous architecture connected by open squares, lanes, streets and parks. It is these structures and urban spaces in which the life of the town has evolved that distinguish the concept of historic town from a group of monuments. Since their demolition or neglect would deprive the town of its essence, a policy for their treatment should be established.*

What Feilden and Jokilehto observe in the historic town is mirrored within the historic quarters of cities and, indeed, by entire cities themselves. As Brand (1994) has written: 'While the regions provide myth, cities express history.' It is this expression of history that gives comfort to people and gives value to urban life, as David Lowenthal (1985) has observed in *The Past Is a Foreign Country*. Our towns and cities then are mostly intensely complex historical documents.

Spiro Kostoff (1991) has noted: 'Cities are amalgams of buildings and people. They are inhabited settings from which daily rituals – the mundane and the extraordinary, the random and the staged – derive their validity ... The city is the ultimate memorial of our struggles and glories.' As inhabited settings, the intimate characteristics of nearly every urban district are a reflection of a vital contest that has taken place over time between socio-economic forces of change and the remarkable persistence of the city's most enduring feature, its physical build. This is the case, block by block, street by street, site by site. This is not just another theoretical way of viewing urban space, it is basic raw reality. It is the 'how' and the 'why' that explain every aspect of physical form in the streetscape – from the 'puzzles of premeditated and spontaneous segments [of urban form], variously interlocked or juxtaposed' to the 'small incident, the twisted street, the rounded corner, the little planted oasis unexpectedly come upon'.

Everyone, it seems, has some innate and instinctive recognition of the value of this developmental complexity in our towns and cities. Peter Larkham (1996), explaining the theoretical approach to townscape management of M.R.G. Conzen, has put it thus:

> *Landscapes embody not only the efforts and aspirations of the people occupying them at present, but also those of their predecessors. In this way, the townscape may be seen as embodying the spirit of society in the context of its own historical development in a particular place ... It becomes the spirit of the place, the genus loci. In Conzen's view, it is an important environmental experience for the individual, even when it is received unconsciously. It enables individuals and groups to take root in an area. They acquire a sense of the historical dimension of human experience ... Viewed in this way, townscapes represent accumulated experience ... and are thus a precious asset.*

ICOMOS's Washington Charter (ICOMOS, 1987) which was concerned with 'the conservation of historic towns and urban areas', noted that such areas 'embody the values of traditional urban cultures'. The Charter advised that the management of historic urban areas 'should be an integral part of coherent policies of economic and social development and of urban and regional planning at every level'. Specifically, it recommended that:

> *Qualities to be preserved include the historic character of the town or urban area and all those material and spiritual elements that express this character, especially:*

- *Urban patterns as defined by lots and streets;*
- *Relationships between buildings and green and open spaces;*
- *The formal appearance, interior and exterior of buildings as defined by scale, size, style, construction, materials, colour and decoration;*
- *The relationship between the town or urban area and its surrounding setting, both natural and man-made; and*
- *The various functions that the town or urban area has acquired over time.*

Active management of historic areas and urban landscapes needs to consider and respect all these many and varied attributes, to be successful and sustainable in its effects.

World Heritage Sites and Cities

The *Convention Concerning the Protection of the World Cultural and Natural Heritage*, more commonly referred to as 'The World Heritage Convention' was adopted by UNESCO in November 1972. At the time of writing, 191 national states have ratified the Convention (UNESCO, 1972).

The Convention requires that a World Heritage List be maintained by an inter-governmental World Heritage Committee. The World Heritage List identifies cultural and natural properties which are to be protected under the Convention. The Convention (Article 1) defines 'cultural heritage' (for instance, Figure 2.10) under three headings:

1 *Monuments: architectural works, works of monumental sculpture and painting, elements or structures of an archaeological nature, inscriptions, cave dwellings and combinations of features, which are of outstanding universal value from the point of view of history, art or science;*
2 *Groups of buildings: groups of separate or connected buildings which, because of their architecture, their homogeneity or their place in the landscape, are of outstanding universal value from the point of view of history, art or science;*

Figure 2.10   The Sydney Opera House is a World Heritage Site.

3 *Sites: works of man or the combined works of nature and of man, and areas including archaeological sites which are of outstanding universal value from the historical, aesthetic, ethnological or anthropological points of view.*

Article 2 of the Convention defines 'natural heritage' (for instance, Figures 2.11 and 2.12) as:

1 *Natural features consisting of physical and biological formations or groups of such formations, which are of outstanding universal value from the aesthetic or scientific point of view; geological and physiographical formations and precisely delineated areas which constitute the habitat of threatened species of animals and plants of outstanding universal value from the point of view of science or conservation;*
2 *Natural sites or precisely delineated natural areas of outstanding universal value from the point of view of science, conservation or natural beauty.*

UNESCO's *Operational Guidelines for the Implementation of the World Heritage Convention* allow for the inscription of mixed cultural and natural heritage sites and, as we have already seen, for cultural landscapes as cultural properties representing the 'combined works of nature and of man' (UNESCO, 2012).

As the description of each category of cultural and natural heritage makes clear, the defining characteristic is that, in every case, the asset or property must be of 'outstanding universal value. This is defined as:

(a)

(b)

Figure 2.11 (a),(b)   Pamukkale in Turkey is an example of a natural site on the World Heritage list.

cultural and/or natural significance which is so exceptional as to transcend national boundaries and to be of common importance for present and future generations of all humanity. As such, the permanent protection of this heritage is of the highest importance to the international community as a whole.

Figure 2.12   Ha-Long Bay in Vietnam is another example of a natural site on the World Heritage list.

Currently, ten criteria are used to establish outstanding universal value. Properties being nominated for inscription on the World Heritage List must meet one or more of the following criteria:

1 *Represent a masterpiece of human creative genius;*
2 *Exhibit an important interchange of human values, over a span of time or within a cultural area of the world, on developments in architecture or technology, monumental arts, town-planning or landscape design;*
3 *Bear a unique or at least exceptional testimony to a cultural tradition or to a civilisation which is living or which has disappeared;*
4 *Be an outstanding example of a type of building, architectural or technological ensemble or landscape which illustrates a significant stages in human history;*
5 *Be an outstanding example of a traditional human settlement, land-use, or sea-use which is representative of a culture (or cultures), or human interaction with the environment especially when it has become vulnerable under the impact of irreversible change;*

6 *Be directly or tangibly associated with events or living traditions, with ideas, or with beliefs, with artistic and literary works of outstanding universal significance;*

7 *Contain superlative natural phenomena or areas of exceptional natural beauty and aesthetic importance;*

8 *Be outstanding examples representing major stages of earth's history, including the record of life, significant ongoing geological processes in the development of landforms, or significant geomorphic or physiographic features;*

9 *Be outstanding examples representing significant ongoing ecological and biological processes in the evolution and development of terrestrial, fresh water, coastal and marine ecosystems and communities of plants and animals;*

10 *Contain the most important and significant natural habitats for in-situ conservation of biological diversity, including those containing threatened species of Outstanding Universal Value from the point of view of science or conservation.*

Clearly, not all these criteria are relevant to cultural heritage assets.

Inscribed cultural World Heritage Sites range from individual monuments and sites through to historic areas and cities such as Bath, Brasilia, Toledo and Venice and the Lagoon (Figures 2.13 and 2.14). In some countries, such assets are provided with additional protection under national planning/development legislation, although it must be stressed that is not always the case.

The Operational Guidelines require that nominated properties 'should have an appropriate management plan or other documented management system which should specify how the outstanding universal value of a property should be preserved, preferably through participatory means', the purpose being to ensure effective protection for present and future generations. The Guidelines also recognise that 'Management systems may vary according to different cultural perspectives, the resources available and other factors. They may incorporate traditional practices, existing urban or regional planning instruments, and other planning control mechanisms, both formal and informal.' However, it is suggested that, to be effective, management arrangements could include:

- A thorough shared understanding of the property by all stakeholders;
- A cycle of planning, implementation, monitoring, evaluation and feedback;
- The involvement of partners and stakeholders;
- The allocation of necessary resources;
- Capacity-building; and
- An accountable, transparent description of how the management system functions.

This is potentially onerous where the World Heritage Site includes numerous properties in private ownership. In the end, as the Guidelines make clear, the State Party is 'responsible for implementing effective management activities for

(a)

(b)

Figure 2.13 (a)–(c)   Venice (with the Lagoon) is an example of a city that is a World Heritage Site.

a World Heritage property', doing so 'in close collaboration with property managers, the agency with management authority and other partners, and stakeholders in property management', As ICOMOS's tourism handbook for World Heritage Site Managers comments, 'The management of urban historic sites is perhaps the most complex of all sites. They are living organisms, often densely

(c)

Figure 2.13   *(Continued)*

populated, with deteriorating infrastructures and enormous development pressures. The management of these sites is often fragmented among various local and national government agencies' (ICOMOS, 1993). In the worst case, this might necessitate direct intervention by a national government to correct ineffective management of a World Heritage Site, if the World Heritage Committee has concluded that the situation is placing the outstanding universal value of the asset in jeopardy.

The World Heritage Resource Manual, *Managing Cultural World Heritage* (UNESCO *et al.*, 2013) addresses many of these issues as well as setting out (in its Appendices) a framework for a comprehensive management plan for World Heritage Sites.

Buffer zones and urban settings to major heritage assets

Increasing attention is being paid to the urban settings of World Heritage Sites, historic monuments and other cultural heritage assets and to their potential to act as part of a planning buffer zone to protect the major heritage asset at their core. While these settings are usually historic areas and sometimes urban landscapes in their own right, in our view, this focus seems likely to intensify still further in the

(a)

(b)

Figure 2.14 (a)–(d)   The City of Bath is a World Heritage site; much of it is also defined as Conservation Areas. In addition, it contains many individually protected scheduled monuments and listed buildings. Photographs (c and d) courtesy of John Bailey.

future. For this reason, we have separated them out for individual consideration in this brief overview of heritage asset types.

This section deals specifically with urban situations. A buffer zone is defined in UNESCO's *Operational Guidelines* as an area surrounding the nominated property which has 'complementary legal and/or customary restrictions placed

(c)

(d)

Figure 2.14 *(Continued)*

Figure 2.15   View across the former Central Docks in Liverpool: The boundaries of World Heritage Sites and their buffer zones can sometimes be complex. Here, the dock space in the foreground, including Victoria Clock Tower to the right, is part of one of six character areas in the Liverpool Maritime Mercantile World Heritage Site. The empty space behind is part of the World Heritage Site's buffer zone. Beyond that, in turn, is another small 'island' of the same World Heritage Site character zone, then another section of buffer zone (where high rise buildings can be seen), and finally in the distance a second character area of the World Heritage Site where the two towers of the Liver Building are just visible. This arrangement makes consideration of settings and management of development impacts highly problematic.

on its use and development to give an added layer of protection to the nominated property' (Figure 2.15). While this is intended to relate only to World Heritage Sites, replacing the words 'nominated property' with 'heritage asset' provides a satisfactory definition for all situations. UNESCO's *Operational Guidelines* go on to expand upon the definition by stating that a buffer zone: 'should include the immediate setting of the nominated property, important views and other areas or attributes that are functionally important as a support to the property and its protection'.

The concept of setting was discussed earlier in this chapter. The settings of urban historic sites (or areas), like all other historic areas, will usually contain numerous individual properties that will be in separate ownership. Management responsibility is thus often split among many individuals and property-owning organisations. Just as with other historic areas, settings encapsulate a multitude of cultural values for the local community.

It is worth repeating the words of Feilden and Jokilehto (1993) quoted above while considering historic areas and urban landscapes:

Often a large part of urban fabric may consist of simple buildings with-out special artistic qualities, anonymous architecture connected by open squares, lanes, streets, and parks. It is these structures and urban spaces in which the life of the town has evolved that distinguish the concept of historic town from a group of monuments.

Obviously, this describes the urban setting of a heritage asset just as well as any other 'typical' historic area. We have suggested in looking at historic areas and urban landscapes generally that 'as inhabited settings, the intimate character-istics of nearly every urban district are a reflection of a vital contest that has taken place over time between socio-economic forces of change and the remark-able persistence of the city's most enduring feature, its physical build' (Kostoff, 1991). Again, that is as true of architecturally mundane settings for major urban heritage assets as it is for large parts of other urban grain.

However, unlike other historic urban areas, for reasons that are arguably both good and bad, the conservation world has come to regard the character of urban settings to more major – often, monumental – heritage assets as being, to a degree, selectively expendable in the interests of 'proper' management of the latter. In simplistic terms, we seek to impose a conceptual relationship of master and subordinate on major historic assets and their urban settings. In theory, this approach risks subordinating the history and values of the setting into being but a subset of the history and values of the more major heritage asset itself. It defines the setting as being principally an attribute of the heritage asset with little value as an organic area in its own right.

Literature and guidance relating to the setting of heritage assets remain in rel-atively short supply, what little there is, expressly or implicitly, reflects this same attitude. Historic England's (2015) guidance states categorically that 'Setting is not a heritage asset ... Its importance lies in what it contributes to the signifi-cance of the heritage asset', while the Venice Charter states that 'conservation of a monument implies preserving a setting which is not out of scale. Wherever the traditional setting exists, it must be kept' (ICOMOS, 1964). Whatever one's sympathy with the intent behind these notions, once again they do imply a mas-ter and subordinate relationship between the heritage asset and the setting. It demands that the ongoing 'vital contest' within the setting (which after all until then has not affected the survival of its 'traditional' nature) be curtailed and sub-ordinated to the perceived needs of the major asset for protection from change and the inappropriate world outside. Of course, the very notion that the setting will be 'traditional' is a solecism. The fact that it is now routine to, for example, define 'traditional housing' as that which was built before 1945 (or sometimes perhaps 1948) adds to the problem with the term, and, of course, begs the ques-tion as to what is the 'traditional setting' of a post-war building or estate.

Every urban space and hence every setting without exception are the result of historical decisions and activity that, according to Larkham (1996), 'embody ... the efforts and aspirations ... of predecessors' and thus, in Kostoff's eyes (1991) represent 'the ultimate memorial of our struggles and glories'. The twentieth-century urban setting of the Tower of London provides a vivid illustration of the serious misrepresentation inherent in this attitude and the dangers that it can bring.

As a composition of fortifications, imposing buildings and spaces, the Tower is an internationally recognised icon of England's heritage. It receives more than 2 million paying visitors each year and there are at least as many again who tarry to admire and photograph without entry. In terms of designation and statutory protection, the Tower's intrinsic worth is well recognised: it is a World Heritage Site, a scheduled monument and virtually every structure within its walls is a listed building in its own right. More potently, perhaps, it is a living symbol of the power of the Crown through almost a thousand years of cultural development. The Tower of London has been at the heart of so much that defines the nation. Its involvement in the history of the state is familiar to many, but it has also been the birthplace and home of many major political and cultural institutions, for instance, the Board of Ordnance, the Ordnance Survey, the Royal Observatory, the Public Records Office, the Royal Mint and, through the Royal Menagerie, even London Zoo. In simple terms, it is one of the most vital and important heritage assets in the land. As such, it should be treasured.

With this as background, it would seem axiomatic that the modern setting of the Tower should be rich in 'sense of place'. Bewilderingly, nothing could be further from reality, for the area has long been epitomised by diminished social and cultural values and wasted opportunity. Despite a number of determined attempts in the past 60 years by those seeking to improve and regenerate, little value has been ascribed or added to the environs of the Tower in the post-war reshaping of this quarter of London until recent alterations have made some improvements to the open space immediately beside the asset. Superficially, it is difficult to comprehend how this situation could have developed. Despite the recent improvements, the architectural amphitheatre and open space surrounding the Tower are blighted by the visual and environmental impact of a dual carriage highway which cuts across the open land immediately to the north of the Tower. The road forms an impenetrable barrier and the pavements alongside it are, for the most part, so narrow that pedestrians are encouraged to use subways for 'safe' passage around the environs. Above ground, the public open spaces are so seriously ravaged by traffic noise and pollution as to feel like the roadside verge. Of course, much the same can be said about the Colosseum in Rome and many other internationally important heritage assets.

However impoverished the current setting of the Tower might be in environmental and aesthetic terms, it is an important historic space in its own right. It just cannot be read as such very easily today. Across many centuries, the primary defensive function (both real and overtly symbolic) of the Tower of London was not to protect the capital from river-borne invasion, but to impose the will of the Crown upon the often reluctant City of London, and its administrators and inhabitants. The history of the development of the surrounding urban area (as distinct from the history of the Tower of London) is a fascinating one. Innumerable examples might be quoted of the continuing open and deep-seated conflict between these two powers from the Tower's construction in the late eleventh century through to the mid-to-late 1800s. During this time, the wider urban area

Figure 2.16 (a)–(b)   The Tower of London and its modern urban setting in 2006 and 2013.

(which also happens to be the setting of the fortress) can be viewed as a political, social and cultural 'battlefield', with the ongoing history of physical development, ownership and rights reflecting the ebb and flow of power and influence between these two forces, as well as the 'efforts and aspirations' of the many generations of local people.

Crucially, the current urban setting of the Tower is the direct inheritance of several generations of part-implemented planned comprehensive solutions to the area's problems. Master plans, developed with the best of intents to address urban blight and squalor in the 1930s, 1950s, 1960s and 1970s, all concentrated on the importance of the Tower and its history to the exclusion of anything else. On each occasion, the Tower was conceived as being a self-contained historic monument that was solely responsible for any significance and cultural value in the wider locality. Its environs were only regarded as the means of approach to the monument, not as being a cohesive and meaningful historic area in its own right (Figures 2.12 (a) and (b)). This attitude has repeatedly pervaded re-planning of its future. The result has been sequential piecemeal yet radical restructuring of the environs as a setting for the Tower of London and no more. In the long term, this approach has been of no benefit. Critically, it has not re-engendered any sense of place. Instead, with each cycle of change, the principal outcome has been merely to leave further residues of discordant and inharmonious elements as a legacy to the future.

This situation is far from unique. On many occasions, there are very real risks in treating the urban setting of a monument as being to some extent subordinate, risking implying that it has lacked a development history of its own, and therefore is open to shaping or stultification of change to suit the perceived needs of its influential neighbour. This approach reinforces the belief that our towns and cities consist, in essence, of isolated historic jewels or cores of elegance (each of which should ideally be protected by an umbra of appropriateness) surrounded by the historically or culturally valueless and dispensable. The lasting effect of this attitude is the total concealment of the importance of the 'vital contest' (between socio-economic forces of change and persistence of the built historic grain) to urban existence. As observed, the importance of buffer zones is already enshrined within the *Operational Guidelines for World Heritage*. At that level, undoubtedly, there is a strong justification for ensuring wider protection of assets of 'outstanding universal value' (although the shortcomings with the setting of the Tower of London – itself a World Heritage Site – must remain an object lesson). The problem is exacerbated, however, when dealing with the need to protect more modest heritage assets from the deleterious influence of unsatisfactory development in their setting. It is conceivable that, in the coming years, pressure will grow to protect some historic urban areas of note by the designation of a setting or buffer zone in which additional planning controls can be applied. At that level, the 'sacrifice' of one area's ongoing organic development to benefit another could well prove hard to justify. The key will be in the nature and derivation of the additional planning controls applied to the setting/buffer zone. If these are built from an understanding of the value and significance of the setting, the arrangement may provide sustainable solutions; if they are based solely upon the significance and needs of the dominant heritage asset, unsustainable and ultimately damaging change will occur.

The foregoing suggests that the management of change in settings to heritage assets and, by implication in protective buffer zones, can be a challenging issue, perhaps more so and for different reasons than is even now recognised, despite the development of helpful guidance on settings in recent years.

Intangible heritage

This book deals with the sustainable management of built heritage. While intangible values are often a vital and significant component of such assets, and will be mentioned further in Chapter 3, an assessment of management issues affecting intangible heritage (for example, language, folklore and assets such as sacred mountains) lies beyond our current scope. For this reason, intangible heritage will not be covered in this brief review of heritage assets.

Owners, managers and management approaches

The analysis of heritage asset types set out above has sought to demonstrate that assets, individually or as an estate, are subject to different management regimes and approaches according to ownership patterns. This is a fundamental point.

Individual property owners or tenants view the act of management and the nature of their management responsibilities in a very different manner to corporate, institutional or governmental asset managers. Among other things, organisations as property managers must often have regard to the influence and expectations of external stakeholders. By and large, individuals manage the buildings they own or lease solely for their own needs and interests. It would be incorrect, as well as being potentially invidious, to suggest that one or other group takes better management decisions or cares more for the special interest of a heritage asset. They are exposed to very different pressures and influences, and manage in contrasting ways.

For as long as their freehold or leasehold interest exists, individual owners or tenants provide continuity in property management. Conversely, the individual is unlikely to perceive their use, care and alteration of the historic building as equating to 'management'. Therein lies the inherent threat that such 'managers' pose to the significance of their property. Without a framework of management policies and strategies, it is unlikely that they will readily associate individual actions with the potential to inflict lasting damage on vulnerable aspects of significance.

The professional manager frequently comes with very different 'baggage'. To some, property management is merely a 9-to-5 job undertaken using someone else's money. While this does not necessarily prevent the care that they give to a heritage asset being entirely professional, for better or worse, it will hardly equate to the devotion applied by a proud home owner. Of course, neither is guaranteed to achieve appropriate sound care of the heritage asset and both can have highly undesirable results. They are, however, fundamentally different management approaches, which are likely to influence the nature of ongoing change in the asset.

Generalist (as in, non-heritage) property managers are no more likely to manage in a way that respects the significance of a historic site than the average individual freeholder or lessee. Often, the application of standard 'one-size-fits-all' management approaches and procedures across a mixed portfolio of building types (in other words, a combination of heritage and non-heritage assets) is likely to result in undesirable or ill-judged repairs or changes to the historic structure. With an individual owner, problems often occur through a lack of understanding of conservation ideas, particularly perhaps in relation to awareness of the cumulative harm that may occur through small, but regular, changes to the fabric, as well the sense that appearance is the primary issue and therefore that the replacement or repair of original material is not contestable as long as the new look likes the old (in other words, that appearance is more important than, or the same as, character).

It might be assumed that heritage management organisations are *per se* better equipped to manage heritage assets in a more caring and appropriate way than generalist property or portfolio managers. It is arguable that this is not always borne out in practice. Heritage management organisations tend to be somewhat idiosyncratic and self-absorbed. They are certainly frequently fraught with unique tensions between those with responsibility for aesthetics, maintenance and works, and commercial and operational managers whose fundamental objective is to get things done to improve the standard of facilities and increase income generation.

There are two fundamental problems that pervade both non-heritage and heritage property management organisations. First, with frequent personnel changes, all are prone to iterative loss of 'understanding' (or institutional memory) about the assets under their control and loss of ownership of planned initiatives. This can lead to weakening of focus, much wasted expenditure, and the tendency to 'reinvent the wheel' with astonishing regularity. Second, the quality of property management is very often seriously compromised by the inability to cascade understanding and ownership down to those whose job is to action day-to-day maintenance and repair tasks. This puts the vulnerable heritage asset at continuous risk of compromise or lasting harm, since works will tend to be undertaken without comprehension of their sensitivity, in a manner which suits the maintenance operative rather than the specific needs of the asset and its significance. Whatever the nature of the manager of a heritage asset, therein lies the challenge to conservation planning as a management approach. Unless the decision-makers and the day-to-day operatives possess shared ownership of the management process and of the assessment of the asset's significance, they are unlikely to reach sound strategic decisions and also implement appropriate physical actions that respect and seek to enhance its wider special interest and value.

References

Australia ICOMOS (2013) *The Burra Charter*. Burwood, VIC, Australia, Australia ICOMOS. Inc.

Bettey, J.H. (1993) *The Estates and the English Countryside*. London, Batsford.

Brand, S. (1994) *How Buildings Learn: What Happens After They're Built?* New York, Viking Penguin.

Byrne, D. *et al.* (2003) *Social Significance: A Discussion Paper*. New South Wales, National Parks and Wildlife Service.

Cameron, D. (2014) *Scotland's Community Land Ownership Story*, available at: https://www.opendemocracy.net/ourkingdom/david-cameron/scotlands-community-land-ownership-story

Country Life (2010) *Who Really Owns Britain?* November 2010 edition Time Inc UK Ltd.

DCLG (Department for Communities and Local Government) (2014) *Planning Practice Guidance: Conserving and Enhancing the Historic Environment*. London, Department for Communities and Local Government.

DCMS (Department for Culture Media and Sport) (2007) *Heritage Protection for the 21st Century*, White Paper. London, Department for Culture Media and Sport.

English Heritage (2008) *Conservation Principles, Policies and Guidance: Sustainable Management of the Historic Environment*. London, English Heritage.

English Heritage (2011) *The Setting of Heritage Assets*. London, English Heritage.

English Heritage (2012) *PPS5: Planning for the Historic Environment Practice Guide*. London, English Heritage.

Feilden, B.M. and Jokilehto, J. (1993) *Management Guidelines for World Cultural Heritage Sites*. Rome, ICCROM.

Fowler, P. (2001) Cultural landscape: great concept, pity about the phrase. In *The Cultural Landscape: Planning for a Sustainable Partnership between People and Place* (eds R. Kelly, L. Macinnes, D. Thackray and P. Whitbourne). London, ICOMOS UK, pp. 64–82.

Fowler, P. (2002) World Heritage Cultural Landscapes, 1992–2002: a review and prospect. In *Cultural Landscapes: The Challenges of Conservation*. UNESCO World Heritage Papers 7. Paris, UNESCO.

Historic England (2015) *Historic Environment Good Practice Advice in Planning 3: The Setting of Heritage Assets*. London, Historic England.

Historic Scotland (2010) *Managing Change in the Historic Environment: Setting*. Edinburgh, Historic Scotland.

ICOMOS (1964) *International Charter for the Conservation and Restoration of Monuments and Sites: 2nd International Congress of Architects and Technicians of Historic Monuments*, Venice, Article 6 (The Venice Charter). Available at: www.icomos.org/en/charters-and-texts

ICOMOS (1987) *Charter for the Conservation of Historic Towns and Urban Areas (adopted by ICOMOS General Assembly, Washington, DC), (The Washington Charter)*. Paris, ICOMOS.

ICOMOS (1993) *Tourism at World Heritage Cultural Sites: The Site Manager's Handbook*. Paris, ICOMOS.

Kostoff, S. (1991) *The City Shaped*. London, Thames and Hudson.

Larkham, P. (1996) *Conservation and the City*. London, Routledge.

Lewis, P. (1979) Axioms for reading the landscape: some guides to the American scene. In *The Interpretation of Ordinary Landscapes: Geographical Essays* (ed. D.W. Meinig). New York, Oxford University Press.

Lowenthal, D. (1985) *The Past Is a Foreign Country*. Cambridge, Cambridge University Press.

Sauer, C. (1925) Morphology of landscape. In *University of California Publications in Geography*. Berkeley, CA, University of California Press.

Scazzosi, L. (2002) Landscape and cultural landscape: European Landscape Convention and UNESCO Policy. In *UNESCO World Heritage Papers 7: Cultural Landscapes: The Challenges of Conservation*. Paris, UNESCO.

UNESCO (1972) *Convention Concerning the Protection of the World Cultural and Natural Heritage.* Paris, UNESCO.

UNESCO (2012) *Operational Guidelines for the Implementation of the World Heritage Convention.* Paris, UNESCO.

UNESCO et al. (2013) *Managing Cultural World Heritage: The World Heritage Resource Manual.* Paris, UNESCO.

United Nations (1987) *Report of the World Commission on Environment and Development (the Brundtland Report).* New York, United Nations'.

Chapter 3

Heritage Values and Cultural Significance

Conservation is about negotiating the transition from past to future in such a way as to secure the transfer of maximum significance.

(Holland and Rawles, 1993)

The conservation of heritage assets in a manner appropriate to their significance is a core planning principle.

(DCLG, 2012)

The Getty Conservation Institute (GCI) report, *Values and Heritage Conservation* observes: 'The creation of cultural heritage is largely derived from the way people remember, organise, think about and wish to use the past and how material culture provides a medium through which to do this' (Avrami *et al.*, 2000, p. 8). But as Zancheti and Jokilehto (1997) observe: 'Conservation is a process that can only exist if society attributes values to the urban structure.'

Much of the literature in conservation refers to the values which are embodied in, or represented by, built heritage, and it uses the idea of protecting these values in order to explain and justify the purpose of conservation and its importance for individuals, groups and nations. The idea of protecting values is fundamental to the notion of conservation activity. The Getty Conservation Institute report, for example, suggests: 'The ultimate aim of conservation is not to conserve material for its own sake but rather to maintain (and shape) the values embodied by the heritage – with physical interventions or treatment being one of many means towards that end' (Avrami *et al.*, 2000, p. 7).

The term 'cultural significance', generally shortened simply to 'significance', is used to refer to the totality of heritage values associated with an asset that together identify why it is important. The Burra Charter (Australia ICOMOS,

Managing Built Heritage: The Role of Cultural Values and Significance, Second Edition.
Stephen Bond and Derek Worthing.
© 2016 Stephen Bond and Derek Worthing. Published 2016 by John Wiley & Sons, Ltd.

2013) suggests: 'Cultural significance is embodied in the place itself, its fabric, setting, use, associations, meanings, records, related places and related objects.' The identification, measurement, protection and enhancement of cultural significance form the basis of what has come to be referred to as 'values-based management' or 'significance-based management' (and as we stated earlier, we will use the latter term in this book).

It is suggested that societies protect certain aspects of the built environment because conservation brings benefits. This assertion raises the question not only of what these qualities are, but how they are identified, by whom, and for what reasons (and who benefits).

It is then the sense that the built heritage embodies and represents a range of, often complex, sometimes conflicting, values that bring benefits, which is behind the idea of conservation. As Mason observes (2002, p. 8), 'Heritage is valued not as an intellectual enterprise but because (as one aspect of material culture) it plays instrumental, symbolic and other functions in society.' This point is reflected in the document *Power of Place* (English Heritage, 2000, p. 4) which states, 'The historic environment is what generations of people have made of the places in which they lived. It is all about us. We are the trustees of that inheritance. It is in every sense a common wealth.'

Benefits of conservation

In his seminal book *The Past Is a Foreign Country*, David Lowenthal discusses the 'benefits and burdens of the past'. He observes that, although there is a general consensus about past-related benefits (and he is concerned not just with the built environment here), they are seldom articulated, and so he sets out these categories (1997, pp. 38–52):

- *Familiarity: The surviving past's most essential and pervasive benefit is to render the present familiar. Its traces on the ground and in our minds let us make sense of the present. Without habit and the memory of past experience, no sight or sound would mean anything; we can perceive only what we are accustomed to.*
- *Reaffirmation and validation: The past validates present attributes and actions by their resemblance to former ones.*
- *Identity: The past is integral to our sense of identity ... Ability to recall and identify with our own past gives existence meaning, purpose and value ... Even traumatically painful memories remain essential, emotional history.*
- *Guidance: The past is most characteristically evoked for the lessons it teaches.*
- *Enrichment: A well-loved past enriches the world around us.*
- *Escape: ... besides enhancing an acceptable present, the past offers alternatives to an unacceptable present. In yesterday we find what we*

miss today. And yesterday is a time for which we have no responsibility and when no one can answer back.

Lowenthal says: 'No sharp boundaries delimit these benefits' and he observes, for example, that a sense of identity is also a mode of enrichment and that familiarity provides guidance. He also observes that some of these benefits are in conflict and gives as an example 'using the past to enrich present-day life is at odds with wanting to escape from the present'. Indeed, escape from the present is seen as a negative aspect of an 'obsession with the past' associated with what Robert Hewison (1987) identified as 'The Heritage Industry' in his well-known and rather polemical book of the same name.

It can be suggested that the benefit of conservation in a general sense might include the five points discussed below.

1   There are significant benefits to the social, psychological and political well-being of individuals, groups and nations – or indeed collections of nations

In essence, the benefits that Lowenthal (1997) refers to are congruent with these social, psychological and political concerns. The notion is that the physical evidence of the past holds meaning for individuals and/or groups. Mason (2002, p. 11) suggests that 'The capacity of a site to convey, embody or stimulate a relation or a reaction to the past is part of the fundamental nature and meaning of heritage objects.' In part, this is related to relatively intangible concepts such as the idea of a collective memory and the sense that the physical remains of the past can embody, represent and stimulate this. The argument is that the ability to connect to the past is important because it, among other things, 'gives existence meaning, purpose and value' (Lowenthal, 1997). This might work at a national level with often symbolic values being at play – the role of the restoration, or in many cases re-creation, of iconic buildings or structures following war or other disasters is an obvious example. But it can of course happen at a smaller group level, where a building can symbolically represent the development or values of particular factions and therefore play a positive role in reinforcing and acknowledging shared values and reinforcing notions of community identity. However, it can have the opposite effect, and polarise and exclude by reinforcing and validating a particular view of the past.

Hubbard, in a paper entitled 'The value of conservation' asserts: 'It is apparent that the townscape must be considered extremely important for stabilising individual and group identities, particularly in times of stress' (1993, p. 266). In addition, he quotes Rowntree's comment that 'loss of cultural identity can be alleviated through the creation of shared symbolic structures that validate, if not actually define, social claims to space and time'. Hubbard suggests that this notion of shared but constructed value is important for community cohesion in a fragmented world. Thus the designation of places as having cultural value means the built environment can have a special function in creating and stabilising group identity. Stokols and Jacobi (1983) suggested that the bond between place and identity can give cultures a sense of historic perspective and belonging, but that the process for doing this may not be necessarily conscious and that the values may be difficult to discern or disentangle. Hubbard concludes that conserved environments generally create a sense of place and that this is imbued by people with cultural meaning, and that 'Conservation must be viewed as an important means by which groups can maintain their socio-cultural identity.' Interestingly, though he also makes the point that 'the public tend to exhibit a profound ambivalence towards the historicity of the townscape'. By implication, this suggests that 'historicity in itself cannot act as an adequate basis for conservation policy' and he suggests that buildings should not be preserved merely for their historicity alone, but because of their value for the wider community. This underlines the importance of involving communities in such processes as conservation plans and heritage impact statements in order to properly understand the value of heritage assets. Again as Hubbard (1993) observes: 'Artistic qualities cannot be abstracted without considering those functional characteristics and the role that these buildings play in the everyday lives of ordinary people.'

The European Charter of the Architectural Heritage (Council of Europe, 1975, p. 1) picks up on some of these themes when it states:

> *The past as embodied in the architectural heritage provides the sort of environment indispensable to a balanced and composite life. In the face of a rapidly changing civilisation in which brilliant successes are accompanied by grave perils, people today have an instinctive feeling for the value of this heritage. This heritage should be passed onto future generations in its authentic state and in all its variety as an essential part of the memory of the human race. Otherwise, part of man's awareness of his own continuity will be destroyed.*

In an essay, entitled 'Do we need a past?', the Swedish philosopher, Sören Halldén, wrote:

> *The intensity of the awareness of life's continuity depends on the extent to which a society is enlivened with history. Monuments and settlement patterns contribute a great deal to the process of enlivening International conservation.*
>
> *Why do we need such an enlivened environment in much the same way that animals need biological territory? With a few exceptions, most living creatures find it rewarding to live in an environment enriched with memories. Knowing what it is all about makes one feel more secure. This very basic biological fact is still valid within environments that we have made relatively safe by other means (by social welfare, for example). In our context, cultural identity is the sense of belonging created by many*

aspects of the physical environment that remind us of links between the present generation and the historical past.

(Halldén, 1983)

The notion that there may also be benefits to groups of nations is also well established (if not necessarily agreed upon). For example, the Council of Europe (2005) refers to the common heritage of Europe, which, it states, consists of:

1 *All forms of cultural heritage in Europe which together constitute a shared source of remembrance, understanding, identity, cohesion and creativity; and*
2 *The ideals, principles and values, derived from the experience gained through progress and past conflicts, which foster the development of a peaceful and stable society, founded on respect for human rights, democracy and the rule of law.*

It has been suggested that 'the cultural heritage of each is the cultural heritage of all' (ICOMOS, 1994) and that 'damage to cultural property belonging to any people whatsoever means damage to the cultural heritage of all mankind, since each people makes its contribution to the culture of the world' (UNESCO, 1954).

At the 1984 ICOMOS General Assembly held in Germany, the Rapporteur, Dr Roland Palsson, spoke of the crucial importance of peace and international co-operation as the basic prerequisites for the conservation of cultural heritage (ICOMOS, 1987a). He recognised that the concept of cultural heritage was widening as the differences in the traditions and context of cultures and societies were taken into account. This increasing awareness of cultural diversity and pluralism gives hope for increased tolerance and respect for ethnic and religious minorities and for local opinions. Most particularly, cultural identity, having dimensions in both time and space, provides an essential framework for people's lives and activities.

The hope for peace and international co-operation is picked up by UNESCO, which operates its World Heritage programmes as a core part of its mission to 'create the conditions for dialogue among civilizations, cultures and peoples ... encompassing observance of human rights, mutual respect and the alleviation of poverty'. Elsewhere, the World Bank has invested in cultural heritage programmes in tandem with making major infrastructure loans to developing and transition national economies (frequently as part of post-conflict rehabilitation), because it sees this as being a powerful way to engender economic stability and growth. Cultural heritage can be a beneficial and benign tool in the search for peace, international stability, communication among and the forging of links between peoples, the sharing of common values, and respect for cultural diversity.

2   *There are significant educational benefits: that we can understand aspects of past societies not only through analysis of the physical remains of the past but also the historic environment is a focus and an opportunity for a less 'expert' engagement with the lives and experiences of previous generations*

In the same way that we suggest that the buildings we construct today reflect the values of modern society, those from the past can help us to understand the political, social, economic and cultural values of previous societies. As *Power of Place* (English Heritage, 2000) observes, 'The historic environment is an incomparable source of information. For people in the distant past and for more recent generations whose history was never recorded, it offers the only route towards an understanding of who they were and how they lived.'

3   *As existing buildings, they are a resource that should be reused for (environmental and financial) sustainability reasons*

Heritage assets are often the focus for, and driver of, regeneration projects. Also, as with all existing buildings, their continued use (or their reuse with a changed function), usually consumes less energy than would be the case in the construction of a new building. That is, the existing building represents the embodied energy (the environmental capital), that has already been expended in its construction, whereas a replacement building, even one that is energy-efficient, will consume non-renewable resources in the demolition of the old and the construction of the new. Also less waste is produced and the development of greenfield sites is avoided.

4   *The historic environment contributes to a sense of place through its character and its visual aesthetic*

In many cases, the built heritage is a strong defining force or anchor for a sense of place (*genus loci*) that can be identified and appreciated by inhabitants and visitors. For some, the extent and intensity of such identification may be determined by the knowledge and understanding of the place that the person or group has, particularly in relation to factors such as present and previous uses or the nature and meaning of events which may have taken place there. The asset may be important as the repository of a cultural memory that reinforces group identity.

5   *Historic buildings and areas attract significant tourist revenue and make significant contributions to local, regional and sometimes national economies and employment*

This point needs little further expansion here, for we have already observed that the World Bank recognises the considerable potential of cultural heritage programmes to assist in the stabilisation and reinvigoration of regional and national economies damaged by conflict. In most such situations, this will be reliant upon the development of a significant cultural tourism industry.

The benefit of both built and natural heritage to stable developed economies is demonstrated by numerous case studies. For example, the Heritage Lottery Fund-commissioned report, *The Economic Impact of the UK Heritage Tourism Industry* (El Beyrouty and Tessler, 2013) stated that the heritage-based tourism economy directly accounts for at least £5 billion in GDP and supports 134,000 jobs, and that once indirect and induced effects are taken into account, then this rises to at least £14 billion and 393,000 jobs.

It is tempting to add the comment that all of the above justifications of the benefits associated with conserving the past may be unnecessary if one accepts the notion that (in a similar vein to Oliver Wendell Holmes' statement: 'I like to pay taxes, with them I buy civilisation'), conserving the past is what civilised societies do. That is, we would suggest that conservation of built heritage, as a notion and an activity, has an intrinsic value. Holden (2004) perhaps has this in mind when he suggests that it is necessary to promote a '"strong" culture, confident in its own worth, instead of a "weak" culture dedicated to the production of ancillary benefits'.

However, there will always remain the question (as with taxes) about whose values and interests are being served, and therefore attempts to measure and articulate benefits in a transparent and understandable manner are necessary both in general and for the particular place, and arguably such a process is usually an aid to understanding the cultural significance of an asset. As Hewison (2003), in pointing out that public value is more than value for money, observes:

> *The measure of Value for Money is Economy, Efficiency and Effectiveness, but you can only judge the economy and efficiency of a work of art once you know its intrinsic, rather than instrumental effectiveness. Effectiveness in art is not measurable by targets, tables and testing. In the arts, there is no equivalence in the implied equation, Value for Money, when value is moral, not monetary, expressive, not instrumental, aesthetic, not utilitarian. There needs to be a new accountability, not of value for money, but money for values.*

The issue was also addressed in a DEMOS report, *Capturing Cultural Value* (Holden, 2004) – albeit about a range of cultural activities – which observed that 'the consequences of cultural engagement are too remote in time and space to be a matter of simple cause and effect'.

In a paper entitled 'The value of heritage', Smith (2010) considers the concept of the 'public value' of heritage which, he says,

> *appears to be an interesting idea for assessing the worth of cultural heritage, and could also, in the fullness of time, evolve into a useable tool. It is, however, important that, as competition for scarce resources becomes*

ever more fierce, we are able to quantify the value of heritage in realistic, responsive, easily understandable and robust ways.

He warns that to simply quantify the value of built heritage in monetary terms is to ignore fundamentally important intangible, essentially humanistic components of value which cannot readily be expressed in this uni-dimensional way. He then goes on to state:

> *there is plainly the need for a recognition within the mainstream of planning, policymaking and public sector funding that conserving heritage pays – even if it is not always easily assessable in financial terms. In order to support this view, it is, of course, necessary for heritage conservers to mobilise sufficient public opinion and political influence to ensure that the initial 'money value only' hypothesis fails. Such a view plainly requires a close understanding of the intangible culturally significant values involved, and an acceptance by those with political power and influence that, even if they cannot be quantified in a deterministic way, proper consideration of these values is an important factor in ensuring the future growth, well-being and stability of a mature and caring society.*
>
> (Smith, 2010)

Whether or not the attempt to marry economic and social benefits with the type of research that suggests that 'The impact of visiting historical sites on wellbeing is statistically significant and the amount of money which provides the same impact on wellbeing as visiting heritage overall is calculated as £1,646 per person per year' (English Heritage, 2014) has an effect on perceptions or decision-making is an interesting debate.

English Heritage (1997) articulated most of these benefits by suggesting that:

> *Historic buildings are a precious and finite asset, and powerful reminders to us of the work and way of life of earlier generations. The richness of this country's architectural heritage plays a powerful part in our sense of national identity and our enjoyment of our surroundings.*

The Charter for the Conservation of Places of Cultural Heritage Value (ICOMOS New Zealand, 1993) states:

> *In general, such places:*
>
> - *Have lasting values and can be appreciated in their own right;*
> - *Teach us about the past and the culture of those who came before us;*
> - *Provide the context for community identity whereby people relate to the land and to those who have gone before;*
> - *Provide variety and contrast in the modern world and a measure against which we can compare the achievements of today;*

- *Provide visible evidence of the continuity between past, present and future.*

In a similar vein, The Burra Charter (Australia ICOMOS, 2013) suggests, 'there are places worth keeping because they enrich our lives: by helping us understand the past; by contributing to the richness of the present environment; and because we expect them to be of value to future generations.'

To a large extent, these are potential rather than actual benefits. For example, realising educational benefit not only requires the active engagement of people but also a commitment by the owners and managers of historic places to inclusive access strategies and the development of objective interpretation strategies.

Power of Place recognised the need to deliver actual benefits in observing that:

> *many feel powerless and excluded [when] the historical contribution of their group to society is not celebrated. Their personal heritage does not appear to be taken into account by those who make decisions ... if the barriers to involvement are overcome, the historic environment has the potential to strengthen a sense of community and provide a solid basis for neighbourhood renewal.*
>
> (English Heritage, 2000, p. 23)

Understanding the cultural significance of a heritage asset

Understanding the cultural significance of a heritage asset and being able to articulate what the values that make up its significance are, – and which aspects embody and represent them – have come to be seen as a crucial task in 'significance-based management' of the built cultural heritage. As Mason (2002, p. 5) points out, 'Assessment of the values attributed to heritage is a very important activity in any conservation effort, since values strongly shape the decisions that are made.' It follows that, to achieve effectiveness, it is important that there is an integration of value-led decision-making at all levels (in the organisation that is responsible for the asset) which addresses the issues of what to protect, how to protect it, how to prioritise and how to address conflicting interests.

We would suggest that the idea of significance-based management should be centred upon:

- The principle that in order to protect and manage a place, you need to know why it is important, and what elements contribute to that importance;
- The point that the importance of an asset (and what it is that contributes to that importance) cannot be inferred or assumed, but needs to be demonstrated by understanding the asset and assessing its significance through a rigorous, transparent and objective process.

Development in the idea of values

We can see that the basis of today's conservation values, at least in a Western, or, perhaps more specifically a Northern European context, were articulated in the Victorian period through the writings of William Morris and John Ruskin. These two men, in inspiring the development of the early conservation movement, articulated the idea of the stewardship of existing resources, the spiritual and educational value of the built cultural heritage and a concern for the fabric of these buildings as a physical manifestation that embodied and represented these values. At the same time, they honoured the skill, artistry and spirit of those who had created them. Such ideas emphasised the sense of the uniqueness of the authentic fabric of historic buildings, which was a physical expression of cultural values and concerns, and a resource for education and social development.

In the UK, despite the concerns of the early conservation movement about the importance of the work of the craftsmen and the value of 'everyday buildings', protection was originally focused on protecting monuments – either empty buildings, ruins or iconic buildings. The idea of protecting a wider range of buildings developed over the first half of the twentieth century, culminating in the setting-up of the listing system in the period following the Second World War – a position that was at least partly influenced by the destruction of (historic) buildings during the air raids. However, the dominant ethos was still one of architectural aesthetics and a focus on individual prestigious buildings of historic value or artistic achievement (based on class and power), combined with notions of protecting pleasing amenity views. It was damage of a different kind, or rather from a different source, that encouraged the setting-up of conservation areas in the 1960s. Their creation was originally, at least in part, a response to the perceived damage to the context, and therefore the integrity, of listed buildings, caused by new roads, slum clearances and urban development projects that often left them physically and 'spiritually' isolated.

In recent years the focus has moved away from what to protect (although the listing of post-war structures has re-ignited that debate) to a development in the ideas about which qualities are to be valued. Perhaps the most important shift in attitude is towards the acceptance of a wider-ranging and more inclusive idea of what is of value. The idea that 'the everyday' (particularly where it traces the development of a wider range of social movements or where it embodies associations and memories for different social groups) might be as valuable as the iconic high points of artistic and historical development has come to be accepted, if not entirely acted upon.

International charters

It is possible to track some of these changes, in ideas of the value and the benefits of conserving the built cultural heritage, through developments in the concerns raised and focused on by various international charters.

After the Second World War, the United Nations and its agencies, such as UNESCO, were formed. Key individuals from UNESCO, the International Centre for the Study and the Preservation and Restoration of Cultural Property (ICCROM) and other internationally focused organisations drafted the Venice Charter, which was adopted by the International Council on Monuments and Sites (ICOMOS) on its foundation in 1965. The Venice Charter reinforced the international nature of the issues of conservation and it laid down a framework that considered the courses of action that were acceptable in deciding on how to protect 'monuments'. It was very much a product of its time: an attempt to deal with individual, usually iconic, monuments, where redevelopment was seen as a severe threat to the historic environment. Although it made reference to 'a common heritage' and referred to more 'modest works of the past which have acquired cultural significance with the passing of time', it nevertheless did seem to emphasise works of art rather than the more 'everyday'. Article 3, which stated that the 'intention in conserving and restoring monuments is to safeguard them no less as works of art than as historical evidence' (ICOMOS, 1964, p. 1), illustrates this point.

The Venice Charter has been criticised for its 'euro-centric' perspective and for concentrating on monuments (although the term has a more inclusive sense in the rest of Europe than it has in the UK). However, the Charter was of vital importance – a seminal document that stressed the requirement to preserve the authenticity and integrity of the 'monument', and the need for proper documentation before, during and after essential interventions.

In the latter part of the 1960s and through the 1970s there was an increasing emphasis on the importance of 'the everyday', and a sense that those assets that were not considered important according to the criteria of art history and age were nevertheless of value. Bell (1997) draws attention to UNESCO's concerns in the 1976 document *Recommendation Concerning the Safeguarding and Contemporary Role of Historic Areas* (UNESCO, 1976) and its emphasis on the importance of recognising the 'significance and message' of the composition of minor buildings in long-established settlements. There was also in this period a growing awareness of the need to place conservation in its wider context, and we start to see it being related to what we now see as issues of sustainability, in relation not only to physical resources, but also in economic and social terms.

Charters such as the Washington Charter of 1987 (ICOMOS, 1987b), which looked at historic towns and urban areas, continued the examination of broader concerns and the need for holistic and integrative policies for conservation which related to wider economic and social development issues and the general spatial planning context. The *Nara Document on Authenticity* (ICOMOS, 1994) reflected the sense of a growing acknowledgement of a range of values associated with the built cultural heritage. This is reflected in that document's statement that:

> all judgements about values attributed to cultural properties as well as the credibility of related information sources may differ from culture to culture and even within the same culture. It is thus not possible to base judgements of value and authenticity within fixed criteria.

The Charter on the Built Vernacular Heritage (ICOMOS, 1999) captured the idea of the social value of heritage when it stated:

> *The built vernacular heritage occupies a central place in the affection and pride of all peoples. It has been accepted as a characteristic and attractive product of society. It appears informal, but nevertheless orderly. It is utilitarian and at the same time possesses interest and beauty. It is a focus of contemporary life and at the same time a record of the history of society. Although it is the work of man, it is also the creation of time. It would be unworthy of the heritage of man if care were not taken to conserve these traditional harmonies which constitute the core of man's own existence.*
>
> *The built vernacular heritage is important; it is the fundamental expression of the culture of a community, of its relationship with its territory and, at the same time, the expression of the world's cultural diversity.*
>
> *Vernacular building is the traditional and natural way by which communities house themselves. It is a continuing process including necessary changes and continuous adaptation as a response to social and environmental constraints. The survival of this tradition is threatened worldwide by the forces of economic, cultural and architectural homogenisation. How these forces can be met is a fundamental problem that must be addressed by communities and also by governments, planners, architects, conservationists and by a multidisciplinary group of specialists.*

Other key developments in the recent evolution of conservation thinking have spread from, on the one hand, Eastern Europe and, on the other, from East and South-East Asia. Political turmoil in many Eastern European countries after 1989 led to the birth (or reappearance) of a number of nations and new cultural alliances. People began to dream of the revitalisation of their cultural roots, as a potent symbol of newly won or regained identity. Basic components of international heritage, which in many cases had been suppressed or prohibited for decades or more, came to be considered as being vital elements in supporting and sustaining people in the process of nation-building (or rebuilding).

At the same time, it became evident elsewhere in the world that economic development strategies designed around Western models could not be applied rigidly or simplistically to communities with very different cultural traditions. At international gatherings, representatives from Pacific Rim countries raised awareness of intangible aspects of heritage, since traditionally these cultures and societies had been permeated with spiritual and other intangible values and associations that were poorly served by the 'monumental' focus of Western-dominated thinking on heritage protection. In the early 1990s, recognition grew that urgent action was needed to protect the region's extensive intangible cultural heritage, which was under threat from rapid social change sparked by strong economic growth.

These two contemporaneous catalysts initiated a period of extensive international debate on intangible heritage issues, much of which occurred within

forums provided by international organisations such as UNESCO and ICO-
MOS. Opinion and accepted wisdom on the nature of cultural heritage and the
value of its intangible aspects have developed radically in the past 20 or so years.
UNESCO's Convention for the Safeguarding of the Intangible Cultural Heritage
acknowledged that intangible cultural heritage (or 'living heritage') is the main-
spring of our cultural diversity and its maintenance proffers a guarantee for continuing creativity (UNESCO, 2003). Over the past 60 years, the Western world
has become increasingly secular and material in its focus, at times, seemingly
besotted by transience and ephemera. As a result, many find it hard to recognise
or appreciate the importance of intangible values. The 2003 Convention provides a marker, reflecting a growing understanding that our intangible cultural
heritage is traditional and living at the same time. It sees intangible cultural heritage as being manifested in oral traditions and language, the performing arts,
social practices, rituals and festive events, knowledge, and craftsmanship. As
such, intangible cultural heritage:

- Is transmitted from generation to generation;
- Is constantly recreated by communities and groups, in response to their envi-
  ronment, their interaction with nature, and their history;
- Provides communities and groups with a sense of identity and continuity;
- Promotes respect for cultural diversity and human creativity;
- Is compatible with international human rights instruments;
- Complies with the requirements of mutual respect among communities, and
  of sustainable development.

The reawakening of awareness of the intangible dimension to heritage has
had a profound effect upon the practice of conservation around the world
in the last decade, including in the United Kingdom. The notion of living heritage and our growing concentration on the concept that the historic
environment involves everything around us are compatible and convergent
views.

   As conservation practice has expanded into this new territory, it has become
clear that different considerations prevail and other management tools are
required. Some 30 years ago, in a conservation world dominated by tangible
elements of heritage and physical acts of preservation, conservation was often
regarded as being an artistic activity aided by scientific and historical knowledge. This notion sits less comfortably when dealing with, say, the management
of change in a cultural landscape, the protection of vulnerable intangible cultural
heritage or even safeguarding the character of a historic urban area threatened
by modern developments such as tall buildings.

   Much of the philosophical bedrock for today's conservation planning can
be seen to emanate from Australia ICOMOS and the Burra Charter. The Burra
Charter (Australia ICOMOS, 2013) was developed in Australia and was first
published in 1979. There have been several revisions with the latest (at the time
of writing) being produced in 2013. Based on the Venice Charter, this has proven

to be an immensely useful document for conservation practice everywhere, providing guidance on the conservation and management of places of cultural significance. The Burra Charter helped to broaden perspectives on what was important and why, and it emphasised the need to first understand and then to use conservation values to explicitly inform and lead management decisions. Perhaps more than any other post-war Charter, it has helped conservation to evolve. As this has happened, the Charter itself has been adapted, with the critical recognition of the less tangible aspects of cultural significance, including those embodied in sense of place, and the meanings and association that places have for people.

In the early years of the twenty-first century, conservation is no longer mainly or solely about the repair and protection of monuments and a philosophy based on the notion of the primacy of art and art history. That aspect of conservation has not been banished to the waste heap of history as a fashion of the nineteenth and twentieth centuries, but, internationally, it is no longer pre-eminent. For many in the Western world, this has involved a dramatically changing conceptual landscape as increasing emphasis is placed upon economic, social and cultural processes. As Feilden and Jokilehto (1993) observe, 'The tendency today is to understand cultural heritage in its broadest sense as containing all the signs that document the activities and achievements of human beings over time.'

Value characterisation: typologies

As we have observed, there has, over the past few years, been increasing debate and a re-examination of a range of cultural, social and economic values embodied in and represented by the built heritage and the means by which these can be identified and evaluated. Value characterisation has always been implicit but until relatively recently there has been little attempt at clearly articulating a common understanding of what those values are and how they might be expressed and utilised.

The values represented by the built heritage are diverse and complex. Older sites have multiple layers of history but newer sites can also be complicated because of the range of values that are or may be represented. Values are also sometimes difficult to 'measure' and it is partly because of this that attempts to do so have been avoided, but there have also been concerns expressed about the usefulness and the possible negative effect of categorising heritage values from both a conceptual and a pragmatic viewpoint. Avrami *et al.* (2000, p. 8) observe: 'Though the typologies of different scholars and disciplines vary, they each represent a reductionist approach to examining very complex issues of cultural significance.'

Despite the difficulties and concerns, we would suggest that it is important to have a range of values stated, rather than a situation where value judgements are clearly being made but where they are not being adequately articulated or made available for discussion and debate. That is, it is necessary to have a clear articulation of the cultural value of a place in order to inform decision-making in the context of 'significance-based management' (as well of course as being necessary to have a more definite reference point for measuring, articulating and justifying the case for suggesting that a particular place is important and should be protected). The other important aspect of this is that clearly setting out a values framework could be the basis for increasing accountability at both the level of identifying places worthy of protection and in respect of managing them, because it would allow more openness and transparency about decision-making by producing better opportunities for debate as well as scrutiny. It would also encourage and allow a greater understanding of the heritage asset for a wider constituency.

A value typology or categorisation needs to acknowledge the range of possible values in a place, to the extent that all stakeholders recognise that their interests are represented, and it follows from this that no one category of value should be assumed to be more intrinsically worthy than another.

There have been various attempts to characterise and categorise heritage values over the years. Some of the differences accentuate the problems of reaching an agreement on the range of values and what constitutes those values (and, indeed, the meanings of specific terms), but the differences also reflect the particular context and the time at which these were developed. Table 3.1 shows some of the better-known value categories that have been developed and proposed by individuals and organisations.

The rationale for which aspects of the built environment we should conserve has been traditionally dominated explicitly by (value) judgements that emphasise age or rarity and the idea of celebrating high art and culture as well as the icons of power and influence. Although Morris and Ruskin referred to age value (Ruskin wrote that 'the greatest glory of a building is its age') and artistic value (Morris referred to 'ancient monuments of art'), they also implicitly set out a wider range of values including educational and social values (Morris, 1877; Ruskin, 1989).

Riegl's (1902) is perhaps the most oft-quoted next attempt to articulate heritage values, and is particularly interesting because of the way in which he links the categories to conservation actions. For example, of age value he wrote: 'in principle it condemns every effort at conservation, every restoration, as nothing less than an unauthorised interference with the reign of natural law', which he saw as being in tension with historical value by suggesting that:

> *Prior disintegration by the forces of nature cannot be undone and should, therefore, not be removed even from the point of view of historical value. However, further disintegration from the present day into the future, as age value not only tolerates but even postulates, is from the standpoint of historical value, not only pointless but simply to be avoided, since any further disintegration hinders the scientific restoration of the original state of a work of man. Thus the cult of historical value must aim for the best possible preservation of a monument in its present state.*

Table 3.1 Examples of cultural value typologies.

Riegl (1902)	Feilden and Jokilehto (1993)	English Heritage (1997)	Mason (2002, p. 10)	Feilden (2003, p. 6)	Throsby (2006, p. 43)
• Age • Commemorative • Use • Newness	Cultural values: • Relative artistic or technical • Rarity Contemporary socio-economic values: • Economic • Functional • Educational • Social • Political	• Cultural value • Aesthetic value • Recreational value • Resource value • Economic importance	Sociocultural values: • Historical • Cultural/symbolic • Social • Spiritual/religious • Aesthetic Economic values: • Use (market) value • Non-use (non-market) values: – existence – option – bequest	• Emotional • Cultural • Use	• Aesthetic • Spiritual • Social • Historical • Symbolic • Authenticity

The Burra Charter Practice Note entitled 'Understanding and assessing cultural significance' (Australia ICOMOS, 2013b) categorises values under the following headings:

- *Aesthetic value refers to the sensory and perceptual experience of a place—that is, how we respond to visual and non-visual aspects such as sounds, smells and other factors having a strong impact on human thoughts, feelings and attitudes. Aesthetic qualities may include the concept of beauty and formal aesthetic ideals. Expressions of aesthetics are culturally influenced.*
- *Historic value is intended to encompass all aspects of history—for example, the history of aesthetics, art and architecture, science, spirituality and society. It therefore often underlies other values. A place may have historic value because it has influenced, or has been influenced by, an historic event, phase, movement or activity, person or group of people. It may be the site of an important event. For any place the significance will be greater where the evidence of the association or event survives at the place, or where the setting is substantially intact, than where it has been changed or evidence does not survive. However, some events or associations may be so important that the place retains significance regardless of such change or absence of evidence.*
- *Scientific value refers to the information content of a place and its ability to reveal more about an aspect of the past through examination or investigation of the place, including the use of archaeological techniques. The relative scientific value of a place is likely to depend on the importance of the information or data involved, on its rarity, quality or representativeness, and its potential to contribute further important information about the place itself or a type or class of place or to address important research questions.*
- *Social value refers to the associations that a place has for a particular community or cultural group and the social or cultural meanings that it holds for them.*
- *Spiritual value refers to the intangible values and meanings embodied in or evoked by a place, which give it importance in the spiritual identity, or the traditional knowledge, art and practices of a cultural group. Spiritual value may also be reflected in the intensity of aesthetic and emotional responses or community associations, and be expressed through cultural practices and related places. The qualities of the place may inspire a strong and/or spontaneous emotional or metaphysical response in people, expanding their understanding of their place, purpose and obligations in the world, particularly in relation to the spiritual realm.*

In 2008, English Heritage proposed a 'family' of values under headings which it explains as follows:

- *Evidential: 'Evidential value derives from the potential of a place to yield primary evidence about a past human activity. Physical remains of past human activity are the primary source of evidence about the substance and evolution of places and of the people and cultures that made them ... Their evidential value is proportionate to their potential to contribute to people's understanding of the past.'*

- *Historical: 'Historical value derives from the ways in which past people, events and aspects of life can be connected through a place to the present.'*

The document observes that historical value tends to be illustrative or associational (i.e. associated with a person, family event or movement).

- *Aesthetic: 'Aesthetic value relates to the way in which people draw sensory and intellectual stimulation from a place.'*
- *Communal: 'Communal value relates to the meanings of a place for the people who relate to it, or for whom it figures in their collective experience or memory and whose collective experience or memory it holds. Communal values are closely bound up with historical (particularly associational) and aesthetic values, but tend to have additional and specific aspects.'*

Categories of values

In our experience of conservation planning, we have found that the following categories of values have been useful and have worked well.

Aesthetic

In the UK, the term 'aesthetic' is sometimes used in this context, mainly in relation to visual perception rather than all the senses. As we have noted, the Burra Charter (Australia ICOMOS, 2013a) uses 'aesthetic' in this wider connotation, as does the aforementioned English Heritage document. The Charter then goes on to suggest that in considering aesthetic value, the questions to be addressed include:

- *Does the place have special compositional or uncommonly attractive qualities involving combinations of colour, textures, spaces, massing, detail, movement, unity, sounds, scents?*
- *Is the place distinctive within the setting or a prominent visual landmark?*
- *Does the place have qualities which are inspirational or which evoke strong feelings or special meanings?*
- *Is the place symbolic for its aesthetic qualities: for example, does it inspire artistic or cultural response, is it represented in art, photography, literature, folk art, folk lore, mythology or other imagery or cultural arts?*
- *Does the place display particular aesthetic characteristics of an identified style or fashion?*
- *Does the place show a high degree of creative or technical achievement?*

The Historic England document (English Heritage, 2008) makes similar points but also observes that aesthetic values can be the result of the conscious design of an asset, but can also be the result of the seemingly fortuitous outcome of the way in which a place has evolved and been used over time.

We are essentially talking about character and what makes a 'sense of place'. Appearance will of course be part of the character of an asset but there is often a real danger that this dominates an assessment of the wider value category. In part, this is because it is easier to measure and articulate what something looks like than is the case with more complex and perhaps less tangible attributes. There are many examples where the appearance of an asset has been 'enhanced' but its aesthetic has been damaged. Sometimes this has occurred because of a misplaced desire to 'tidy up' and 'improve' it, but often because the use and feel of the asset – and its noises, smells and activities – have neither been understood nor their importance appreciated.

Scenic and panoramic

These are closely associated visually aesthetic values. Panoramic value belongs to sweeping *outward* vistas, whereas scenic value may be related more to beauty in a reasonably confined setting and may include the subject place or be experienced looking from it.

Architectural/technological

Architectural value is concerned with innovation, development and perhaps pinnacles of achievement (as in 'the finest example of …') in relation to architectural ideas and movements, and also in the work of individuals. This value would also embrace the work of craftsmen and the development of materials. Some of the architectural values might be related to developments and high points in technical achievement, but a place may have technological value represented by structures, etc. which would fall outside the concept of architecture – an obvious example would perhaps be a bridge.

Because architecture and technology (or indeed art) are not created in a vacuum, the social, cultural, political and economic context that informed their development will also be represented by the architectural and technical achievement.

Historical

Clearly the concept of historical value is of primary importance in the notion of built cultural heritage, and to a large extent it underpins and validates many of the other values. Here we are concerned with, as Mason puts it, 'The capacity of a site to convey, embody or stimulate a relation or reaction to the past is part of the fundamental nature and meaning of heritage objects' (2002, p. 11).

Historic England refers to 'the perception of a place as a link between past and present people' (English Heritage, 2008), and clearly historical value is closely linked to social value and associational values.

Associational

Clearly an asset may be important because of its associational links with a person or event. But how symbiotic that link is needs to be considered: that is, the link should be substantial and generally it should not be transitory. An important issue might be the extent to which there is some evidence that the asset had an impact on the activity or work of the person or on the event(s) in question. How intact the asset is in relation to the period and activity related to the association is also an important consideration. The Burra Charter observes, however, that 'some events or associations may be so important that the place retains significance regardless of such change or absence of evidence' (Australia ICOMOS, 2013a).

Archaeological

As *Conservation Principles* (English Heritage, 2008) observes, archaeological value is linked to educational value and relates to the ability of an asset to be a source of information about the past through scientific investigation. As it states, 'In the absence of written records, the material record, particularly architectural deposits, provides the only source of evidence about the distant past (as well as of poorly documented aspects of the more recent past).'

The value derived from an understanding and interpretation of the archaeological record is of course not just a one-off process, as even the best-known and apparently well-investigated and well-documented place can sometimes continue to reveal new information. A good example of this is the moat at the Tower of London, which has continued to reveal important evidence about the development of the medieval fortress and its entrance in recent years, despite the amount of attention that has been paid generally to the archaeology of the site over many decades. However, the converse of this must be appreciated just as well. As has often been stated, archaeological excavation is a destructive process – once something has been 'dug out', the capability of future generations to learn more from the same archaeological strata and material is either greatly reduced or erased altogether.

There is another, in some ways more esoteric, value, in the archaeology which is buried and remains essentially unseen but which has a mystery and therefore an almost spiritual value.

Economic

This can be seen at a very simple level as pertaining to the quantification of how much money is generated by heritage places, either directly through admissions and sales of services and goods at the site, or indirectly in the sense of visitors to a place purchasing goods and services in the wider area. The effect of heritage value on attracting visitors to the wider region, or indeed a particular country, is also an economic value that can be measured in terms of direct and indirect investment and employment opportunities and realities. This important value is of course, as we have mentioned previously, not necessarily without negative effects for the place itself.

Another way of measuring economic value is by asking people what they are prepared to pay for it – whether it be how much they are prepared to pay to enter a particular place or how much public money they think they would be prepared to see spent on it (in the context of perhaps higher taxes or in relation to other things of public value such as healthcare or street cleaning). Throsby (2006, p. 41) refers to this latter point of gauging a person's willingness to pay to preserve (*sic*) the heritage when that same person is not gaining a direct benefit from it (in the same way as a visitor), and identifies them as 'non use values'. He suggests that these may relate to: the asset's existence value (people value the existence of the heritage item even though they may not consume its service directly themselves); its option value (people wish to preserve the option that they or others might consume the asset's services at some future time); and its bequest value (people may wish to bequeath the asset to future generations).

But there is also a more prosaic economic value, and that is the value of the place as real estate, including its development value. The issues that a valuer might take into account will vary depending on whom they are valuing it for, but often the fact that a place is protected may reduce its monetary value because of perceived restrictions on how it can be managed and developed. Clearly also, the potential development value may lead owners and users to propose changes that damage its cultural value. However, the potential to develop the place through a new use may be what actually effectively protects the place, as long as the new use is compatible with its cultural significance.

Educational

In part, educational value is derived from the historical value of the place. This can work at an informal level, in that a place may invite and stimulate a person's interest through curiosity. That person may then go away and, through other media, investigate the asset, its context and the society that created it. To a certain extent this may be triggered by how powerful or astonishing the atmosphere of the place is – Machu Picchu is a good example of this. Or it may be a combination of wonderment of the atmosphere combined with interest in the artistic or even technical achievements, such as engendered by, say, a cathedral or perhaps the Alhambra Palace or Sydney Opera House to name but a few places at random. But that curiosity is also likely to be stimulated by wanting to understand more about less grand places that the person is unfamiliar with but with which they feel some connection or association. However, and as we have already observed, in many instances, educational values will only truly be realised through effective interpretation strategies.

Recreational

Clearly, many built heritage assets are enjoyed as sources of recreation, in which an engagement with the past may be a primary or a secondary reason for the visit. Their value is essentially that of an amenity.

Historic England has suggested that 'the historic environment plays a very significant role in providing for people's recreation and enjoyment. Increasingly the past and its remains in the present are a vital part of people's everyday life and experiences' (English Heritage, 1997).

Artistic

This again may be closely related to historical and educational value. Artistic value may be related to the work of a particular person or an artistic or architectural movement, and may be important because it is a unique example or it may be pivotal or representative.

Social

This is largely about the meaning that an asset might have for individuals or groups because of some kind of association they have with it, or with events that occurred there. It refers to the benefits of social cohesion and group identity. Social value may be related to events that occurred in the relatively distant past and which are connected to the present through oral history traditions anchored by and to the place in question, but the events and the association may also be relatively recent or ongoing.

Historic England (English Heritage, 2008) suggests that the 'social value is associated with places that people perceive as a source of identity, distinctiveness, social interaction and coherence'. They make the important point that some places:

> *may be comparatively modest, acquiring communal significance through the passage of time as a result of a collective memory of stories linked to them. They tend to gain value through the resonance of past events in the present, providing reference points for a community's identity or sense of itself. They may have fulfilled a community function that has generated a deeper attachment, or shaped some aspect of community behaviour or attitudes.*

This sense of a heritage asset reinforcing group identity and social cohesion may work at a relatively small local scale but it may also of course be a focus of regional or national identity.

The category of social value is often closely linked to symbolic value. There can of course be a negative aspect to this where, particularly in a multicultural society, symbols of national identity are associated by some groups and communities with feelings of being excluded rather than embraced.

Commemorative

These are different from associational values in that the commemorative asset may or may not be located where the event actually took place. War memorials are an obvious example of this (see Case Study 4 in Chapter 9).

Symbolic/iconic

Very often the symbolic values that a place holds are interpreted differently by different groups. In some cases, different interpretations are relatively harmonious and positive and reinforce its importance, but sometimes they are negative, particularly where they are seen by, for instance, minority groups, as celebrating past events which oppressed or damaged them. There can be benefits in conserving places precisely because they are reminders of past wrongdoings, attitudes and events that are to be condemned. Whether that benefit is realised will depend on perceptions and interpretations.

In a slightly different way, the very human sense of belonging can attach symbolic or iconic value to an asset both for individuals and also arguably for whole sections of a community. The sense of home is important to many people. Irrespective of the amount of time they have lived at the place that they feel to be 'home', people may experience the warmth of homecoming every time they approach or see a particular landmark, scene, vista or place that they associate with their journey home. Sometimes that symbol of home may be many miles away from the place itself. While this is a very personal value, in towns and cities, by the very nature of things, many people may associate precisely the same symbolic trigger with the same value (albeit that a different 'home' is the object of that symbolism). In some ways, this implies there is also a separate value to do with 'belonging', not the symbolic attachment to a place other than home as part of the ritual of homecoming, but the strong value felt when standing in the 'bosom' of one's community, or perhaps the cameo view of the world gained from your own window, or the value many people place in their birthplace or first home.

Related to this form of symbolic value is the importance that many people, when travelling, place on landmarks and the like as symbols of arrival at a gateway. An example of this is the Wellington Monument, the UK's tallest obelisk standing at the end of a dominant range of hills overlooking a busy motorway in the south-west of England. Many thousands, perhaps millions of travellers associate the Monument with arrival to and departure from the area. This is an extremely powerful symbolic value placed on this asset.

Spiritual and religious

The Burra Charter (Australia ICOMOS, 2013a) suggests that to appreciate the spiritual value of a place, one might ask:

- *Does the place contribute to the spiritual identity or belief system of a cultural group?*

- *Is the place a repository of knowledge, traditional art or lore related to spiritual practice of a cultural group?*
- *Is the place important in maintaining the spiritual health and well-being of a culture or group?*
- *Do the physical attributes of the place play a role in recalling or awakening an understanding of an individual or a group's relationship with the spiritual realm?*
- *Do the spiritual values of the place find expression in cultural practices or human-made structures, or inspire creative works?*

At the most obvious level, places of worship are likely to have spiritual value to both worshippers and other members of society, including (sometimes) adherents of other religions. Equally, an asset such as London's Highgate Cemetery may well have spiritual value to many visitors, including atheists, as well as being important for its artless beauty and its historical, associational, commemorative, social and educational values. All of these combine together to create its essential 'sense of place'.

It is also important to observe that those without any religious conviction can experience spiritual value. As Mason (2002, p. 12) observes: '[These] spiritual values can emanate from the beliefs and teachings of organised religion, but they can also encompass secular experiences of wonder, awe, and so on, which can be provoked by visiting heritage places.'

The cultural values, 'religious', 'spiritual' and 'inspirational' are closely related to each other, but may be experienced concurrently or individually. They are appreciably different, but belong to one family of intangible values. Not all inspirational assets have spiritual value. Arguably, atheists do not personally experience religious value, but they will find spiritual value in certain spaces and places.

In some ways, spiritual value is one of the harder intangible values to pin down – it is so very personal. What is a spiritual mountain to millions in a Pacific Rim country is but a mountain to even more people elsewhere around the world, albeit, quite possibly an awe-inspiring, panoramically or scenically valued piece of natural heritage.

Inspirational

As with the spiritual and religious, this is a cultural value that can be hard to define unambiguously and with precision, because of its very personal nature. Nonetheless, millions of people may derive enormous inspirational drive or emotions from the same place. The contrast between inspiration as a driver and as an emotion is interesting and is key to appreciating that, perhaps more than most other values, inspiration can be gained from an astoundingly diverse group of places and assets. Sometimes inspiration is to be connected with the 'awe-inspiring'; at other times, it is not a sense of positive or wondrous awe, but a very different drive to do good or better that is derived through inspiration. Thus, an unscientific poll of friends and colleagues when writing this text produced the following disparate list of places or assets exhibiting powerful inspirational value: Angkor Wat, Machu Picchu, the Taj Mahal, the Great Wall of China, Stonehenge, the terracotta warriors at Emperor Qin Shihuang's Mausoleum in Shaanxi, Mayan ruins, the Pyramids of Giza, Eisenman's 2005 Holocaust Memorial in Berlin, Auschwitz and Dachau, the Parthenon, Chartres Cathedral, Coventry Cathedral, the complex of Hue monuments in Vietnam, and the Washington Monument.

This list illustrates the different forms of inspiration that can be felt by different people on different occasions. Assessments of significance need to be able to explore such diversity, but reaching conclusions on relative values when inspiration is involved can be extremely problematic.

Ecological

Ecological values are perhaps easier to understand and assess in terms of relative importance than something as intangible as inspiration. Conversely, assessments of significance produced for built cultural heritage assets in the UK, including those to be found within conservation plans, have often dealt with ecological significance very poorly, since such assessments tend to focus over-much on traditional building conservation themes like archaeology and history and not tackle value holistically.

Environmental

Environmental value is often confused with ecological interest, but they are and should remain quite distinct. Landscapes can have environmental value without being ecologically significant; equally, a park in a city can also provide important environmental value to the local community, not least by acting as a 'green lung' to reduce pollution. As with ecological value, this has often been undervalued and under-represented in assessments of significance.

Some examples of assets and their values

As we have suggested, any given place will have a number of cultural values. As an example, we can imagine what the range of values might be for the following places.

- *Sydney Harbour Bridge* (Figure 3.1) is significant among other things for its iconic status, as an entry to and symbol of Sydney and Australia, its place within panoramic views, as an architectural composition, socially for communication and linkage value, as an economic driver related to tourism, and so forth.
- *The Eiffel Tower* (Figure 3.2) similarly has strong iconic, panoramic/scenic and economic values, arguably technologically it is more significant than Sydney Harbour Bridge and it has particular associational value.

Figure 3.1   Sydney Harbour Bridge.

Figure 3.2   The Eiffel Tower.

- *Coventry Cathedral* (Figures 3.3 (a)–(c)) is a post-war building that stands alongside the ruins of the old Cathedral which was bombed in 1940. The 'new' Coventry Cathedral is a post-war Grade I listed building (Figure 3.3 (a)). It contains many specially commissioned works of art, including Graham Sutherland's tapestry of Christ (Figure 3.3 (b)). The ruins of the medieval Cathedral were incorporated into the new design (Figure 3.3 (c)). There are obvious

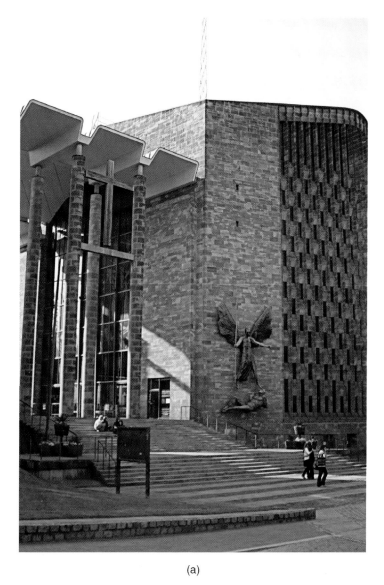

(a)

Figure 3.3 (a)–(c)   Coventry Cathedral. The 'new' Coventry Cathedral is a post-war Grade I listed building (a). It contains many specially commissioned works of art, including Graham Sutherland's tapestry of Christ (b). The ruins of the medieval Cathedral were incorporated into the new design (c).

(b)

(c)

Figure 3.3   *(Continued)*

spiritual, commemorative and historical values represented here, as well as architectural and artistic ones.

- *The Royal Botanic Gardens at Kew* (Figure 3.4), a World Heritage Site, is particularly strong in educational, ecological and recreational values, as well as being important for its historical, architectural and associational significance.

Figure 3.4   The Palm House at Kew Gardens.

- *The Byker estate* in Newcastle upon Tyne (Figures 3.5 (a) and (b)) has strong architectural and townscape value and social value related to its concept and execution, including the way that the community was involved in the design and planning process.
- *St Paul's Cathedral* (Figure 3.6) is a particularly iconic building with extremely powerful associational, symbolic, inspirational, historical, architectural and townscape values.
- *The Bauhaus*, Dessau (Figures 3.7 (a) and (b)), is one of the most iconic buildings of the twentieth century. It has powerful architectural, historical, symbolic and commemorative values, in relation not only to the 'art, craft and architecture' of the Modern Movement but also its associated social and political ideas and ideals.

(a)

(b)

Figure 3.5 (a),(b)   The Byker Estate in Newcastle upon Tyne.

Figure 3.6   St Paul's Cathedral, London.

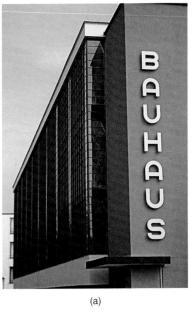

(a)   (b)

Figure 3.7 (a),(b)   The Bauhaus, Dessau.

Figure 3.8   The Radiator Building (foreground) and the Empire State Building, New York.

- *The Radiator Building and the Empire State Building* (Figure 3.8) in New York are both iconic buildings which represent architectural, technological, historical and symbolic values, particularly in relation to the confidence and energy of American capitalism in the period between the two world wars.
- *The Lutyens War Memorial* (Figure 3.9) on Tower Hill in London also has powerful associational, historical and architectural values, but beyond this it has a very strong commemorative significance.
- *Parkhill* (Figure 3.10) in Sheffield Park Hill is a housing estate built between 1957 and 1961. It is a Grade II* listed building. Its design was inspired in part by Le Corbusier's Unité d'Habitation. It has clear social, architectural, historical, iconic and aesthetic values.

Figure 3.9   Lutyen's Great War memorial on Tower Hill in London.

Figure 3.10   Parkhill housing estate, Sheffield. The estate consisted of nearly 1000 dwellings in a 'streets in the sky' design inspired by the work of the architect Le Corbusier. The photograph shows the existing structure alongside recent 'remodelling' work.

The list could go on. We do not pretend that the foregoing assessment is scientific, objective or comprehensive – our purpose in providing these rough-and-ready 'pen portraits' of ten well-known heritage assets is merely to make one vital point. In the end, through careful analysis, significance can be identified and, in a comparative way, quantified. This helps to build up a picture of the holistic value of an asset which, at least to a degree, can be likened to a unique 'fingerprint' that defines its special interest to society today. If you understand and can define that 'fingerprint', you can begin to make rational management decisions that build upon the asset's real value to society.

References

Australia ICOMOS (2013a) *The Burra Charter: The Australia ICOMOS Charter for Places of Cultural Significance*. Burwood, VIC, Australia, Australia ICOMOS Inc.

Australia ICOMOS (2013b) *Understanding and Assessing Cultural Significance*. The Burra Charter Practice Note. Burwood, VIC, Australia, Australia ICOMOS Inc.

Avrami, E., Mason, R. and de la Torre, M. (2000) The spheres and challenges of conservation. In *Values and Heritage Conservation: Research Report*. Los Angeles, The Getty Conservation Institute.

Bell, D. (1997) *The Historic Scotland Guide to International Conservation Charters*. Edinburgh, Historic Scotland.

Council of Europe (1975) *European Charter of the Architectural Heritage*. Available at: www.international.icomos.org/charters.htm

Council of Europe (2005) *Framework Convention on the Value of Cultural Heritage for Society*. CETS Number 199. Available at: www.coe.int

DCLG (2012) *Conserving and Enhancing the Historic Environment*. Planning Practice Guidance, National Planning Policy Framework. London, Department of Communities and Local Government.

El Beyrouty, K. and Tessler, A. (2013) *The Economic Impact of the UK Heritage Tourism Economy*. Oxford, Oxford Economics.

English Heritage (1997) *Sustaining the Historic Environment*. London, English Heritage.

English Heritage (2000) *Power of Place: The Future of the Historic Environment*. London, English Heritage.

English Heritage (2008) *Conservation Principles, Policies and Guidance for the Sustainable Management of the Historic Environment (Second Stage Consultation)*. London: English Heritage.

English Heritage (2014) *The Value of Heritage. Heritage Counts 2014*. London, English Heritage.

Feilden, B. (2003) *Conservation of Historic Buildings*. London, Architectural Press.

Feilden, B. and Jokilehto, J. (1993) *Management Guidelines for World Cultural Heritage Sites*. Rome, ICCROM.

Halldén, S. (1983) *Behövs der Förflutna?: en bok om det Gåtfulla Vardagslivet*. Stockholm, LiberFörlag. [Do we need a past?][In Swedish].

Hewison, R. (1987) *The Heritage Industry: Britain in a Climate of Decline*. London, Methuen.

Hewison, R. (2003) Money for values. In *Valuing Culture*. London, Demos.

Holden, J. (2004) *Capturing Cultural Value*. London, Demos.

Holland, A. and Rawles, K. (1993) Values in conservation. *Ecos* 14(1), 14–19.

Hubbard, P. (1993) The value of conservation. *Town Planning Review* 64(4), 359–73.

ICOMOS (1964) *International Charter for the Conservation and Restoration of Monuments and Sites* (The Venice Charter). Available at: www.international.icomos.xorg/charters.htm

ICOMOS (1987a) *ICOMOS Monograph: 7th General Assembly and Symposium, Rostock–Dresden, 1984.* Berlin, VEB.

ICOMOS (1987b) *Charter for the Conservation of Historic Towns and Urban Areas* (The Washington Charter). Available at: www.international.icomos.org/charters.htm

ICOMOS (1993) *The Charter for the Conservation of Places of Cultural Heritage Value.* Auckland, ICOMOS.

ICOMOS (1994) *The Nara Document on Authenticity.* Available at: www.international.icomos.org/charters.htm

ICOMOS (1999) *Charter on the Built Vernacular Heritage.* Available at: www.international.icomos.org/charters.htm

Lowenthal, D. (1997) *The Past Is a Foreign Country.* Cambridge, Cambridge University Press.

Mason, R. (2002) Assessing values in conservation planning: methodological issues and choices. In *Assessing the Values of Cultural Heritage, Research Report* (eds E. Avrami, R. Mason and M. de la Torre). Los Angeles, The Getty Conservation Institute, pp. 5–30.

Morris, W. (1877) *The Principles of the Society (for the Protection of Ancient Buildings) As set Forth upon its Foundation.* Available at: www.spab.org.uk/html/what-is-spab/the-manifesto/

Riegl, A. (1902) The modern cult of monuments: its essence and its development (trans. Karin Bruckner with Karen Williams of *Der moderne Denkmalkultus*) In *Historical and Philosophical Issues in the Conservation of Cultural Heritage* (eds N.R. Price, K. Talley Jr and A.M. Vaccaro). Los Angeles, The Getty Conservation Institute, pp. 74–6.

Ruskin, J. (1989) The lamp of memory. In *The Seven Lamps of Architecture* (reprint of 1880 edition). New York, Dover Publications, Chapter 6.

Smith, A. (2010) *The Value of Built Heritage.* Occasional Paper Series, Reading, College of Estate Management.

Stokols, D. and Jacobi, M. (1983) The role of tradition in group environmental relations. In *Environmental Psychology: Directions and Perspectives* (eds N. Fiemar and E.S. Geller). New York, Plenum Press.

Throsby, D. (2006) The value of cultural heritage: what can economics tell us? In *Capturing the Public Value of Heritage.* London, English Heritage.

UNESCO (1954) Convention for the Protection of Cultural Property in the Event of Armed Conflict with Regulations for the Execution of the Convention 1954 (The Hague Convention).

UNESCO (1976) *Recommendation Concerning the Safeguarding and Contemporary Role of Historic Areas.* Paris, United Nations Educational, Scientific and Cultural Organization.

UNESCO (2003) Convention for the Safeguarding of the Intangible Cultural Heritage. Paris, United Nations Educational, Scientific and Cultural Organization.

Zancheti, S.M. and Jokilehto, J. (1997) Values and urban conservation planning: some reflections on principles and definitions. *Journal of Architectural Conservation* 1, March, 37–51.

Chapter 4

Assessing Significance

In Chapter 3, we looked at the nature of heritage values and the theory of significance. In this chapter, we will look at the process of identifying and assessing significance, before moving on to its application for management purposes.

Put simplistically, the significance of a heritage asset is the summation of all the heritage values that can be properly attributed to it and which make it of interest and importance to society. Thus, in any one case, the process of identifying an asset's significance entails the unearthing and further consideration of the complete range of heritage values that pertain to it. That task can be far from simple – a proper assessment of the values residing in an asset always takes time and resources and can be a complex matter. Moreover, it is not always easy for one person to understand how and why someone else values something as being part of their heritage. Value is often a very personal thing and may not be widely shared. That in itself does not disqualify or diminish the value that is involved.

The assessment of significance can usefully be regarded as a two-stage process, involving:

1 Establishing an understanding of the asset, its development through time, and its characteristics, dynamics and contextual relationships;
2 Then using this to distil an appreciation of the values that are enshrined within it.

Establishing and analysing the origins and development of an asset

This is often a key part in the understanding of an asset's values and is concerned with determining significance through tracing the asset's origins and how it has changed over time. It is a process that involves gathering material that informs

Managing Built Heritage: The Role of Cultural Values and Significance, Second Edition.
Stephen Bond and Derek Worthing.
© 2016 Stephen Bond and Derek Worthing. Published 2016 by John Wiley & Sons, Ltd.

an understanding of the asset and its social, historical and environmental context, as it was and how it has developed. This information is then analysed in order to determine the significance of the asset and how this is embodied in and represented by its various elements. The elements in question will include the buildings, structures, spaces and objects that constitute the physical manifestation of the asset. It will also be necessary to reach an understanding of the interrelationships between the various elements, and between the asset and its wider setting. In addition, understanding the various uses of the asset and its associations over time will be necessary.

It is also important to understand and analyse the geographical context because, as Pearson and Sullivan (1995) observe:

> *Heritage places exist in two contexts – they are part of the physical landscape and they relate very closely to it ... factors such as transport, arable land, access to natural resources are important in the placement and pattern of early settlement. A prerequisite for a meaningful survey is a general understanding of the physical landscape and the relationship of the places to it.*

Gathering evidence about significance

> *Conservation of cultural heritage in all its forms and historical periods is rooted in the values attributed to the heritage. Our ability to understand these values depends, in part, on the degree to which information sources about these values may be understood as credible or truthful. Knowledge and understanding of these sources of information, in relation to subsequent characteristics of the cultural heritage and their meaning, are a requisite basis for assessing all aspects of authenticity.*
>
> (ICOMOS, 1994)

Most related guidance stresses that before the significance of an asset is assessed, all the evidence relating to its significance needs to be identified, gathered and analysed. It is essential that sufficient time be allocated for this critical preliminary understanding phase before any assessment of significance is made. As was noted at the outset of this chapter, for a large and complex asset, this process can take a significant amount of time and resources.

It is extremely important that all aspects of the asset are investigated and that its relative importance is not assumed. There is perhaps an expectation that in dealing with some assets, particularly those that are well known, their significance is already properly understood and fully documented and that, accordingly, this part of the process can be either missed or its rigour or breadth and depth curtailed. This is potentially a dangerous assumption. It may be that the manner of gathering and interpreting the evidence on long-established sites means that the process of assimilating cumulative material was not carried out effectively. Moreover, new material may have been accepted or rejected (or even sought out) on the basis of whether or not it conformed to the established understanding of the development of the asset – or indeed the particular interests of those in receipt of such information. Also, the chance to review holistically how the integration of material accumulated over time has affected perceptions may not have been taken. An overriding point, however, is that, as we have said before, ideas of what is valuable and why are subjective and change with time. There are many examples where the implementation of a rigorous, focused and holistic approach to preparing a new assessment of significance has revealed new or changed aspects of significance involving assets that it was assumed were already well understood.

In gathering information, it is obviously important to know where relevant material might be stored and how it can be accessed. But this should not be confined just to the obvious: lateral and divergent thinking, objectivity and imagination in identifying sources are important.

Information sources include:

> *all physical, written, oral and figurative sources which make it possible to know the nature, specificities, meaning, and history of the cultural heritage ... Depending on the nature of the cultural heritage, its cultural context, and its evolution through time, authenticity judgements may be linked to the worth of a great variety of sources of information. Aspects of the sources may include form and design, materials and substance, use and function, traditions and techniques, location and setting, and spirit and feeling and other external and external factors.*
>
> (ICOMOS, 1994)

Evidence gathering will consist of identifying and retrieving the documentary material and carrying out an interpretation of the evidence embodied in and represented by the buildings and structures on the site. Kerr (2013) emphasises the importance of paying proper attention to both sources and to their interactions because, as he suggests, 'neither can be neglected as each corroborates and complements the other'.

The development of an understanding of the significance of an asset should be as objective a process as is possible. It should, however, be borne in mind that it will always be an assessment carried out by a particular (generally, small) group of people, with individual interests, knowledge and skills, who are operating in a specific cultural context and at a precise point in time. It is therefore important that the process is not only rigorous but can be seen to be rigorous through its approach and recording. The methodologies and processes that are adopted should be set out and explained. Any areas or aspects of the asset that could not be documented should be highlighted and all source material should be referenced.

The extent and breadth of coverage of research required depend entirely on the asset and specific circumstances, so it is dangerous to rely on prescriptive lists of topics rather than considering each asset and its context afresh.

However, as guidance for those starting out on this process for the first time, it is perhaps helpful to note that the 1999 guidelines to The Burra Charter (Australia ICOMOS, 1999) suggested that the information that needs to be collected might include:

> *The developmental sequence of the asset and its relationship to the surviving fabric.*
>
> (a) *The existence and nature of lost or obliterated fabric.*
> (b) *The rarity and/or technical interest of all or any part of the asset.*
> (c) *The functions of the asset and its parts.*
> (d) *The relationship of the asset and its parts with its setting.*
> (e) *The cultural influences which have affected the form and fabric of the asset.*
> (f) *The importance of the asset to people who use or have used the place, or descendants of such people.*
> (g) *The historical content of the asset with particular reference to the ways in which its fabric has been influenced by historical forces or has itself influenced the course of history.*
> (h) *The scientific or research potential of the asset.*
> (i) *The relationship of the asset to others. For example, in respect of design, technology, use, locality or origin.*
> (j) *Any and all other factors relevant to an understanding of the asset.*

It must be emphasised that this Burra Charter list is reproduced merely to show that considerable research is frequently required as part of the process of assessing significance and that it may demand coverage of a wide range of subjects. It should not be assumed to be comprehensive. The requirements for each individual asset will need to be assessed at the start of the process and kept under review throughout, as information gathered begins to highlight issues, reveal new avenues of research that may be of relevance and importance, and show up gaps in knowledge that must be filled to produce a rounded understanding that can be used as a platform for consideration of heritage values and significance.

Research and types of evidence

Documentary evidence

It is not the place of this book to provide a comprehensive account of all documentary sources or to examine in depth research issues and methodologies. It is important, however, to highlight some of the matters that need to be considered as a core part of the process of exploring and assessing significance.

Documentary evidence can be taken to mean written or graphic evidence that helps to build a picture of an asset, including the way in which it has developed over time. Depending upon the asset and the type and source of the documents, some specialist skills and knowledge may be necessary in identifying, sourcing, reading and interpreting the materials.

There are two categories of documentary evidence: written/graphical and oral. Documentary material about a heritage asset may be available from a variety of sources. Obviously the quantity, quality and veracity of the available material will be variable, depending on a number of factors, including the age and perceived importance or relevance of the asset, the record-keeping activities of the different owners and occupiers over time, etc. Some of the material will be 'primary' and some of it will be 'secondary'.

In this context, primary source material can be taken to mean original documentation. It might include the original deeds or grant for a building or land, the original drawings or contract details, or letters between clients, tenants, owners and contractors. Although, in many countries, there is a wealth of information that is available in archives stretching back to the medieval period (and before), access may sometimes be restricted to these documents because of their fragility or condition. Some documents only survive in part, due to conditions of storage or subsequent events, for example, in the UK, many First World War service records, which are now available to researchers in the National Archives at Kew in west London, were damaged by bombing during the Second World War. In addition, where material is openly accessible, it is sometimes a skilful task for a specialist just to decipher the text, requiring the reader to have a knowledge of medieval and church Latin, Norman French or medieval English, for example. Fortunately, many such documents are available as printed copies, and occasionally as translations.

Typically, secondary sources are the books and articles that have previously been written about aspects of the asset or its locality. They may have been derived from the original primary documents or be based on other secondary writings. Generally, there is a great deal of such material around. For example, in the UK, in the eighteenth and nineteenth centuries, there was considerable interest among the educated wealthy classes in 'antiquities' of all sorts. Investigating old buildings, including churches and their records, was a popular activity, just as it is today. The results of such investigation and study were, and are, sometimes published by local publishers, interest groups or individuals. Clearly, one problem with using secondary material is the reliance that has to be placed on the quality and thoroughness of the research and analysis that underpin it. Unless research has been carried out in a rigorous and objective manner and the fruits of that academic effort have been interpreted and synthesised correctly, the secondary record may be seriously flawed or biased. However, original material can also at times be misleading, for instance, a contemporaneous report may not be a truthful or full account and, as is encountered so many times in practice, a building may not be built exactly as it is shown on a plan or in an illustration. Inevitably, secondary sources are often the starting point because of their immediate availability and accessibility; hopefully, they will draw attention to original documentary sources, including some which may no longer be available.

In conducting research, all material, whether it be primary or secondary evidence, should be treated initially with a discerning and sceptical eye. Reliance should never be placed on received data – the interpretation of which may prove of great importance – until corroboration from further sources can be achieved. This is a pitfall for the unwary. Unbridled enthusiasm and an understandable 'desire' that something that is unsubstantiated should prove to be true (simply because it tells a 'good' story or fills in a frustrating blank) have often led inexperienced researchers to make very wrong assumptions and jump to seriously flawed conclusions. A legion of instances might be cited from the field of ever-popular family history research. For example, working back from the present day, people have made a leap of faith about lineal descent as a result of studying parish records (especially when dealing with common surnames in densely populated cities), and, thereby, unknowingly have 'changed horses' and begun to explore the family history of someone else's eponymous kinsfolk. It would be heartening to suppose that this kind of error does not blight professional historic research and assessments of significance, but experience suggests otherwise. It is a considerable problem and risk, and a trap that can catch many research 'veterans' in an unguarded moment of 'blind certainty'. The point is, quite often, it only needs one flawed building block to be assumed and used in constructing a story from research, for the whole to be substantively compromised and open to criticism from peers. Management of heritage assets based on the platform of a weak assessment of significance, built on subjective interpretation of data or imperfect research, can prove to be very bad management and may lead to damage to or increased vulnerability of the asset's significance.

As we have already noted, it is not our intention to give a detailed and comprehensive account of the areas of research that may be required as part of the process of assessing significance. The following discussion of types of typical documentary material that may have to be sourced and consulted is undoubtedly partial, but, it is hoped, will provide a flavour and some useful pointers and advice. Although this discussion relates to the UK, the principles and general points made are applicable to many countries, with suitable adjustments to terminology and recontextualisation as necessary.

Primary source material

Illustrations, including paintings

These can be extremely useful, although they are often associated with relatively prestigious sites and have been commissioned by wealthy owners, who may not have appreciated the 'warts and all' keen veracity of the artist's eye. As a result, one of the problems with such illustrations is that they may not be accurate representations – obviously, the primary purpose of art is not one of recording. Also, images of buildings (both internally and externally) and landscapes may be incidental to the purpose of the picture and, therefore, rendered inaccurately. For instance, in portraits, the focus was generally on the people, or at least the principal subject of the picture, and the building (often part of its interior) would merely form a backdrop where accuracy was either unimportant or needed to be sacrificed in order to present the subject with greater clarity. Alternatively, the building or landscape may have been deliberately changed to enhance the aesthetic or the 'message' of the image (or the status of the owner).

Registrations of births, baptisms, marriages, deaths and burials/cremations

Before 1837 in England and Wales, and 1855 in Scotland, registers of baptisms, marriages and burials were kept by the established Church and, in the latter years, some non-conformist religious denominations as well. The amount of information provided by such records varies enormously over time and from place to place. Depending upon the type of record, information may, typically, be gained on parentage, domicile, occupation of father and age, as well as the occupation of the groom, bride or deceased person. Parish records of this kind are generally found in County Record Offices (but occasionally in the parish or at the chapel concerned), although partial transcripts may be found in local libraries (especially in local studies sections), in the library of the Society of Genealogists, and elsewhere.

From 1837 onwards, civil registration has recorded births, marriages and deaths. These records are available at a variety of locations including libraries, the National Archives and online from subscription-based and pay-as-you-go commercial services.

Particular pitfalls to be avoided are inaccuracies – often numerous – in transcripts (which are essentially secondary sources of data), which have occurred through misinterpretation of handwritten records. It is worth being aware that commercial online services have also suffered occasionally from erroneous transcriptions of data from official but handwritten registers. The subtle difference between birth/baptism and death/burial records can also lead to errors for the uninitiated. Pre-nineteenth-century records can be bedevilled by gaps, omissions, lost and damaged registers, and the lack of interest of particular church incumbents in keeping accurate or timely records. Sometimes, registers were only filled in from memory and from scrawled notes many months after the relevant event – usually just in advance of the local bishop's visit to the parish.

Registration data of this kind can be important for tracing people associated in one way or another with the heritage asset. Sometimes, this information is directly relevant to the process of assessing significance; at other times, understanding relevant dates can be vital for use indirectly in obtaining other information that is pertinent to the study.

Correspondence, reports, minutes of committee meetings, specifications of work, contractor's invoices, etc.

Such evidence might include written material produced by individuals or the organisations who commissioned, designed, built and occupied (and changed) the asset over time. Depending on the asset and its uses, such evidence may range from official material stored in public authority archives to more personal documentation, such as letters and diaries, possibly held by friends and relatives or given to museums or local societies. Many, particularly public, organisations such as government departments, hospitals, local authorities, etc. will keep records not only of the site and buildings and how they have evolved over the years, but they will also have accounts of the factors that drove and influenced the creation of and changes to those buildings. It is important here, as elsewhere, to link the physical evidence – what happened to the asset – to the organisational and socio-economic drivers for change and evolution.

The survival of original detailed specifications of work can be very important, but it must never be assumed without further verification that what was specified was actually ordered or built in the way intended. For instance, the survival of the original Bills of Quantities and Specifications for the former Public Record Office in Chancery Lane, London, proved invaluable in understanding the construction and fixings of rare zinc ceilings found in the reception hall and Round Reading Room during conversion of the empty building for use as a library for King's College, London, in 2001/2002. Those records included letters from the supplier to the architect, explaining the problems that had been experienced during erection of the prefabricated ceiling sections, following their importation from France. This opened up other lines of enquiry that shed more light on the asset and its significance. However, the same specification that contained detail of the form and fixings of these ceilings, also dealt with another zinc ceiling which appears never to have been built. All such records require very careful interpretation.

Census returns

Census records exist in a number of countries. In the UK, detailed, largely complete, decennial census data are available for the years 1841–1911. Partial information is also available for the years 1801, 1811, 1821 and 1831. This data is available as primary evidence through the original enumerators' scheduled returns and microfilms/microfiches of these in the National Archives, and in some County Record Offices and public libraries/local studies libraries. The same data (give or take!) is also available as secondary source material through transcripts of varying extent, quality and accuracy in libraries and other collections and, as with birth/baptism, marriage and death/burial records, is online through searchable subscription-based and pay-as-you-go commercial services.

The information provided in census entries depends upon the year and location. Typically, this might include the address, listings for other occupants living at the same address (giving an idea of the number of rooms or size of the property), make-up of the household, ages, occupations or employment information such as the number of people employed by the same person, details of servants and visitors on census day and their place of birth. Official (government) and unofficial (research) analyses of census returns are also available as secondary sources, giving invaluable statistics and insights into demography and employment, among other matters.

The potential uses of census evidence are wide, including: mapping change in an area (population, housing densities, employment, occupations, class, construction of new roads and housing, renaming of roads, slum clearance, and so forth); identifying individuals and tracking (some of) their movements and changes of occupation, means etc.; and establishing occupiers of property at given times. Researchers need to bear census data in mind at all times and think laterally about the possibilities that such information might offer in any given circumstance. It is strongly advised that, for those unused to accessing and interpreting such data, further reading is undertaken to understand the peculiarities, problems and limitations of using census material (for instance, Herber, 2004).

Trade directories

Commercial and trade directories were, in many ways, the forerunner of telephone directories – these, too, are now being consigned to history. Although various eighteenth-century directories survive for London, most towns and cities (and some rural areas) have some extant coverage from the 1830s and often a good run of annual directories from the 1870s onwards. These are often available in County Record Offices and local studies libraries, although some university libraries and the British Library also have partial – sometimes good – coverage. A small number of directories are available as scanned images online.

The information contained in commercial and trade directories does vary according to publication and date, but, generally, commercial occupiers are listed by name and nature of business, and sometimes the names of the heads of household are given for every residential property as well. Some later nineteenth-century directories for parts of cities like London give less, not more, information per entry, just because there were so many people and therefore the publishers had to greatly restrict the information that they gathered. Directories also require careful interpretation, partly as a result of this, but also because some relied on out-of-date information from previous years, so that the closure of a business or the move/death of a person did not work through to show on the printed page for several years. Despite these limitations, our experience has been that commercial and trade directories offer an invaluable resource for study in preparing assessments of significance and that their potential is often underplayed or entirely unrealised by researchers.

For example, in research for a historic area analysis of part of Liverpool, it was found that two important conservation commentators had written that, to paraphrase, 'no direct contemporary evidence could be found to establish the date of construction of ten roads of late 19th century terraced housing' which lay on either side of a reasonably major arterial road and was the subject of regeneration proposals including potential partial clearance. Further study revealed that, while it was correct that no other documentation furnishing this information appeared to survive within the local archive, an incomplete run of commercial and trade directories from 1860 to 1910 in the local studies library (filled in for the remaining years at the British Library in London) provided firm dating evidence for the first appearance of streets and occupiers of residential and commercial premises. With this knowledge, substantiation could be attained and the story fleshed out by occasional articles that appeared in the contemporary local newspapers for the area. Similarly, a comprehensive record of use of two adjoining properties in Russell Square, London, from 1870 to 1968 has been collated from directory entries for use within a conservation statement in recent years – information that had proved difficult to obtain from other sources.

Maps

Maps of various places of course go back to at least Roman times. There is a wealth of map-based information available in the UK, covering both rural and urban areas, particularly from about 1850 onwards. Often maps from this time on were updated at relatively short intervals, which may be particularly useful in tracing the development of a site. Before that time, tithe maps, estate plans and various maps of towns and cities can provide invaluable comparative or specific data, although the purpose for which they were prepared needs to be kept in mind to assist with interpretation.

There are a number of useful sources of information on maps and the location of relevant archives, including sections in Herber (2004) and Beech and Mitchell (2004). The locations of maps will depend upon the subject matter and may include the National Archives, County Record Offices, local libraries, university libraries and private archives.

Map regression is an extremely valuable technique for use in building up an understanding of the origins and changes that have occurred at mapped assets over time. Sequential historic maps for the relevant area (from the earliest available through to the present time) are used to analyse change that has occurred to the asset and in its setting. This can be linked to interpretive information from other documentary evidence and from an analysis of the built fabric or present-day landscape with their 'fossil' traces of previous activity, use and change. Often, overlays to maps can be used to good effect in both analysis and in the presentation of findings/data.

Plans

In the UK, the Public Health Acts of the 1800s led to the preparation of record drawings of buildings showing how they would be improved to comply with the Acts. Likewise, plans showing local authority and statutory proposals for the introduction of various services, such as sewerage, gas and electricity to new and existing developments may be of use in tracing the development of the asset (and, of course, simply being able to date the introduction of the services themselves may add important information). Building regulation and planning drawings from more recent times will also provide information of latter-day changes, and will also show the state of the asset at the time of the application.

Photographs and postcards

The increasing use of photography from about 1900 onwards means that photographic evidence can sometimes be quite extensive. Unlike paintings and drawings, generally, an old photograph will provide an accurate record to the extent that it is decipherable. But photographers can and will choose what to photograph for various reasons and therefore place emphasis on certain aspects to the exclusion of others. Aerial photographs will often provide valuable evidence as well as clues for further investigation, and are useful because they obviously provide a particular perspective that is normally not available. Clearly, aerial photographs are a product of recent times, but are not uncommon from the 1920s onwards. Relatively good coverage has sometimes been driven by particular events, for example, the extensive aerial photography carried out by the Royal Air Force in 1946–1948 in order to assess the extent of bomb damage in the Second World War.

Surveys

Surveys have been routinely carried out in many urban areas in the UK since the second half of the nineteenth century. The purpose of these varied from being a matter of record to design and planning proposals. Such records will vary in detail, scope and accuracy, quality and quantity (as will their survival/availability). Other record surveys have been created in response to public works, including the provision or improvement of drainage, sewerage, gas and electricity supplies – and, in recent times, cable television – and may provide more general evidence of development than just these utilities.

Local newspapers and journals

It can be debated as to whether contemporary newspapers are primary or secondary sources or an amalgam of both. In the end, it might be argued that the distinction hardly matters. For ease, we have included local newspapers here, and alongside these should be placed long-running journals. In the UK, examples of the latter include *Country Life*, which is useful for architectural reports and commentaries, and *The Builder*, the forerunner of today's *Building* magazine, which provides unrivalled contemporary information on many nineteenth century construction issues and buildings.

Although some journals were published at a strikingly early date – for instance, the *London Journal* from 1665 – the great era of local newspapers began in the mid-nineteenth century. Many early newspapers were short-lived, but they often had meteoric impact (some essentially crusading on single issues such as the corruption of a local Poor Law Union) and, for the local historian or property researcher, they contain invaluable information as well as gossip. The trick can be working out which is which.

By 1800, there were around 100 provincial newspapers in the UK. The abolition of stamp duty on newspapers in the 1850s led to a massive growth in numbers. Local newspapers of the age covered meetings, building work, slum clearance, the doings of the Great and the Good, the wretchedness of the poor, fires and accidents, murders, deaths, criminal cases, and so forth – the list of topics covered is seemingly endless. As such, they can provide essential direct and indirect evidence that may be vital for the developing an understanding of an asset and of how its significance has changed over the years.

Historic newspapers can be found in local studies libraries, County Record Offices and the British Library's Newspaper Library at Colindale in north London, where journals such as *The Builder* can also be studied, as well as online through subscription-based and pay-as-you-go commercial services.

Some other primary sources of direct and indirect information on built assets and land are:

- Wills and the evidence of bequests of property;
- Fire insurance plans and other documents;
- Tithe awards;
- Estate records;
- Land registration;
- Title deeds;
- Mortgage deeds;
- Leases;
- Inland Revenue valuations and surveys;
- The National Farm Survey, 1941–1943;
- Place and field names;
- Electoral registers;
- Poor Law records, including Settlement examinations and orders;
- Glebe terriers;
- Records of trades, businesses and professions, including guilds and livery companies;
- Licensing of inns and various shops and businesses;
- Taxation records, including seventeenth-century hearth and seventeenth- to nineteenth-century window taxes and land tax records;
- Civil and Ecclesiastical Courts' records, especially those of the Court of Chancery, Criminal and Magistrate Courts, and Quarter Sessions;
- Coroners' records;
- Trade catalogues and pattern books (as with others, depending upon circumstance, these may be primary or secondary sources);
- Archaeological excavation and scientific reports;
- List descriptions, Register of Parks and Gardens, etc.

It must be stressed that this analysis does not claim to be and is not comprehensive. Further information on sources can be obtained from a number of texts, including Herber (2004) and Porter (1990).

Secondary material

As has already been suggested, secondary material is often more readily available, but, given that it is based on information that has been 'processed' by others, considerable judgement needs to be applied to its acceptance and use. A list of secondary source material would be long and out of place in this book and hence will not be attempted. Typical sources, however, that might be consulted during research include:

- Books and indexes;
- Histories;
- Architectural commentaries;
- Transactions of archaeological societies;
- Archaeological and other treatises;
- Historic environment records;
- Previous assessments of significance, conservation plans, research and professional reports, dissertations and theses.

Research takes time, and good research takes practice. At all times, the researcher needs to be cautious of becoming sidetracked by interesting but, in the great scheme of things, irrelevant facts and discoveries. Good research requires balance and constant objectivity. Too many assessments of significance are fundamentally flawed through poor research and interpretation of data, which, as has already been noted, can lead to skewed assessments of relative significance and, on the back of that, poor management decision-making in the future.

The researcher also needs to be aware of the inbuilt law of diminishing returns. An assessment of significance does not require – in fact, specifically does not need – everything there is to know about the asset and its associated personalities. There comes a time when further research is unlikely to provide anything of value to the specific objective in hand – which is different to saying that there is no place for comprehensive analysis, for that is patently untrue. There is considerable skill involved in deciding when the appropriate balance of evidence and information has been attained. Thereafter, the need for ongoing research into remaining aspects of interest (which, if an appropriate balance has been achieved, should be unlikely to impact on the assessment of the asset's significance in any substantive way) can form an important recommendation for the management process itself.

The balance between inadequate, sufficient and excessive research material and data is a delicate one, as the example below demonstrates.

Example: a North of England church

A conservation plan was commissioned of a long-redundant church in the north of England to form the backbone of a feasibility study into reuse of the site. Background research into the history of the asset and the wider area was commissioned from a professional researcher who had worked as part of many similar teams. The researcher investigated primary source material at the County Record Office relating to the construction of the church in 1835 and its extension in 1858. Surviving records of the Building Committee from 1857/1858 were found, which provided useful information on the architect, contractors and the considerations of the Committee in planning the extension. Unfortunately, no records appeared to survive relating to the original construction of the church only 23 years before. The researcher resorted to comparison with other church and public buildings in the locality in the 1820s and 1830s to make suggestions regarding the identity of the earlier architect and he backed this up with information obtained from a very incomplete series of early trade directories for the area. He did not investigate other available contemporary documentation – especially local newspapers and census records.

The manager of the assessment process was slightly concerned about this paucity of contemporary source material about the original church and undertook some very brief research of her own. She looked first in contemporary local newspapers held at the local library. While this provided no information on the completion of the church in 1835, it did turn up a number of articles from the laying of the foundation stone of the extension in 1858 to a report of a service and a tea party held to celebrate the opening of the extended church later that year. These included quotations from the extension's architect in which, contrary to the supposition of the first researcher, he told the congregation that he had designed the original church. Subsequent research of census records and registrations of death revealed that the architect had died in 1863.

Using this information, the plan manager was able to find various newspaper obituaries which filled out information about other local buildings that the architect had designed or worked on. Additionally, examination of newspapers for the 50-year anniversary of the building of the church provided a wealth of information on its design objectives and brief, which had clearly been collated at the time from then extant primary source material that had since been lost.

This illustrates that even experienced professional researchers, however skilled and talented, sometimes get the balance of research wrong. Moreover, it almost certainly highlights another significant, but rarely mentioned, problem. We all come with baggage that tends to distort the sources of information we use. As just one instance of this, a number of academic researchers appear to be suspicious and, to a degree, dismissive of family historians, regarding their work as a debased and poor relation of true academic research. There is a natural inclination in these circumstances to tend not to use primary sources that are regarded as being the province of family historians, for example, decennial census data and contemporary local newspapers. Bias is a risk that confronts us all. The researcher needs to guard against this risk at all times, giving frequent consideration to the developing products of research and considering alternative sources that might be used to fill in vital gaps.

There is a danger in listing possible sources, in that it reinforces the idea of a standard set of information. Clearly there is a danger that, in looking for evidence, the researcher only goes to the obvious and usual sources. It is important when searching for evidence to think laterally and to follow other leads and possibilities. Research data should be corroborated from alternative sources, including, where appropriate, the record of the built fabric itself.

In writing up the documentary evidence, it is important for reasons of credibility, transparency and accountability that certain criteria are followed:

- It is made clear what information and evidence was drawn upon, and how it was analysed and interpreted. It should also be shown how competing ideas, contradictory information, etc. were dealt with.
- All sources used in the report are cited with sufficient precision to enable others to locate them.
- All sources consulted are listed, even if not cited.
- All major sources or collections not consulted, but believed to have potential usefulness in establishing significance, should be listed and the reasons why they were not used explained.

Interpreting the building/physical remains

In addition to the use of documentary evidence, an understanding of the historical development of an asset can also usually be derived, at least in part, from an analysis and interpretation of the physical evidence provided by its buildings, structures and landscape at the site. This is evidence that derives from the asset itself – the way that its fabric and layout, its landscape and immediate setting and/or the building(s) and its/their use, have changed over time.

Traditionally, conservationists have placed great emphasis on the importance of protecting the fabric of significant places and on valuing the evidence of changes in the fabric. In this instance, it must be remembered that, for the purpose of interpretation, fabric may also include the immediate landscape as altered by man, for this can be read too.

Conservation principles (which are discussed in more detail in Chapter 8) emphasise the importance of keeping accurate records of how and why changes to the built fabric occur (although generally the equivalent potential of the landscape is sadly overlooked). The reason for such emphasis on record-keeping is that historic fabric contains vital archaeological information about the asset and its past use and change. If properly interpreted, these physical remains can reveal critical information, not only about architectural and constructional detail of the evolution of the asset, but also the wider socio-economic and cultural story of human habitation, use and interaction with the place and how it has evolved over time. As Kerr (2013) asserts, the fabric of an asset is the most accurate (though often incomplete) document of its history. He suggests that the physical evidence 'tells the story of what actually happened rather than what someone intended should happen or believed did happen'. English Heritage (2008) reinforce this by stating: 'The fabric of any place, however recent, is the primary record of its evolution.'

The process of interpreting the historic fabric will involve the study of the development of architectural form, layout, construction technique, and the materials and services used in construction, along with indications of change held within the accessible fabric in the form of the remnants of redundant elements, vestigial traces of removed structures, straight construction joints, and other archaeological evidence. Physical evidence of changing uses and the processes that occurred there should be sought in order to understand the specific functions that took place within the asset and on its site.

Hopefully, the results of documentary research and physical analysis of the built fabric or landscape will complement and reinforce each other, leading to increased confidence in interpretation. Equally, when things work well, positive evidence from the one can often help fill in gaps in the other. In practice, of course, complex assets are rarely so compliant. Therefore, it must be anticipated that the study will end up in a developmental history that can be partly read and interpreted, but which contains a number of frustrating lacuna and some bits of documentary or more often physical evidence which cannot be placed with certainty anywhere in the 'jigsaw'.

Reading and interpreting built fabric and landscapes take time and practice. They are not skills that can be learnt from a book or generally by an individual in isolation. For complex assets, the professional and academic rigours of archaeology, architectural history or landscape and garden history need to be combined. It is human nature that many building and landscape analysts believe that they can deliver all such skills on their own. In reality, this is rarely the case – different disciplines require different attributes – especially, different ways of looking at things – and these are not often combined in one person.

This book is not about interpreting fabric and it is therefore not possible to discuss the various techniques and tools that are used in the process. However, it is worth pointing out that, in addition to visual analysis, an increasing range of non-destructive analytical tools is now available. These all have strengths and shortcomings, and investment in the hire of equipment or specialist contractors for such work should not be made until the suitability of the method for the purposes intended and the circumstances involved is assured. On occasion, it can be beneficial to follow up visual and non-destructive analysis with targeted and limited opening up of the fabric to clarify critical uncertainties. This approach should never be adopted lightly and without consideration of the impact on the historic fabric and its integrity. If the site carries statutory protection such as listing, prior consent for opening up may be necessary from the relevant authority, depending upon circumstances.

Establishing and analysing the character, dynamics and setting of the asset

The foregoing deals with some very tangible matters that may need to be understood, considered and appreciated in reaching an assessment of significance for a heritage asset. There are other, often less easily defined, characteristics of an asset that need to be understood, too – for example, the idea of a sense of place. It is fundamental to recognise that these are not just 'nice to have' components of the assessment process – sometimes, they are of overriding importance to a balanced consideration of significance.

The character of an asset may consist wholly or largely of comfortably tangible elements, but frequently that is not the case and intangible attributes are involved. Identifying and understanding these require an open and receptive mind and senses, and often take time. Sights, sounds and smells can be critically important, as can diurnal or seasonal variations. Those analysing an asset as the first step in making an assessment of significance must approach their task with an awareness of such possibilities. For example, in assessing the inner city and dockland character of Liverpool as part of its successful nomination as the Liverpool Maritime Mercantile City World Heritage Site (inscribed in 2004), the City Council observed that the city is distinctive for attributes such as its historic and modern commercial astuteness, internationalism, innovation, creativity and risk-taking, but more than anything they came to appreciate that it is defined by its 'edginess'.

Identifying the dynamics of a place is critically important, but it is not an easy process to describe, as the far from comprehensive range of factors mentioned in the preceding paragraph demonstrates. Using one's senses to map out vital characteristics such as sights, sound and smells is one thing – detecting and appreciating something like 'edginess' for what it is requires a very different analytical approach. And there are so many possible intangible characteristics apart from these. The identification of these is a challenge that must be taken on when approaching the understanding of a heritage asset and assessment of its significance. There are many things that contribute to a sense of place. Managing an asset to protect and even enhance its sense of place, if indeed it is found to be an element of profound significance to the asset, can be a delicate issue, for intangible values can be vulnerable when essentially they are 'invisible'. Currently, a dominant school of thought in the western hemisphere seems to be that what needs to be grasped and dealt with are the *physical attributes* of intangible values. We are not convinced about that. To stick with the dockyard theme, it is evident that part of the sense of place of a historic dockyard may be the saltiness of the air, the insistent cries of seagulls, the sounds of water lapping against the wharf edge or dock gates and of traffic on the sea or river close by. The physical manifestations of these characteristics, deposited salt crystals from evaporation or corrosion on old iron dock fixtures, the transitory presence of individual birds in a view across the space, the water and the boats themselves are arguably not the things that matter, are not the essence of the sense of place. In fact, as noted, many of these positive attributes keep moving and may spend almost no time in the setting of the asset itself. Yet, in terms of future management of change, these key contributors to the dockyard's sense of place may well be at risk. New tall or dense development along the wharf edge is unlikely to eradicate the saltiness of the air or silence the noise of the gulls, but within the redeveloped historic dockyard it may act as an impenetrable baffle to the sounds of lapping water and the dull chugging of boat engines. The process of learning about the asset, identifying its essential characteristics and assessing significance must always be capable of picking up on these and all other intangible values and establishing the relative magnitude of the contribution of each to the significance of the asset, irrespective of whether or not the value manifests key immovable physical attributes within the place or its wider setting. A similar issue sometimes arises with historic areas which are 'tidied up' and become gentrified. It is often the case that while the physical assets remain (albeit sometimes in an over-restored state), the sights, sounds, smells and atmosphere are changed as one group of people and their activities move out and another moves in.

There can also be an overarching difficulty in relating intangible issues, such as the emotional draw of an asset that is associated with memories, to the physical aspects of the site. In relation to this issue, English Heritage (2008) has observed:

> *Compared with other heritage values, social values tend to be less dependent on the survival of historic fabric. They may survive the replacement of the original physical structure, so long as its key social and cultural characteristics are maintained; and can be the popular driving force for the re-creation of lost (and often deliberately destroyed or desecrated) places with high symbolic value.*

and

> *The social values of places are not always clearly recognised by those who share them, and may only be articulated when the future of a place is threatened. They may relate to an activity that is associated with the place, rather than with its physical fabric. The social value of a place may indeed have no direct relationship to any formal historical or aesthetic values that may have been ascribed to it.*

In Chapter 2, we observed that is a fundamental principle that all heritage assets have a setting and that these settings constitute an integral part of an asset's historical and cultural significance. It should be apparent, therefore, that in developing an understanding of an asset, its setting and the disposition of that setting within the wider historic environment must be explored, characterised and subsequently considered as part of the process of assessing the asset's significance. It is the contribution that the setting makes to the significance of the asset that must be defined. As English Heritage's (2011a) and Historic England's (2015) guidance make clear, the setting of a heritage asset can enhance its significance, whether or not it was ever designed to do so. Given what has been said already, it should be obvious that the evaluation of an asset's setting also needs to consider intangible characteristics that may be a fundamental contributor to significance.

It should be evident that views can play an important part in the contribution that the setting makes to the significance of a heritage asset. This is reflected in current guidance, with Historic Scotland (2010) noting that settings might include, *inter alia*:

- The visual envelope, incorporating views to, from and across the historic asset or place;
- Key vistas, framed by rows of trees, buildings or natural features that give an asset or place a context, whether intentional or not;
- The prominence of the historic asset or place in views throughout the surrounding area;
- General and specific views, including foregrounds and backdrops.

In terms of the process of assessing significance, Historic Scotland (2010) recommends:

> *Key viewpoints to, from and across the setting of a historic asset should be identified. Often certain views are critical to how a historic asset was approached and seen, or understood when looking out. These views were sometimes deliberately manipulated, manufactured and/or maintained. Depending on the historic asset or place in question these could include: entrances, specific points on approaches, routeways, associated farmland, other related buildings, monuments, natural features, etc.*

That, of course, is right, but, in our view, placing too great an emphasis on 'key viewpoints' can diminish the understanding of the valuable contribution that is sometimes made by 'general' views. The assessment process should ensure that a thorough and balanced appreciation is achieved of all contributory views and vistas. For clarification, a 'vista' is usually defined as a scene experienced through or along a viewing corridor, such as an avenue of trees, whereas, somewhat more generally, a 'view' is regarded to be a scene or prospect gained from a particular position. Of course, views can be designed or accidental; they will either be fixed/static or dynamic/kinetic (that is, changing with the movement of the viewer). In assessing the contribution that they make to the significance of a heritage asset, it is also critical to remember that views may well be subject to seasonal and diurnal variations. This analysis should be built into the assessment process.

Historic England's guidance on setting notes that: 'The setting of any heritage asset is likely to include a variety of views of, across, or including that asset, and views of the surroundings from or through the asset' (Historic England 2015). The identification and assessment of views and vistas can in consequence be a complex and time-consuming process. It must be stressed that it is not simply views of (that is, directionally towards or across) the asset that may be of interest for the contribution that they make to significance. Views across and from the asset that do not include the built element of the heritage asset must also be given equivalent consideration. Accidental or intentional inter-visibility between two or more heritage assets in the locality or between a heritage asset and natural or topographic features in the wider environment can also be important contributions to significance.

Identifying and characterising views and vistas in order to understand the contribution that they make to significance take practice, but this is an important skill to learn if management through significance is to be carried out proficiently. It is not always necessary to undertake a formal views analysis, of course, but for complex situations it should be regarded as being essential. In 2011, English Heritage published its guidance, *Seeing the History in the View: A Method for Assessing Heritage Significance within Views* (English Heritage, 2011b), which explains the concept of qualitative visual assessment of views. While this is overly complicated for use in many assessments of significance, the general principles it promotes are of value. The guidance rightly emphasises that there are two very distinct components that must be understood in every identified view:

1 individual heritage assets that are included within it; and
2 the value of the view as a whole.

Whatever degree of formality is adopted in analysing views as part of the process of assessing significance, it is important to rationalise and be able to justify the reasons for selecting particular viewing places and the particular views therefrom. Critically, the history of the view from each viewing place should be understood, as this is a key factor in appreciating the changing contribution to significance that the view has made over time.

Assessing community values

Local communities need to be involved in the process of assessing significance because what happens to the asset may have a material effect on them, and they may well attribute important tangible and intangible values of their own to the heritage asset, irrespective of who owns it. It is important, however, that liaison with the local community is not just a case of keeping them informed about decisions, but that it also actually involves them in making decisions (which is of course one of the benchmarks of sustainability) – particularly in identifying what is valuable about the asset. The community (and, importantly, others who have or have had, an association with the asset – including those who have worked at the site) may be a useful source of written, visual and oral material, which can add to an understanding of the asset because they may know how it was used and how it worked. That is, they may be able, because of their first-hand experience, in giving oral evidence, to help to complement the evidence from elsewhere and, in addition, they may be able to explain, interpret and validate the written and visual documentary evidence (or perhaps question its validity). In addition, it is important to acknowledge, and take account of the fact, that people's memories and associations with the asset are also an important part of the make-up of what contributes to its significance. In a sense. they are effectively the repository of the contemporary social value of the place. The significance of an asset essentially resides in how it is valued by people, particularly in relation to such issues as identity and belonging.

Stakeholders therefore need to be identified and involved in the determination of significance. This will include the past and present owners and occupiers of the asset and also past and present members of the community who used, or were associated with, or associated themselves with, it. We are concerned here with those for whom the asset has memory or ties because of its physical or its symbolic presence. In many cases, the insights that are added are related to the 'intangible' aspects of the atmosphere and 'the spirit' of the place.

This is a particularly important aspect of establishing significance, not least because conservation activity is often actually justified on the basis that society chooses to value certain things, whereas in reality 'experts' – and often experts drawn from certain strata in society – have decided what is valuable and why. As Blunstone (2000) observes: 'Getting at the meaning of places should not reside with professionals alone but with the people that use and visit and construct their own meanings out of places.'

It can be argued that the incorporation of stakeholders' memories and associations has been better prioritised in recent years, but it is still an area where much more can be done. In part, the problem is related to the 'mindset' or perhaps the willingness, or otherwise, of those involved in the assessment process (including the client) to engage with stakeholders, but, in part, it is also an issue related to available resources – skills, time and money. As Sian Jones (2014) observes:

> *Yet while all values are ultimately historically and culturally situated, for many heritage professionals the new emphasis on contemporary value and benefit introduces a dangerous element of subjectivity, transience and instrumentalism. It also contributes to a fundamental tension between the idea of heritage as something that is fixed, tangible and of the past on the one hand, and something that is mutable, intangible and very much of the present on the other.*

Although worthwhile and important – and actually we would suggest essential to an understanding of significance – community values can be quite a difficult issue to deal with effectively. The sort of issues that arise might include:

- How to identify what constitutes the appropriate community/stakeholders. It is relatively easy to map who will be affected by decisions, but less easy to identify (and sometimes contact) those whose memories and associations can contribute to the idea of significance. This is particularly so as communities are more mobile and more dispersed and less homogeneous than they used to be – and meaning is now perhaps more than ever lost between generations.
- There is of course power in the process of identifying who the stakeholders are, and therefore it is important that this is viewed as holistically, objectively and, as the process evolves, as dynamically as possible.
- Mapping, recording and articulating some kind of community vision may also be difficult when it may be necessary to interpret competing associations and memories, or, indeed, conflicting memories. A difficulty may also arise when some aspects of the significance of the asset may be important only for a small and politically unsophisticated or disenfranchised group.
- The question of how to deal with powerful groups who may distort or dominate the process is sometimes problematic.

As we have observed, community values are very often concerned with memories and associations. Memories can of course be distorted and 'the truth' filtered through nostalgia, which can cause problems of verification and 'authenticity'. It should, however, be remembered that the important connection for people to the past does not necessarily rely on historical accuracy, but is important for its symbolism and its sociological and psychological value. The smells, sounds, sights, atmosphere (and even things that cannot be directly sensed) are important characteristics which connect people to the asset and should be treated as seriously as the more easily 'measured' aspects. Nevertheless, this can present problems where the memories, values and the sense of what is important held by the community contradict or are in tension with the 'fact-based' investigation of the asset through documentary and physical evidence gathering. Similarly the community may see their relationship to the asset, and therefore its significance, as being represented by buildings that are seen by the experts as being less architecturally or historically important. In allocating relative significance, the experts may find this problematic, especially where it means that they may have to adjust their interpretation of what is important and why.

There can also be an overarching difficulty in relating intangible issues such as the emotional draw of a place associated with memories to the physical aspects of the site. Indeed, English Heritage have observed that:

> *Social value can also survive, and may even encourage, replacement of the original structure, so long as its key social and cultural characteristics remain intact ... Compared with other heritage values, social values are thus less dependent on the survival of historic fabric.*
> (English Heritage, 2008, p. 29)

It should be noted, however, that for those who see the fabric as being the primary attribute of significance, this disconnect between value and the fabric of the asset can cause fundamental 'philosophical' problems.

There is also a judgement to be made about the relative importance of a particular event in relation to the overall significance of the asset. An example might be where a recent or dramatic event associated with the asset has had a big impact on the community. The community may see the event as being a, or even the, major reference point of significance, rather than appreciating it as one of a series of impactful events that have occurred over time. Memories may be vivid but related to incidents that, while they may be of immediate impact, are highly temporal and will be blurred in the minds of the next generation. Of course, such a situation reinforces the general point that significance changes over time. The opposite problem might occur, where some people's memories associated with an asset may be painful and unwanted and they are antagonistic to plans to conserve it. An example might be places of hardship associated with poor and/or dangerous employment such as cotton mills or mining. A similar but slightly different issue can arise with more modern buildings, where the social and perhaps the aesthetic values of places, such as post-war social housing estates, might be contested. It is interesting, and pertinent, to observe that in the case of recent buildings (such as post-war social housing estates), there is often a reluctance to attribute social values. Possibly this is because it is more difficult, and also perhaps because it is more contentious particularly where estates are perceived to have 'failed' architecturally and socially. In these instances, the case for protection is often met on largely less contentious, though still contested, grounds. The problem here is that if the 'true' or one of the key criteria is not openly acknowledged and debated, then that value can be lost in decisions on management and change.

The community may of course be aware of, or indeed involved in, plans to develop the site. If the community is in favour of the plans, this may affect their perception of the importance of the place which can be problematic if the proposals have the potential to damage its significance.

As we have said, community value is often an important component in the process of the assessment of significance, requiring more attention than it is usually given. There are good examples where the active involvement of a community has not just added to an understanding of significance, but has changed the appreciation of how significant the place is and in which attributes of the asset significance resides. As Pearson (Pearson and Sullivan, 1995) observes, 'Local communities have a more holistic view of the elements in their environment that they value and they can clearly articulate the contemporary relevance and significance of those elements.'

Analysing significance

The cultural significance of the asset will be assessed and determined by an analysis of the physical and the documentary and oral evidence (including community values) gathered about the site. The analysis will be used to interpret and articulate meaning and significance from the evidence. There can be a tendency when undertaking value assessments to put a substantial amount of effort into gathering the evidence of the history of the asset, but less into the analytical stage. It is important, therefore, in the evidence-gathering stage, that the purpose of the exercise – to understand what is important about the site rather than to produce an exhaustive history – is borne in mind. In the evidence-gathering stage, it is both inevitable and useful that some analytical work occurs. The process should be seen as an iterative one (which should also always keep the aims and objectives of the exercise in mind). Such interaction will help in focusing and rationalising the evidence gathering and should save time and resources. However, it is important that it does not exclude material relevant to an understanding of significance, or stifle a divergent approach which seeks out and is open to the validity of a variety of sources. It may well be that the analysis highlights gaps or deficiencies in the material, which may make it necessary to revisit some material and/or expand on its scope.

It is important that the integration and analysis are carried out, as for any type of research project, with rigour, clarity and transparency in order to ensure credibility. The methodology used to synthesise and interpret the evidence should be stated and justified. It should be made clear what evidence was drawn upon both directly and indirectly (it should also be properly referenced) and how, if at all, it was weighted or conflicts in evidence were resolved. Any assumptions made should be indicated as such, and the basis on which they were made should be clearly set out. If there were any gaps in the information-gathering stage – evidence that cannot or has not been retrieved and analysed – this should be made clear.

In addition, to this perhaps prosaic explanation, it would be useful to set out the 'philosophical' underpinning used in the assessment. Such rigour is necessary to justify the judgements being made and to allow others to understand, and perhaps challenge, the basis of such judgements.

Assessing significance: comparisons and relativity

In Chapter 3 we gave examples of some of the value typologies which are in use. It is important that no one particular value category should be assumed to be more intrinsically worthy or important than another, and should not be allowed to dominate the assessment of significance of a particular place or decisions flowing from it. That is not to say that for a particular asset certain attributes and therefore values will not emerge as dominant characteristics because, obviously, that is the aim of assessing significance. Rather we are emphasisng that the task should not be approached with subjective assumptions that, say, architectural values are inherently or automatically more important than, for example, social values. Following on from an assessment, this balance needs to be maintained to ensure that one set of values does not obscure other values in terms of either celebrating the place or managing it (and it is in the management of the asset that values are likely to be 'lost'). It is, for example, not uncommon for age value to dominate to such an extent that more recent aspects of the site are seen as relatively insignificant.

This assumption that all value categories should be considered to be of equal standing is the working premise when approaching an assessment of significance as should be the assumption, initially at least, that the full range of values might be represented. The process of assessment should then normally follow these procedures:

1 The identification and assessment of the overall and particular values embodied in and represented by the asset.
2 An evaluation of the asset's importance compared to others.
3 An evaluation of which aspects and elements of the asset contribute to overall significance, and how they do so.
4 Following from the above, an evaluation of the relative significance of the various aspects and elements of the asset.

It can be seen that at the heart of this process is an assessment of value which is looking outwards at comparisons and looking inwards at relativity.

Comparative significance is best expressed by using a hierarchy of ascending or descending levels of value. A number of different hierarchical systems are in use today, but the three most common would appear to be a traditional structure built around international/national/regional/local levels, high/medium/low grading or several variants of a hierarchy proposed by Kerr (2013) which typically might consist of:

- *Exceptional*: features of exceptional/international significance or which contain elements with a significance beyond national boundaries.
- *Considerable*: features of considerable/national significance, possibly reflected in statutory designations such as Scheduled Monument, Listed Building or equivalent nationally graded sites (including those of ecological and nature conservation value).
- *Some*: features of some significance, important at regional level either individually or for group value.
- *Limited*: features of limited/local significance.
- *Unknown*: features of unknown significance resulting from a lack of sufficient information on which to base sound analysis of its value.
- *No*: features of no significance.

In many cases, a further category – 'negative significance' – is also identified in this kind of hierarchy in order to identify features that are thought to have such a deleterious effect that they detract from the overall significance of the asset, or from elements of it.

It would be remiss not to recognise that some people feel uncomfortable with the idea of relative significance, in the sense at least of actually classifying and grading elements, particularly when the relative significance of aspects, elements or components is assessed not only to help in articulating the overall significance of the asset, but also in order to make decisions about managing change. Fabric may be lost as a result of these decisions stating which elements absolutely must be protected and which are less important.

It is clearly important that the categories 'unknown' and 'no' are not treated as being more or less one and the same. 'Unknown' clearly indicates that it is a position that has been arrived at because of lack of information, whereas 'No' implies that this judgement has been arrived at after an objective and thorough investigation of the asset and its range of values. There is a concern about deciding that something has no significance. Documentary evidence may not be available about every aspect of the place (it may have been lost, overlooked, or there is no evidence because it was not thought important in the past – even though it may be now). This raises the question of whether, in an evidence-based assessment, a lack of evidence supporting the significance of something means that it is not significant. As the traditional aphorism has it, 'absence of evidence is not evidence of absence'. It could be argued that 'the precautionary principle' should apply and that elements should only be placed in this category if it can be actively demonstrated that they are not important, rather than assuming they are not just because there is no evidence to support their value. Schaafsma (1989) suggested that 'Our problems in cultural resource management persist because we have failed to develop means to identify insignificant sites satisfactorily.' For him, the historic resource was significant until proved otherwise. While such an approach may not be practical, it is perhaps a valuable 'mindset' to adopt in that it adds to and reinforces the notion of rigorous assessment.

Likewise, negative significance implies that this judgement has been arrived at through analysis and interpretation including taking account of the views and perspectives of all the stakeholders. It should also be borne in mind that an element that is considered less significant than another may still be vital to an understanding of the value of the more significant element because it might be contextually important.

Despite the need for caution as expressed above, the attribution of relative significance is important because it will highlight areas where change can take place at a site without reducing significance. Also it should be borne in mind that, as English Heritage (2008) observe, 'Some elements of a place may actually mar or conceal its significance ... Eliminating or mitigating negative characteristics may help to reveal or reinforce heritage values of a place and thus its significance.'

It should of course be borne in mind that the elements that have no or negative significance will possibly have a function which is difficult to relocate, but at least the no/negative value can be taken into consideration in future decision-making.

Whichever hierarchical system is chosen, it is vital that the levels are fully explained in the introduction to the assessment of significance so that readers can comprehend the adopted gradings unambiguously. There is a real danger in trying to read out and compare one assessment of significance to another, although in our experience this is occasionally attempted.

The issue of how a range of values, sometimes co-existing and reinforcing each other, but sometimes competing with each other, can be clearly identified and accommodated, and then protected and enhanced, without producing something which lacks coherence and cohesion, can be difficult to resolve. If such a situation occurs, then not only will it be a source of confusion and probably controversy, it will be impossible to produce an effective management regime.

The assigning of a relative value is not a quantitative exercise and is not meant to be a scoring system – it is rather a means of making comparisons. It is important to assign 'soft' criteria which, while differentiating, do not give the impression of absolutes or the sense that such things can be easily measured, particularly as we are dealing with comparative judgements. Kerr suggests (2013, p. 19): 'The hierarchy developed to present the level of significance should [therefore] be chosen to suit the place and that it should be explained with clarity.'

It is this area, the extent to which ideas of relative significance can be agreed upon, that can cause the most difficulties, both conceptually and in practice, but upon which the success of any plan or process arising out of an assessment of significance will, to a large extent, rest. This is because, in effect, its purpose and role are derived from the idea that a significance-based approach to managing the built heritage acknowledges that there may be different values embodied in the asset, and that these might be embodied both alone and in various combinations, in its different elements, aspects and qualities. The key to an effective management process is that it is an attempt to identify values as separate, while understanding and celebrating their connections and intricacies and the way that they contribute to the whole – but nevertheless at the same time judging and balancing their worth in order to provide the substance of a single cohesive and coherent process which allows decisions on managing change to take place. As the Burra Charter observes, 'Relative degrees of cultural significance may lead to different conservation actions at a place' (Australia ICOMOS, 1999).

Comparisons

To a large extent, assessing the overall significance of a place is based on comparisons. Therefore, it is all about relative significance, particularly in terms of what we might call traditional conservation criteria (e.g. the best example of an architectural period, the first time such and such a technique was used, etc.). But it is arguably less so with other perhaps newer criteria in that, for example, you cannot really measure the value of an asset to one community compared to the value of a similar asset to another community, though you can, of course, measure how many people value it, etc. Therefore, part of the process of assessment may well involve a knowledge of comparative information about, say, building types, for example, how does this nineteenth-century workhouse compare in terms of, say, its design, layout and use in relation to other workhouses regionally and nationally? Other examples might be:

- Is it the most complete?
- Does it perhaps have a design and layout which represent or illustrate some change in social policy regarding how the poor were regarded by society and how they were treated?
- Is it a representative example of its type (which might be the most valuable quality)?
- If it is the work of a particular architect, does it represent, say, an early example of their work, or a particularly fine example of it?
- If it is good example of a particular style of architecture – say, Arts and Crafts or Modernism – is it the only known example in that area or a pioneering example?

Such comparisons provide a context that will help to assess and then to justify, explain and illustrate significance. However, it is important that such comparisons do not produce too much of a straitjacket for the assessment, which could overshadow the unique qualities and values of the particular asset.

Kerr (2013) suggests that the quality of the assessment of significance will depend on the assessor's contextual and comparative knowledge of the subject and period. He refers to the need, among other things, to establish to what extent an example is:

- Early
- Seminal
- Intact
- Representative
- Rare, or
- Climactic

We would suggest that these categories are extremely useful for comparative purposes in helping to assess importance (and some are, of course, explicit or implicit values), and we would make the following observations on Kerr's list (to which we have added age and vulnerability):

- *Age*: The fact that something is old is often considered as in itself demonstrating value. Indeed, in some countries such as the UK, age is an overriding factor in determining whether a building should be listed. Whether something should be automatically considered valuable simply on the basis of its age is clearly a debatable point – and has been since the time of William Morris. The point that the emphasis on age is one of the factors which increases the vulnerability of more recent buildings of cultural value, particularly perhaps from the post-war period, is an obvious one but nonetheless important.
- *Early*: Obviously the quality of being an early example is a different concept to age, as it can just as easily mean an early example of a telecommunications site as it can an early example of a medieval timber-framed farmhouse.
- *Rarity*: The characteristic of something being rare is another reference point for demonstrating its importance. The sense that just because something is unique it is valuable is generally accepted, although it is interesting to reflect on why this should be necessarily so. There is perhaps a distinction to be made between something which is now the only remaining example of an important building type or place and something which is rare because it was the only one of its kind – in which case, we might value its uniqueness because this might tell us something about a society or the forces that created a 'one off'. If it is a less important object, it might be considered a 'curiosity' and therefore of interest rather than of significance.
- *Vulnerability*: The question of whether we value something that is in immediate danger of being lost more highly than we otherwise might is interesting.
- *Completeness*: The extent to which something is complete or in good condition will make it valuable because of what we can learn and understand from the whole (physical) picture. But many sites are valuable because they are incomplete. Pompeii and Machu Picchu are examples where the atmosphere created by the ruins is arguably as important as the story to which the ruins testify.
- *Representativeness*: This is an important characteristic and some have argued that it is more important than significance. It can be viewed at two levels. One is the sense of being representative of its type – in which case (as Kerr suggests), the extent to which it is complete may be important. The other is related to a perhaps more fundamental issue about identifying what should be protected and why. In turn, this is related to the point that, if one of the purposes of

conservation is for present and future generations to understand more about past societies, then, for example, when the iconic or rare is favoured over that which represents the ordinary and the everyday, the picture is distorted.

- *Seminal*: Places or buildings that influenced and shaped ideas will clearly be significant (for example, in relation to an architectural movement, or in representing and illustrating changes in public policy in, say, the treatment of offenders, care of the mentally ill, etc.).
- *High point*: That which is considered perhaps the developmental peak of, say, architectural or technical achievement, or perhaps a social idea which is reflected in the built form.

Some issues in value assessment

> *Objects, collections, buildings and places become recognised as 'heritage' through conscious decisions and unspoken values of particular people and institutions and for reasons that are strongly shaped by social contexts and processes.*
>
> (Avrami *et al.*, 2000)

The sense that value is a subjective judgement clearly raises issues not only about the benefit of conserving the built heritage but also about the process(es) by which certain elements of the built environment are chosen as being worthy of protection (and by implication some are said to have little or no value), and how those elements are protected and managed.

Value typologies need to be understood in terms of both meaning and intent by a range of groups. They should also reflect a variety of perceptions of what is valuable and why, and not just reflect how 'experts' and professionals view heritage. A value typology, therefore, needs to acknowledge the range of possible values in a place to the extent that all stakeholders recognise that their interests are represented. Therefore, there needs to be a development and use of value categories which are more wide-ranging, holistic, pluralistic and inclusive (particularly in acknowledging the views of those who have associations with the site) than the sort of typology that even in recent times favoured the art-historical and elitist view of what constituted cultural heritage. This is a situation that, in part at least, can be seen to have been due to the fact that decisions about what should be protected, and why, were decided by a relatively small, and some would suggest, elite group of experts, drawn from a relatively narrow constituency.

Value categories should be conceived of as being fluid and not mutually exclusive. The value of categories is in having a reference point, but they should be designed and intended to stimulate divergent thinking. The intention should be to help order thinking about the place, but not to restrict it. It is also important not to oversimplify – complexity needs to be acknowledged and worked with.

The fact that, in most cases, an asset will have multiple values will usually reinforce its importance and therefore the case for its protection. However, multiple values will also probably mean that different individuals or groups see the importance of the asset as being embodied in or represented by different elements or aspects of the asset. Also where the values of a place are represented by a particular object or element, a situation can arise where different groups see the same thing as important but for different reasons. Both of these examples of differing perspectives can, in practice, cause problems in the management and protection of a place because while sometimes these different values (and perspectives) complement and reinforce each other, sometimes they can be in tension or conflict. There are many examples where the protection of one aspect of the value of the asset leads to damage to other aspects. Experts may also implicitly (or explicitly) favour certain aspects or interpretations of the past over others, no matter what their relative merits – for example, the dominance of the age value often means that some conservationists attach a higher value to older artifacts or buildings than they do to, for example, more recent architecture. The Burra Charter Practice Note, under the heading, 'Avoiding preconceptions', observes:

Assessing cultural significance requires a careful process of analysis. It is not sufficient to make judgements based on rules of thumb or conventional wisdom. In assessing cultural significance, it is essential to be open to knowledge and values expressed from different perspectives and cultural contexts. Be prepared to conduct deeper research beyond 'the mainstream'.

(Australia ICOMOS, 2013)

Also the credibility or the value attached to different types and different sources of evidence may vary between different cultural groups in the community, between the community and the experts, and possibly between experts with different backgrounds and perspectives. That is, different disciplines within conservation will give different priorities and see things in different ways. There may also be problems with interpretations of terms and even meanings. So it may seem that different groups perceive the same value as being embodied in the same aspect or element of the place (say, aesthetic value), but in reality they conceive and interpret that value in different ways.

This emphasises the fact that the attitude of and make-up of the team which is undertaking a value assessment are important, and it reinforces the point that the process of value measurements, as well as the results, needs to be open and democratic – and as objective as possible.

The articulation of values into a typology is never going to be an 'absolute' definition of the cultural significance of a particular asset, but its usefulness is as a framework which can be an organisational tool and a reference point while being fluid and flexible. A typology should broadly acknowledge a range of values that ought to be considered in most situations and which allows for common reference points and comparisons as a starting point, which will be modified to take account of the particular qualities of an asset. That is, the typology should not be used in a way that assumes that all the values do or should exist at a particular site, nor, more importantly, that any typology encapsulates all aspects of value. Most commentators suggest that the values statements are useful frameworks, but which probably need to be broken down into more precise categories as knowledge and understanding of the site increase.

We can suggest that the typology categories should be further defined and refined in response to the characteristics of the particular asset. That is, for any given asset, the typology should be used to engage with it and tease out its particular characteristics and attributes. Although they may have to be 'deconstructed' and developed for the particular situation in order to make a better fit, there is clearly a conceptual and practical use in setting out a typology which effectively categorises a range of values that may contribute to the significance of an asset. Mason (2002) suggests that the purpose is to 'move conservation stakeholders closer to having a *lingua franca* in which all parties values can be expressed and discussed'. He also suggests that devising and debating the typology are a means of stimulating participation.

It is important to understand the following points about values and value typologies. What is regarded as valuable about a particular asset will not only vary between individuals and groups but will change over time, as will value categories themselves. That is, significance is dynamic and subjective and evolves within the context of changing social, cultural and political contexts. In other words, changing social perceptions considerably influence the value that we put upon our historic environment. For example, most generations struggle to appreciate the architecture of their own period along with that of their immediate predecessors. For example, in the UK, Georgian architecture was reviled by the Victorians, yet arguably it is appreciated more than any other age/style today. Most of the high Gothic Victorian architectural masterpieces that we acknowledge today were decried forty years ago as monstrosities. Current debates about the value of twentieth century buildings reinforce this point. It is extremely difficult to predict how and when such a reappraisal of value may occur, but consideration of this is an important part of the equation in seeking to optimise benefits accruing today without compromising the value that might be placed on that asset by future generations.

In looking at how conservation was discussed in the relatively recent past, an attitude can be perceived among some that the buildings and sites in question were self-evidentially valuable (and that the values are now self-evident because the sites are designated); that is, they were treated as though there were some intrinsic value involved. However, cultural values are not intrinsic in the sense of being fixed or absolute. Essentially, places, sites and objects become culturally significant because people – often from a rather small and narrow constituency – have ascribed values to them. Value in this sense is essentially a social construct that can vary between people and over time. As Avrami *et al.* (2000) observe:

> *Objects and places are not in and of themselves what is important about cultural heritage; they are important because of the meanings and uses that people attach to these material goods and the values that they*

*represent. These meanings, uses, and values must be understood as part
of the larger sphere of socio cultural processes ... As a social activity, conservation is an enduring process, a means to an end rather than an end
in itself. The process is creative and is motivated and underpinned by the
values of individuals, institutions and communities.*

It is important then to remember that cultural values are in fact dynamic, relative
and subjective (as are the value typologies). It is worth noting, however, Mason's
(2002) observation that '[This] intrinsic value argument in heritage conservation
would be analogous to the "intrinsic" argument in environmental conservation,
through which it is assumed that "natural" characteristics (wildness) are intrinsically valuable.' There are, in one sense, widely accepted values – age and rarity,
for example (at least in Western cultures, although even in Europe the notion is
not uncontested) – and of course some characteristics that are considered to be
of value may be intrinsic to particular sites or buildings. However, the idea that
conserving something, for example, just because it is old is a social construct.
Significance, then, is an articulation of what people feel about the historic environment and how they respond to it, rather than reflecting any inherent qualities
of the place. We should 'understand significance as growing out of the needs of
contemporary societies rather than existing independently, within the relics of
past cultures' (Carman, 1996). Consideration of the idea that we are not dealing with absolute values also emphasises that what we choose to protect is not
a means of preserving the past *per se* (particularly by choosing some elements
and not others), so much as it is the holding up of a mirror to our present-day
concerns and our selective interpretation of what we deem to be important. As
Lowenthal (1997) states:

*However faithfully we preserve, however authentically we restore, how-
ever deeply we immerse ourselves in bygone time, life back then was based
on ways of being and believing incommensurable with our own ... we cannot help but view and celebrate it through present-day lenses.*

However, it is worth acknowledging that, as Impey observes (2006), values 'are
liable to evolve along with changes in people's own perceptions and interests
although longstanding attachment of value to places itself confers a species of
value and adds substance to the idea of "established" value'.

Sensitivity to change

We have made the point that attributing relative significance to the elements that
make up the asset is a useful, and indeed necessary, task which allows change
to be managed in a way that causes least harm to significance (and indeed may
improve it where there is negative significance). Another way of conceptualising
the assets and its various elements is to consider their sensitivity to change. Pearson and Marshall (2005) refer to the level of sensitivity to change being based

on the vulnerability of the component to loss of heritage values through change, and give the following example from a Conservation Plan that they wrote for the National Library of Australia:

- *High sensitivity: High sensitivity to change occurs where a change would pose a major threat to a specific heritage value of the component affected, or the Library as a whole. A major threat is one that would lead to substantial or total loss of the heritage value.*
- *Moderate sensitivity: Moderate sensitivity to change occurs where a change would pose a moderate threat to a specific heritage value of the component affected, or would pose a threat to a component of heritage significance in another part of the building. A moderate threat is one that would diminish the heritage value, or diminish the ability of an observer to appreciate the value.*
- *Low sensitivity: Low sensitivity to change occurs where a change would pose no appreciable threat to a specific heritage value of the component affected, and would pose no appreciable threat to heritage significance in another part of the building. Components of the Library with no individual identified heritage values are likely to have a low sensitivity to change (rising to moderate if the proposals affect adjacent areas having values).*

And they go on to explain:

The level of sensitivity will depend on the specific values of the space involved, and any one space might have a range of heritage values that have high, moderate or low levels of sensitivity to the same proposal. Assessment of proposals should therefore consider all values. An example would be a proposal to refurbish a significant reading room. The heritage values of the reading room might include its long-term historical use as a reading room, the design values of its wall cladding and fitout, and its being part of a rare suit[e] of rooms reflecting the original design of the Library. If a proposal to reclad the reading room in new materials were made, the room would have high sensitivity to change in relation to the design of its wall cladding, high to moderate sensitivity in relation to its impact on a suit[e] of rooms, and low sensitivity in relation to use (which would remain unchanged).

Understanding the relationship between values and impacts of change will help in modifying proposals and avoiding loss of significance.

We would suggest that the idea of identifying sensitivity to change is an extremely useful concept which complements assessments of relative significance and highlights the fact that there could be a position where elements of an asset which have relatively high significance may nevertheless be relatively robust, whereas something of relatively lower significance may be relatively sensitive to change. In the same way, we would suggest that, for example, and perhaps counterintuitively, a Grade I building (in England) may be less sensitive to change, i.e. more robust, than a simple Grade II building

References

Australia ICOMOS (1999) *The Burra Charter: The Australia ICOMOS Charter for Places of Cultural Significance*. Burwood, VIC, Australia, Australia ICOMOS Inc.

Australia ICOMOS (2013) *Practice Note: understanding and assessing cultural significance*. Burwood, VIC, Australia, Australia ICOMOS Inc.

Avrami, E., Mason, R. and de la Torre, M. (2000) The spheres and challenges of conservation. In *Values and Heritage Conservation: Research Report*. Los Angeles, The Getty Conservation Institute.

Beech, G. and Mitchell, R. (2004) *Maps for Family and Local History*. Richmond, Surrey, The National Archives.

Blunstone, D. (2000) Challenges for heritage conservation and the role of research on values. In: *Values and Heritage Conservation: Research Report* (eds E. Avrami, R. Mason and M. de la Torre). Los Angeles, The Getty Conservation Institute.

Carman, R.J. (1996) *Valuing Ancient Things*. London, Leicester University Press.

English Heritage (2008) *Conservation Principles, Policies and Guidance for the Sustainable Management of the Historic Environment*. London, English Heritage.

English Heritage (2011a) *The Setting of Heritage Assets*. London, English Heritage.

English Heritage (2011b) *Seeing the History in the View: A Method for Assessing Heritage Significance within Views*. London, English Heritage.

Herber, M.D. (2004) *Ancestral Trails: The Complete Guide to British Genealogy and Family History* (2nd edn). Sutton, Stroud.

Historic England (2015) *Historic Environment Good Practice Advice in Planning 3: The Setting of Heritage Assets*. London, Historic England.

Historic Scotland (2010) *Managing Change in the Historic Environment: Setting*. Edinburgh, Historic Scotland.

ICOMOS (1994) *The Nara Document on Authenticity*. Available at: www.international.icomos.org/charters.htm

Impey, E. (2006) Why do places matter? In *Capturing the Public Value of Heritage*. London, English Heritage.

Jones, S. (2014) *Conservation and social value :an ambivalent relationship*. Context issue 133. London, Institute of Historic Building Conservation.

Kerr, J.S. (2013) *The Conservation Plan* (7th edn). Sydney, The National Trust of Australia.

Lowenthal, D. (1997) *The Past Is a Foreign Country*. Cambridge, Cambridge University Press.

Mason, R. (2002) Assessing values in conservation planning: methodological issues and choices. In *Assessing the Values of Cultural Heritage: Research Report* (eds E. Avrami, R. Mason and M. de la Torre). Los Angeles, The Getty Conservation Institute, pp. 5–30.

Pearson, M. and Marshall, D. (2005) *National Library of Australia: Conservation Management Plan*. Canberra.

Pearson, M. and Sullivan, S. (1995) *Looking After Heritage Places*. Melbourne, Melbourne University Publishing.

Porter, S. (1990) *Exploring Urban History: Sources for Local Historians*. London, Batsford.

Schaafsma, C.F. (1989) Significant until proven otherwise: problems versus representative samples. In *Archaeological Management in the Modern World* (ed. H. Cleere). London, Unwin Hyman, pp. 38–51.

Chapter 5
Using Significance in Management Tools and Processes

Introduction

The identification of why an asset is valuable is, explicitly or implicitly, at the heart of deciding which buildings and sites are worthy of protection but it can, and should, also be at the heart of devising and implementing management strategies and processes. That is, the concept of significance can be the basis of an effective management tool, but it requires development from a generalised idea that an asset is worthy of protection to a position where values are identified, assessed and articulated. As we have already observed, one of the problems in the past has been that what makes an asset significant has not always been articulated.

In Chapter 4, we considered the process of identifying heritage values and preparing an assessment of significance for a heritage asset. In this chapter, we will consider how the assessment of significance can and should be used as a front-end 'plug-in' to a range of management documents and processes, acting as a platform to inform management decision-making and the planning of use and change affecting the asset and its setting. The key point is that essentially the same assessment of significance can be used in this way to make a major contribution to management documentation including:

- Conservation/heritage/archaeological/landscape management plans;
- Organisational management plans;
- Historic/conservation area appraisals and management plans;
- Master plans;
- Asset management programmes;
- Heritage statements for development planning purposes;
- Development guidance and briefs;
- Care and design guidance;

Managing Built Heritage: The Role of Cultural Values and Significance, Second Edition.
Stephen Bond and Derek Worthing.
© 2016 Stephen Bond and Derek Worthing. Published 2016 by John Wiley & Sons, Ltd.

- Tenancy agreements;
- Local management/heritage partnership agreements;
- Impact assessments (environmental, development and other impact assessments);
- Historic fabric audits and historic building records;
- Various briefing documents.

In order to avoid repetition, this chapter does not look at the use of the assessment of significance as a 'front end' to each and every one of the management tools. Instead, it concentrates on reviewing issues relating to the use of significance to inform:

- Conservation and management plans;
- Historic and conservation area appraisals;
- Characterisation studies;
- Heritage impact assessments;
- Heritage statements for development planning purposes;
- Local management and heritage partnership agreements;
- Care and quality standards guidance.

The conservation plan

A conservation plan is:

> *a document which sets out what is significant in a place and, consequently, what policies are appropriate to enable that significance to be retained in its future use and development. For most places it deals with the management of change.*
>
> (Kerr, 2013)

In simple terms, a conservation plan is a tool for managing heritage assets based on the key idea that in order to manage effectively, it is vital that an understanding of why the site is significant and how the different elements of that site contribute to that significance are set out, explained and justified. A conservation plan is based on the premise that you cannot protect and manage an asset unless you know and can articulate what it is about that site that is important (and why).

The key elements in a conservation plan are:

- An assessment and articulation of significance;
- Identification of the extent to which that significance might be vulnerable;
- Development and implementation of policies and practices which will mitigate that vulnerability, and will protect and enhance significance.

Conservation plans require that significance should be assessed, attributed and compared (through the articulation of relative significance) in a coherent and transparent manner that allows the assessment to be understood and debated.

A conservation plan is also based on the premise that heritage assets will evolve (even if the overarching principle applied to the asset is one of preservation). Therefore, the challenge, which the conservation plan should address, is how to manage change while protecting and enhancing the values that are embodied in and represented by the asset – that is, its significance. As Kerr (2013) observes: 'A clear understanding of the nature and level of the significance of a place will not only suggest constraints on future action, it will also introduce flexibility by identifying areas which can be adapted or developed with greater freedom.'

The conservation plan embodies the fruits of a significant amount of research that has to be undertaken into the asset. However, once finalised, the conservation plan should have developed into a working document rather than a research study. Put another way, the focus should always be on information gathering for a purpose and not as an end in itself.

A conservation plan is a means by which the asset is understood, but this is of no real use unless it is followed up by effective strategies and processes. It needs to be understood as, and used as, a dynamic entity that provides a picture of an asset at a particular time and which needs to be monitored and reviewed at regular intervals. The plan has to have a single definable goal – the identification and evaluation of the significance of the place so as to facilitate advantageous management in the future. In order for this to happen, the articulation of significance must become the framework, the focus and the driver for all policies and procedures within the management organisation that is responsible for the asset. The conservation plan should articulate and reflect the implications of this. Both the idea and its consequences must be accepted and integrated vertically and horizontally at all levels within the organisation that manages the asset.

It is sometimes suggested that conservation plans are most useful for 'complex' assets. We believe, however, that significance can, and should, be used as the lynchpin for managing all types of heritage assets, and a conservation plan (or, at the very least, a reduced conservation statement) will always be an appropriate tool for its assessment and management. Many important plans deal with assets that are not complex. As but one example, the Australian Antarctic Program's 2001 conservation plan for Mawson's Huts at Cape Denison, Commonwealth Bay, Antarctica, demonstrates the enormous benefits to be attained in sound management of historic resources at an unusual, but otherwise far from complex, site by establishing guidelines for future care and use based on a thorough assessment of heritage values. Undoubtedly, however, the conservation plan can prove an invaluable management tool where mixed heritage assets are involved on a single site. A powerful example of this is provided by a fascinating historic property owned by a charitable trust in the west of England.

The trust that has owned this site for some 50 years, taking ownership after the death of the last member of the immediate family, which had occupied the estate for over 400 years. The historic house itself is of no more than modest interest, being much reduced from its former glories. Today, it is leased as office accommodation to various public sector organisations. The house is surrounded by around 40 hectares of parkland and 10 hectares of woodland, within which are concealed the traces of a potentially important eighteenth-century pleasure garden, including various somewhat enigmatic garden buildings and structures. With little appreciation of the possible historic significance of the garden, the woodland was leased to a wildlife trust to form a nature reserve around 30 years ago.

The origins of the house and its estate immediately before the English Civil War are unclear, due to the absence of contemporary documentary source material. However, it seems evident that the house was purchased as part of the local manor in the mid-seventeenth century and then occupied by succeeding generations of the same family for 400 years. The estate in its heyday was undoubtedly much larger than it is today. Enforced sales of parcels of land, farmhouses and cottages occurred from around 1800 onwards as the family over-reached itself financially in a bid to nurture and sustain its local standing and as a result of the expensive pursuits of successive profligate heirs. In its prime, the estate was undoubtedly of some regional note and, by the end of the eighteenth century, it appears that two generations of the family had created an important and influential Arcadian landscaped park, which may have influenced the development of others nearby (although undoubtedly itself being influenced by Hoare and Flitcroft's masterwork at Stourhead in Wiltshire).

The problem for the charitable trust as owner of the estate today is that, as a result of leasehold agreements struck when there was little understanding of the importance of the historic landscape, significant parts of the management responsibility for the property lie outside its control. In order to create suitable habitats for particular wildlife, the potentially significant historic gardens have to be kept overgrown (Figures 5.1 (a) and (b)). While the historical development and importance of the site are far from clear, it seems possible that modern management of the woodland incorporating the eighteenth-century pleasure gardens as a reserve will not prove compatible with the management ethos that needs to be implemented to protect a nationally important historic garden and landscape.

The conservation plan offers the best hope of resolving such conflicts. But, critically in this instance, to be effective, the conservation plan must explore, evaluate and reconcile some potentially conflicting disparate aspects of the estate's cultural significance. It seems evident that, although now barely recognised or visible, in their time the historic gardens and parkland were of considerable regional and perhaps even wider importance. Conversely, today, the site is undeniably also of considerable significance as a nature reserve, being designated as a County Wildlife Site because of its indicators of ancient woodland and because it supports a remarkably wide range of habitats. It has over 100 species of fungi and a population of great crested newts: an internationally important species that is also Britain's most strictly protected, but most rapidly declining, native amphibian.

Hopefully, the management dilemma is clear. The site has substantive significance both for its historic and modern environments. While it is all well and

(a)

(b)

Figure 5.1 (a),(b)   Important historic landscape features in an overgrown state within the reserve.

good proclaiming that the historic environment forms an intimate and intrinsic part of our modern world, there are times when a profoundly stark management 'fault line' exists between the two. In this instance, it is improbable that a greater management focus on the protection and public interpretation of all or part of the site's historic environment can ever be achieved without compromising elements of the very particular modern environment that has been nurtured at the site in recent years. For instance, the surviving centuries-old trees in the woodland, which are so crucial to an appreciation of the development of the historic landscape and its use, are of relatively little value to the habitats that are vital to the reserve. It is not in the immediate interests of the wildlife trust to manage the asset in ways that specifically perpetuate the survival of this diminishing population of very elderly trees. Instead, reserve management is focused on introducing very different species of trees and some undergrowth that blur and obscure the otherwise crucial eighteenth- and early nineteenth-century planting regimes. Thus, in one way or another, the asset and its significance must be regarded as being extremely vulnerable to compromise or damage from active or passive future management. This is a taxing conservation management dilemma. A robust and holistic conservation plan is the very best management tool for establishing a platform from which sustainable solutions can be reached in this kind of situation.

Kerr (2004) suggests that conservation plans provide:

- Ready advice necessary for care and management, or for the preparation of detailed management and master plans;
- Appropriate requirements and opportunities to guide the planning of new work;
- A basis for assessing proposals to change or further develop the place;
- A reassurance to heritage and funding agencies that projects are pointed in the right direction;
- A valuable aid in the reduction of conflict – particularly because of the consultation processes built into the preparation of the plan.

Genesis of an idea

As we have said, the idea of using significance and vulnerability as a driver and framework is the basis of conservation plans. The conservation plan, as it has developed in the UK, has, to some extent, been based on the recontextualising of ideas used in the management of natural sites. Here, concepts of environmental capital (what you have got) and environmental capacity have been used as a means of describing and evaluating the value of the asset to its owners, users and wider society. Environmental capacity is defined as the capacity of the environment to absorb or accommodate activity or change without irreversible or unacceptable damage (English Heritage, 1997). This assessment of capital and capacity is then used to derive a plan of action. Also, the idea of developing 'management guidelines' – which include an agreement about the relative significance of elements, and were developed as a response to the concerns of owners and investors in listed commercial buildings – helped in driving and consolidating the idea within the UK.

However, as we have observed elsewhere, the biggest influence on the development of conservation plans has undoubtedly been the Burra Charter, which was produced by Australia ICOMOS in 1979. The Burra Charter emphasises the importance of identifying the cultural significance of the asset and then using this idea as the focus and driver for making management decisions (Australia ICO-MOS, 2013). The book, *The Conservation Plan*, by James Semple Kerr (2013) is an extremely useful reference which takes the basic premise laid out in the Burra Charter and develops both management concepts and detail further.

Organisational drivers

For many organisations with a property portfolio that includes heritage assets, conservation plans are increasingly being seen as an essential tool. Such plans not only provide the basis for the effective management of this stock, but also demonstrate an organisation's commitment to the protection of the public value and interest represented by these assets and for which they are responsible. Many heritage organisations in the UK have produced conservation plans for some of their own assets and are encouraging others to do so. Likewise, many public bodies at local and national level are taking a lead in demonstrating 'corporate responsibility' by reflecting the endorsement of the important role of conservation plans by government.

However, in many cases, the reason that conservation plans are produced is to fulfil a requirement of either a funding body (such as the Heritage Lottery Fund in the UK), or a statutory consent authority within the context of a development proposal.

Some owners intending to develop their heritage asset will commission a conservation plan as a way of discovering which possible further or alternative uses might be appropriate. Conservation plans have also been initiated as part of environmental impact assessments in large projects, including regeneration schemes. There is clearly a potentially difficult problem when a conservation plan is produced as a reaction to a development proposal, particularly a very detailed one. There is a danger that the establishment of significance will be developed in such a way as to merely reinforce the feasibility of the scheme, resulting in damage to the value of the asset. Another possible situation, where there may be a tendency to restrain or distort the development of an understanding of cultural significance, is where an organisation wants to downplay significance because conservation and the future management of the site will be difficult or costly to achieve.

It is inevitable that where a proposal for change prompts a conservation plan, then this will influence its scope. But, ideally, conservation plans should be produced without such pressures and influences, particularly to the extent that they may adversely affect the time and energy given to key elements such as the measuring of values expressed by the community.

Of course, all conservation plans are produced in an environment where constraints and opportunities have to be taken into account, but this reinforces the need to produce plans which ensure that significance is assessed in a rigorous and transparent way and that the policies produced by the plan do not take any constraints implied by the development proposal as a given. It is important therefore that the asset itself is what sets the agenda through a process that seeks, as a first step, to understand what is important about it.

Format and content of conservation plans

Since every heritage asset is unique, the standardisation of conservation plans is a possible danger because it might do the following:

- Produce a formulaic approach to determining significance which fails to appreciate, or indeed ignores, information from non-standard sources;
- Fail to take into account the particular context of the asset and its use;
- Fail to maximise the synthesis of the conservation plan policies with the needs and requirements of the organisational culture and policies of the owners and users, leading to it being a generalised 'wish list' rather than a focused and practical management tool.

Because each asset is unique, it is important to acknowledge that the detail and contents of a plan should be determined by both the characteristics of the site and its operating context, and therefore the process of creating a conservation plan must not be rigid and formulaic in its approach. Nevertheless, it is possible to define an overall framework. The Burra Charter (Australia ICOMOS, 2013) states that the procedure for making decisions must be appropriate to the asset and circumstances, but that it always involves some key steps:

- Understand significance;
- Develop policy;
- Manage in accordance with policy.

Kerr (2013) suggests that the plan should consist of a two-stage approach: the first stage being that of understanding the asset through the gathering and analysis of evidence, and the second being that of developing conservation policies and evolving strategies for the implementation of those policies.

A key factor in the suggestion of a two-stage approach is the idea that significance should be assessed 'away from extraneous pressures and without regard to those practical requirements which must subsequently be taken into account when developing policies' (Kerr, 2004). This clearly makes sense from an objective point of view (and will avoid the problem referred to earlier about development proposals skewing assessments). Such an approach will add to a sense of rigour and objectivity in the process. It is also clearly an approach which mirrors good planning practice in other areas where the question, 'Where do we want to be?' is, in the first instance, answered, irrespective of any known or perceived constraints in order that the plan might be as creative as possible. This is not to say that a conservation plan should not engage with the constraints and opportunities related to the site and its context, as well as the needs and requirements of the organisation that occupies the place – if it did not do so, it would not be effective. However, the two-stage approach ensures that the determination of the significance of the asset is not distorted by predetermined outcomes.

It must be remembered that the two stages, although carried out separately, are not independent – in the sense that stage one has no real value (at least in this context) if stage two is not carried out properly, and stage two is operating in a void if it is not derived from the logic and understanding arrived at in stage one. A sense of disconnection is not uncommon in conservation plans, and one of the 'tests' of a good plan is to be able to 'read it backwards' – that is, to be able to easily trace back the processes and policies set out in the second part of the assessment to the evidence of significance in the first part.

A typical step-by-step structure for a plan therefore would be as shown in Box 5.1.

Box 5.1 Structure for a plan

Stage 1: Significance and vulnerability

Step 1 Understand the asset by gathering information, including documents and physical evidence, in order to present an overall description of it and an understanding of how it has developed through time.

Step 2 Assess the asset's significance, both generally and contextually and in detail for each of its main components. This will include comparative significance (to other places), as well as how each element of the asset contributes to its overall significance.

Step 3 Define issues that are affecting the significance of the asset or that have the potential to do so in the future, in other words, assess the asset's vulnerability to deleterious change.

Step 4 Write a statement of significance – a short accessible summation of what is significant about the asset and why (and a description and justification of the sources used and methods adopted in arriving at the assessment).

Stage 2 Conservation policies

Step 5 Develop conservation policies and processes that will ensure that the significance of the asset is respected and retained and, where possible, enhanced in its future management. This will include identifying and appraising options in the light of opportunities and barriers, including the assessment of vulnerability.

Step 6 Apply the conservation policies and processes at all levels of the organisation.

Step 7 Develop and implement policies and processes for monitoring, reviewing and readjusting the conservation plan. As with all good practice in planning, there needs to be a monitoring system that asks 'How are we doing?' Therefore, a timetable to the action plan is needed which can provide measurable benchmarks. In addition, it is important to acknowledge that conservation plans are time-specific, because circumstances change, as do perceptions of significance (new evidence may also emerge that affects the understanding of the significance of the asset). Even if this were not so, the sense that conservation plans are a management tool – and not a documentation of the past – means that they must be dynamic and therefore reviewed and updated at regular intervals in order to ensure their continuing validity and usefulness.

These steps are not mutually exclusive and the process of developing the conservation plan must be iterative. However, each step does represent a logical progression from the proceeding one. The appropriate range of conservation management policies can only be established once a comprehensive understanding of the asset's significance and its vulnerability to change have been developed. This is a long way away from the earlier notion that conservation policies should be automatically focused on minimising intervention with historic fabric at all times, whatever the circumstances and however mundane the material involved.

Although the effectiveness of this approach will ultimately rely on the integrity, sensitivity and skills of those writing (and commissioning) the plan, it does provide a framework which is logical, coherent and robust.

The process of developing a conservation plan is described in Clark (1999, 2001). In Clark (2001: 62), the assessment of significance (Step 2 in Box 5.1) is described as using 'the understanding of the site as a basis for a clear statement of the values that make the site important'. This forms the heart of today's approach to conservation management. The value to society of a heritage asset is not just the amount of historic fabric that it contains. Indeed, this may be entirely irrelevant to the asset's significance.

Who should be consulted?

There are three categories of stakeholders who need to be consulted and involved in the development of a conservation plan (in addition, of course, to the owners and occupiers):

- Those stakeholders and interested parties who might be affected by the conservation plan and/or who might have an impact on an ability to actually deliver the plan. The range of such stakeholders will vary from asset to asset but are likely to include: the local community; the business community; the local planning authority and other appropriate statutory bodies; advisory bodies, local conservation groups; and possibly, depending on the nature and status of the site, national conservation bodies. In part, such consultation will be necessary because of possible statutory requirements that might affect the delivery of the plan. However, involving stakeholders from the beginning and throughout the development of the plan may also actually be the key to successful conception and implementation. It will be important therefore to identify the other two categories of stakeholders, which are listed next.
- Those individuals and groups who may have documentary evidence that may help to inform and clarify issues relating to the establishment of significance.
- Those individuals and groups who because of their association and involvement with the asset have memories and insights which are actually part of its significance and which should be assessed in conjunction with the other values of the asset.

Who should write the conservation plan?

To a large extent, the make-up of the team writing the plan should reflect the intricacies and qualities of the asset and the circumstances and specific purposes of the plan itself. For complex assets, there is clearly an argument for a multi-disciplinary team, but this should be chosen more on the basis of specific skills and qualities rather than narrow concepts of professional discipline – and particularly so as each asset is likely to produce its own specific issues and conundrums. It is important to take account of Kerr's (2004) observation that 'the more disciplines and people involved, the more difficult it is to evolve a coherent product'. To some extent, this is an argument about the efficiency of the process. But there is also the possible impact that having too small or narrowly focused a team might have on the integrity of the product especially as, when dealing with the determination of significance, we are already addressing a subjective concept. A multi-disciplinary approach has the potential of being more rigorous and objective, and also the team may be better placed to think creatively, or at least more holistically, about how to gather evidence and interpret significance from it. However, if the team is not well managed and cannot work effectively together, then there is a danger that the result will be an ill-focused and fragmented document. It is perhaps an obvious point, but there will need to be a clear project leader with skills in people management and interaction. Although the issue of the precise make-up of the team will be determined by the type of asset in question, it also, to some extent, reinforces the importance of the client producing a clear brief that identifies the contextual circumstances affecting the asset, the reasons for producing the plan, its intended use and therefore the issues to be addressed.

Whether or not the conservation plan is written in-house or by a consultant may be decided solely on an assessment of available skills, but the use of an outside consultant may have value in terms of objectivity and a 'fresh pair of eyes'. This, however, should be balanced against the value of an in-house team's understanding (hopefully) of the culture and the policies and processes of the organisation owning and/or occupying the asset. Whatever the make-up of the team, it is important that all understand the purpose of the plan to ensure that they are working towards the same goal. Research carried out in recent years as part of a master's dissertation by a UK-based student revealed that a very large percentage of conservation plans are prepared without meaningful input from the estate management staff of commissioning property management organisations. As a result, the very people who will be responsible to a significant degree for implementing the plan's management policies on the ground have almost no understanding or ownership of its objectives, contents or management approach.

As we have said, the range of skills necessary to write a plan will vary from asset to asset and will be determined not only by the characteristics of the asset but also by its complexity and other factors such as its completeness. It is important to understand that complexity is not just a characteristic of the age and the extent of development of an asset. Very old places with multiple layers of development may still be relatively easy to analyse, whereas some more modern places may represent more complex and perhaps competing values that are challenging to measure and analyse.

Skills and knowledge of construction and structures will be important, not just in terms of understanding the history and therefore the significance of the asset but also in determining its present condition. Clearly, at least for Step 1, the team must have good research skills and experience. However, it is also important that the team has the skills and knowledge, and, perhaps crucially, the motivation to engage with and understand the culture, policies and processes of the organisation that owns/occupies the asset in order that:

- The institutional memory within the organisation might be part of the evidence gathering;
- The policies to protect the cultural significance of the asset can be made more effective by being synthesised, as far as possible, with the aims of the organisation.

Developing the plan

The Historic England document, *Conservation Principles* (English Heritage, 2008), states: 'Understanding a place and assessing its significance demands the application of a systematic and consistent process, which is appropriate and proportionate in scope and depth to the decision to be made, or the purpose of the assessment.' It goes on to say that the process involves the following, shown in Box 5.2.

Box 5.2   The assessment process

Understand the fabric and evolution of the place

To identify the cultural and natural heritage values of a place, its history, fabric and character must first be understood. This should include its origins, how and why it has changed over time (and will continue to change if undisturbed), the form and condition of its constituent elements and materials, the technology of its construction, any habitats it provides, and comparison with similar places.

Identify who values the place, and why they do so

To provide a sound basis for management, the people and communities who are likely to attach heritage values to a place should be identified, and the range of those values understood and articulated, not just those that may be a focus of contention. This involves engaging with owners, communities and specialists with a sufficient range of knowledge of the place, subject to the need for proportionality.

Relate identified heritage values to the fabric of the place

An assessment of significance will normally need to identify how particular parts of a place and different periods in its evolution contribute to, or detract from, each identified strand of cultural and natural heritage value.

Consider the relative importance of those identified values

It is normally desirable to sustain all the identified heritage values of an asset, both cultural and natural; but on occasion, what is necessary to sustain some values will conflict with what is necessary to sustain others. If so, understanding the relative contribution of each identified heritage value to the overall value of the asset – its significance – will be essential to objective decision-making. A balanced view is best arrived at through enabling all interested parties to appreciate their differing perspectives and priorities.

Consider the contribution of associated objects and collections

Historically-associated objects can make a major contribution to the significance of an asset, and association with the asset can add heritage value to those objects.

Consider the contribution made by setting and context

'Setting' is an established concept that relates to the surroundings in which an asset is experienced, its local context, embracing present and past relationships to the adjacent landscape. Definition of the setting of a significant asset will normally be guided by the extent to which material change within it could affect (enhance or diminish) the asset's significance.

Compare the asset with other assets sharing similar values

Understanding the importance of an asset by comparing it with other assets that demonstrate similar values normally involves considering:

- How strongly the identified heritage values are demonstrated or represented by the asset, compared with those other assets;
- How its values relate to statutory designation criteria, and any existing statutory designations of the asset.

Articulate the significance of the asset

A 'statement of significance' of an asset should be a summary of the cultural and natural heritage values currently attached to it and how they inter-relate, which distils the particular character of the asset. It should explain the relative importance of the heritage values of the asset (where appropriate, by reference to criteria for statutory designation), how they relate to its physical fabric, the extent of any uncertainty about its values (particularly in relation to potential for hidden or buried elements), and identify any tensions between potentially conflicting values. So far as possible, it should be agreed by all who have an interest in the asset. The result should guide all decisions about material change to a significant asset.

Undertaking a conservation plan: understanding the asset and assessing significance

Perhaps the first task is to clarify the brief and set out the background and purpose of the plan and how it will be used – that is, why is it being undertaken, what is to be achieved and how will this achievement be measured? Setting out a vision for the asset and aims for how it may evolve in both the long and short term are vital in achieving an effective plan.

The second task is to understand the asset as it appears today by recording it, and by developing an understanding of some of the general issues that do, and will continue to, affect it. Such issues include the location of the asset and its context, related to local geography and the surrounding environment, as well as sociopolitical and economic factors. This might include understanding and then describing:

- The wider context in terms of the political, social and economic environment in which the asset is operating, and the extent to which these might affect the aims and objectives of the plan both in terms of opportunities and threats;
- How the conservation plan might relate to, or be affected by, other policies and decisions in both the wider context – for example, planning strategies for other historic assets – as well as the wider spatial planning issues related to the area, including any regeneration, redevelopment or master planning issues that might involve the asset or may have an effect upon it;
- The specific issues that need to be addressed by the conservation plan, for example, perhaps in relation to new developments, changes of use, improving facilities and interpretation approaches for visitors;
- Clarifying ownership and interests in the asset, how it is managed and the uses to which it is put.

Describing the asset, as it is now

This will be a written and visual description of the asset as it is at the present time, including its buildings, other structures and its open spaces. The process is an important part of beginning to understand the significance of the asset by assessing 'what we have got now'. Much of the information may of course be available already.

The buildings and open spaces should be described in terms of their functional relationships, both holistically (that is how they relate to each other and to the overall function of the site) and as individual elements. The individual elements – both buildings and spaces – should be described in terms of their layout and how they are used.

Contents should be described where they are key to either the function of the space or perhaps more importantly to the architectural style or design of the building – for instance, the furniture in an Arts and Crafts building or artworks such as the Sutherland tapestry in Coventry Cathedral – or some perhaps more intangible aspects of the significance of the space.

The main methods of construction should be noted, as well as the architectural style and the key materials used in the structures.

The condition of the physical aspects of the asset should be assessed in outline in both general and relative terms. A more detailed assessment may or may not be needed later in order to clarify issues of vulnerability: there may be particular defects which are in urgent need of attention because they may be endangering known and unknown elements of significance.

It would also be useful to carry out an initial assessment of character in terms of the nature of the quality of the asset and the factors that affect its character (e.g. atmosphere, use, activities, as well as architectural qualities, materials, etc.).

The different types of heritage that exist should be described, including, where appropriate, the natural heritage. This would cover buildings, archaeology, collections, historic landscapes and gardens.

The (physical) limits of the asset should be shown and its topography and setting should be described and illustrated. Of course the significance of the asset may also be tied up with other sites. This is an important point because it could affect an understanding not just of the asset but also of adjacent sites and structures, that is, there may be a symbiotic relationship which is more than just contextual.

Establishing and analysing the historical development of the asset and gathering and analysing evidence about its significance

The issues and the processes involved with this important part of the production of the conservation plan were set out and discussed in depth in Chapter 4. This section of the plan is, as we said there, concerned with gathering material that informs an understanding of the asset and its social, historic and environmental context, and analysing this information to determine its cultural significance. It is important to explain how significance is embodied in and represented by the elements – the buildings, spaces, objects, structures (and their relationships) that constitute the physical manifestation of the asset – and by its uses and associations.

Vulnerability

Once the site has been understood and its significance assessed in the manner set out in Chapter 4, it is important, before policies are developed to protect and enhance significance, that there should be an assessment of which factors might possibly damage or detract from what is valuable about the asset. That is, it is important to understand the extent to which the values inherent in the asset are at risk of compromise or diminution now or in the future. The conservation plan needs '[to] set out the issues facing the heritage and the problems that need to be solved to find a long-term sustainable future for it' (Heritage Lottery Fund, undated).

The way in which an asset and its values may be vulnerable can be multifaceted; some of the factors may be intertwined and relatively complex to address. Others, such as a lack of financial resources, may be simple to identify but extremely difficult to address adequately.

It is important to understand that, although the plan may be reviewed at regular intervals, it should itself be a relatively visionary document and therefore the anticipation of possible threats should look at the medium and long term as well as issues that may cause immediate problems. This may not determine priorities, of course, as something which is potentially a threat that will not be realised for, say, 5 years may still have to be addressed straight away.

The factors that might affect vulnerability are obviously case-specific to the asset in question, but the sort of issues that will need to be addressed by the plan might include, for example:

- The poor physical condition of the asset (which may require funds, but might also be just, or mainly, as a consequence of poor maintenance management);
- Management of the asset generally;
- Lack of financial resources and/or lack of certainty, to the extent that there is little ability to plan effectively;
- Socio-economic factors that affect the viability of the asset, which might mean that there will be a need to find new uses for it;
- The functional suitability of the site and its buildings for its present use;
- Traffic volumes producing levels of atmospheric pollution that will cause unacceptable levels of deterioration to the fabric;
- Changes to the natural environment (flood levels, coastal erosion, etc.). Heritage bodies from a number of countries, as well as UNESCO at an international level, have recognised the threats posed by climate change to built heritage and the issue needs to be addressed in the asset-specific assessment of vulnerability;
- Loss of context and meaning to the asset because of developments taking place externally and which detract from an understanding of the aesthetic value of the asset;
- Vandalism;
- Tourism levels, which are unsustainable because of physical degradation or because of damage to the atmosphere and a sense of place;
- Insufficient access (generally and for specific groups, such as the disabled);
- Lack of development land for expansion (perhaps to deal with a need to increase visitor numbers or provide for better interpretation facilities);
- Incompatible policies or actions of the users which do or may detract from the significance of the place.

One of the common themes in the analysis of existing conservation plans is the tendency to look inwards and not take sufficient account of external threats or indeed opportunities, particularly those that might arise in the medium to long term (see, for example, 'A future for the past: a new theoretical model for sustainable urban environments' (Landorf, 2011).

Clearly it is imperative that the vulnerabilities that have been highlighted by the process are dealt with as far as possible. The question of how to remove or at least mitigate these threats should be addressed by appropriate policies which focus on each and every one of the issues highlighted.

Integrity of the asset

The integrity of the asset should be understood as 'the ability of the property to secure and sustain its significance over time' (Stovel, 2007). In assessing vulnerability, there may also be the possibility of addressing negative impacts of perhaps a minor nature that can help to improve the integrity and the cohesiveness of the asset and which will serve to protect and enhance its significance.

Pearson and Marshall (2005) elaborate on the idea of integrity by defining it as 'the degree to which a place or component of a place retains the form and completeness of its physical fabric, historical associations, use or social attachments that give the place its cultural significance'.

Examples include a consideration of the appropriateness and the impact of functional operations and activities in terms of their interaction with significance. This might then lead to a consideration of whether those functions could be performed in other areas (either within or without the asset) where there is no likelihood of causing harm to significance. For example:

- Does a particular function detract from the character of a particular asset or part of it? This might be due to perhaps:
  - the noises associated with that function, the equipment necessary to perform it or the intensity of use associated with it, for example, the type of equipment or the way it is laid out detracts from the visual understanding or appreciation of a room. Apart from what we might call noise pollution, there may also be incidences of odour and light pollution that may detract from the significance of the asset.
  - the incompatibility of the spiritual or emotional significance of the asset and the activity taking place there.
- Does the impact of the function, including the number of people using the asset, have an avoidable effect in terms of wear and tear on the fabric, which could be mitigated through changing function or controls on use?
- Does the way that services have been added to the buildings, internally and externally, have a detrimental impact on significance, either in respect of the fabric or in their visual impact? Could this have been handled in a different way, for example, through re-routing, using different designs or materials, or by minimising their impact by avoiding more culturally sensitive areas (including changing the function of certain spaces)?
- Are activities and uses, including temporary ones, appropriate to the significance of the asset? An example might be corporate parties or events which work against the 'sense of place' (weighed against the income generation).
- Are the designs of recent buildings or structures appropriate? Do they add to or detract from the understanding or the atmosphere of the asset?
- What is the impact on integrity of vehicular access, circulation and parking? These factors may have an important impact on the atmosphere of the asset, but they may also exacerbate deterioration rates in significant materials (for example, through wear and tear, danger of impact, the visual effect of their presence and the possible effect of their emissions on the

fabric, e.g. from oil spills or increased damage to stonework or other materials).

Developing policies for the conservation plan

The development of sound conservation policies for the asset is the fundamental objective of the conservation plan process. Too often, the policies section of a plan appears to have been added as an afterthought – almost literally tacked on at the end after the 'interesting bit' (the academic research and telling the story of the asset) has been finished. This reflects the discomfort that many in the conservation world feel with the notion of 'management'. It is, after all, only a few short years since the process of conservation has been more widely acknowledged to be one of management of change rather than 'simply' one of skilful repair.

Since effective management is the focus of the conservation plan, the drafting of conservation management policies needs to be undertaken with care. Appropriate time must be dedicated to the process, again, it should not be a rushed afterthought. Policies need to be tailor-made for the asset and for its management organisation. They should not be taken off the shelf or cobbled together from work done previously for very different assets or, worse, for very different management situations. It goes without saying that, given that policies need to reflect the capacity and capability of the management organisation that will implement them, those responsible for drafting the policies in the first place need to have an intimate understanding of that organisation, its culture and its limitations. Surprisingly few conservation plan teams take the time to gain this understanding. The result is the potential for dislocation between intent and actual implementation of the conservation management policies. That may well prove to be an inherent weakness in the management that is delivered from the conservation plan platform.

Policies should be tightly drawn and unambiguous. All policies must be practical and capable of implementation. Policies should flow from the assessment of significance, and the evaluation of vulnerability, i.e. they should deal with issues that might potentially affect the asset and its significance. The temptation to throw in 'general' or arbitrary policies on the basis that it would be 'good for the organisation' should be avoided. If the policy does not flow logically from the assessments of significance and vulnerability, its place in the conservation plan is open to challenge and that weakens the logic and conceptual basis of the whole plan. Management organisations and individuals within organisations will not take ownership of policies if they cannot see the logical basis for their adoption and implementation. Each policy should be supported by a simple and lucid explanation of the rationale that lies behind it. The corollary to ensuring that all policies flow from the assessments of significance and vulnerability is also important. As we have said, every aspect of vulnerability raised should either lead to a policy for its mitigation or risk management, or to a statement explaining why this is not considered necessary (or possible). Again, maintenance of the internal logic of the plan process is vital in winning over the hearts and minds of the sceptical owner or experience-hardened manager (to mention but two crucial stakeholders).

Policies are not generally well drafted by committee. Experience suggests that they are best developed by one or two people intimately associated with the conservation plan process, after initial consultation with managers and before circulation of a draft for consideration and discussion.

Policy development should be an iterative process. In our opinion and experience, it is unlikely that all policies can be developed and drafted successfully in a single phase. If the first draft of policies passes through the consultation process without challenge and debate, there is a strong chance that those who will be responsible thereafter for adopting and managing their implementation have no ownership of the process and the policies, and perhaps no intention of putting them into practice in any meaningful way. If that is the case, rigorous efforts must be made to re-engage the managers in the whole process, otherwise the effort and funding put into development of the conservation plan will have been wasted.

The significance of the foregoing should be recognised. The conservation plan does not deliver a comprehensive management plan, this is why the term 'conservation management plan' is ambiguous and, in our view, potentially dangerous. The conservation plan delivers a set of conservation management policies that seek to address vulnerability and other issues of potential risk that need to be carefully managed. The conservation plan – with its policies – can then be used as a platform for developing other management tools, including a comprehensive management plan for the asset (see below). It is not possible to manage every aspect of a complex asset on the basis of the conservation policies contained in the conservation plan alone and, furthermore, in most instances, conservation plans are not developed to a level of detail that includes specific actions. Therefore, the conservation plan should not try to wear the guise of a management plan. This is why policies in the conservation plan should address issues raised in the plan and go no further – otherwise, there is a serious risk that it will 'fall between two stools', having neither the conceptual strength that flows from the step-by-step logic of a conservation plan nor the rigour or depth of a fully developed management plan. It must be stressed again that one of the principal failings of conservation plans to date in the UK has been the lack of ownership in the process by those who will take on the day-to-day implementation of its recommendations. Unless ownership can be cascaded to all those who have a hand in management (and all those who are subsequently given that responsibility but were not part of the conservation plan development process), the benefits flowing from investment in the plan will be very limited and most likely of very short duration. Significance-based management can only work when those who manage the asset understand, respect and approve the purpose and product of the conservation plan. That is a major challenge. Engagement in policy drafting can help, but, by itself, will never provide the level of common ownership of the process that is essential if conservation management is to be effective.

Having said that policies should be written to suit the specific circumstances, it is useful nonetheless to suggest the type of policies that are likely to, or may, appear in conservation plans. This should not be taken as being comprehensive or used as a guide for policy drafting, for, as we have already observed, policies must flow logically from the unique assessment of significance and issues of risk and vulnerability that each conservation plan contains. With that caveat in mind, typical policy areas found within conservation plans include:

- *Use and management of the asset*:
  - retention in current use to safeguard its status;
  - development and review of the management plan for the asset;
  - development of other management tools such as historic area appraisals;
  - revision of management structure to improve protection of significance;
  - conservation safeguards in contracts and tenders;
  - development of a risk-based resource allocation plan;
  - maintenance of the balance between needs of different users;
  - acquisitions, disposals and leasing strategies;
  - environmental management policies and actions.
- *Records*:
  - development of a comprehensive database of accurate architectural records (site plan, floor plans, elevations, sections, rectified photographs of interiors, building archaeological survey);
  - maintenance of the archive of the asset's historical development;
  - creation of a permanent and accessible written record of all interventions in the historic fabric;
  - development of a catalogue of important contents/collections.
- *Conservation principles and the management of change, for example*:
  - adoption of standard principles as an approach to different parts of the asset: benchmark standards; maintenance standards to be applied;
  - ongoing review and revision of the conservation plan;
  - maintenance of heritage values and significance;
  - restrictions and potential for change across the asset or on an elemental basis;
  - protection of the asset's setting;
  - training of staff and contractors in conservation approach;
  - management of the buried archaeology and the building's archaeology;
  - management of flora and fauna;
  - establishment of monitoring procedures to identify effects of change on the asset and its significance.
- *Maintenance management*:
  - implementation of a planned maintenance regime;
  - development of long-term and annual maintenance plans;
  - implementation of periodic condition surveys of the asset;
  - development of a detailed work's history record.
- *Disaster management*:
  - commissioning of disaster and safety audits;
  - implementation of new regime;
  - training of staff and emergency services, etc.;

- development of a disaster plan for the asset;
- review of security arrangements;
- training of salvage team.
- *People management:*
  - upgrading of orientation and signage;
  - improvement of facilities;
  - resolution of conflicts between the needs of different users;
  - improvements in access for all people to the site.
- *Communication, education and interpretation:*
  - improved dissemination of information regarding asset;
  - encouragement of outreach (including through wider use of the internet);
  - upgrading and development of interpretation;
  - involvement of local communities in the asset's future;
  - establishment of community and stakeholder forums and development of an engagement policy;
  - exploration of the potential of strategic partnerships.

Once the iterative process of drafting, refining and amplifying policies has been taken as far as is practicable and meaningful within the context of the conservation plan, the plan itself should be ready for its final round of consultation and, in due course, adoption by the management organisation or key interested parties. We are aware of a number of instances where consultation has been restricted by the responsible management organisation to the pre-policy draft of the conservation plan on the basis that external oversight of and intervention with its policies would be unacceptable. While such insularity and determined control are – to a degree – understandable in certain circumstances, this management approach flatly contradicts the notion that the significance and value of heritage assets transcend simple property ownership patterns. Owners and managers are guardians of heritage assets for the nation as a whole as well as for future generations.

In most cases, formal adoption of a conservation plan by the asset's owners, managers or other key parties is critically important – it is not just an administrative nicety. On the one hand, it signals a positive and transparent intent to manage the asset on a day-to-day basis in accordance with the evaluation of significance and vulnerability and the thrust of conservation management policies that have been defined within the plan. It also triggers implementation of the plan's policies – establishing a clear starting date from which a change of management approach should be perceivable to all and can be monitored for impact and effectiveness. Formal adoption can also be an important component in the vital strategy of ensuring that ownership of and a willingness to comply with the plan's conservation management policies are cascaded throughout the organisation to reach those involved in taking or implementing day-to-day asset management decisions. This issue has already been referred to earlier in this chapter, where it was noted that, while broad engagement in policy drafting can help, this alone will not engender the degree of common ownership of the process that is essential if conservation management is to be effective. Once the management organisation has formally adopted the conservation plan, steps need to be taken to begin to nurture and, thereafter, safeguard this common ownership, so that the significance-based management approach becomes second nature to everyone involved in the care of the asset. This is a major challenge. Conceptual ownership and, as a consequence, interest (and vice versa) can tend to decrease in management organisations towards lower levels in the line management hierarchy. Equally, ongoing staff changes over time will dilute recognition of the existence and importance of the conservation plan, unless rigorous procedures are set in place to ensure appropriate training of new recruits to the workforce and occasional training updates for all. Internal review cycles for conservation plans can be used as an opportunity to involve staff afresh in the plan's content and recommendations, although this is a process that needs to be actively planned and managed if it is to be of real benefit.

This brings us to the final key point that needs to be made about conservation plans. Our knowledge base of the historic environment changes over time, sometimes dramatically within short periods due to new research opportunities or the re-discovery of additional sources of information. Ongoing management action may inadvertently or intentionally change the cultural significance of an asset, as may transformations or trends and perceptions in society as a whole. Also the vulnerability of an asset or its significance may increase or lessen markedly with changes in external causal factors. Conservation management policies, through their positive and successful implementation, may sooner or later become redundant (or, at the very least, come to be in need of redefinition). No conservation plan should be regarded as being 'fixed in stone' forever – or even for a long time. For good reasons, as a general rule of thumb, it is normally suggested that, conservation plans should be reviewed quinquennially, but this advice should not be adopted blindly. In some circumstances more rapid review is desirable, even essential; in other cases, little disadvantage will occur through carrying out a major review after, say, seven years rather than five. Yet at all times, managers must bear in mind that taking management decisions on the basis of out-of-date information and policies is a counterproductive and potentially damaging matter. The concept permeating this book is that asset management without the platform that is provided by an understanding of significance and vulnerability introduces increased risk of compromise and permanent reduction in the value of the asset. The corollary is that management decisions and action fashioned around outdated assessments of significance, vulnerability and conservation management policies can be equally harmful. Ongoing change in the asset and its wider context needs to be monitored and understood so that satisfactory cycles for review of the conservation plan can be established.

With the adoption of the conservation plan and its conservation management policies, attention can be turned to the next steps in the use of the conservation plan as a platform for the development of a management plan which will develop and co-ordinate management processes and actions, as the foundation for logical and sustainable decision-making.

The management plan

As we have observed, the management plan is a device for putting strategies and broad policies into action. It is important, for the reasons already stated, that the management plan is prepared separately from (and following on from) the assessment of the values inherent in the asset. In particular, the need to be able to consider significance without the constraints or drivers of existing processes, proposals and plans is vital. Where preparation of a management plan has been informed by the existence of an up-to-date conservation plan for the asset, it should be possible to follow readily a detailed trail backwards through the policies and procedures to the detailed articulation of its significance.

In such circumstances, it is important that the main thrust of the management plan is the development of clear integrated policies, strategies and procedures, which, among other management responsibilities, will include a focus on the protection and enhancement of the significance of the asset. These may be generated independently or as further development of conservation policies in a pre-existing conservation plan. The conservation-related policies need to be integrated with other issues, including the requirements and aspirations of the owners, occupiers and users of the asset. Pearson and Sullivan (1995) observe: 'Significance assessment alone does not and cannot dictate management decisions, which are constrained by a whole range of factors, such as conflicting land use options, financial considerations, technical conservation problems or legislative or social concerns.'

An important difference between a conservation plan and a management plan is that the latter develops this wider set of policies in a practical manner through to implementation with an action plan.

Preparing a management plan

The sequence for preparation of the management plan built from a conservation plan might be as follows:

1 Reaffirm the statement of significance.
2 Consider opportunities and constraints in relation to the asset itself, its setting and its sociopolitical and economic context.
3 Develop further policies to protect and enhance significance, including and as mitigation against vulnerability.
4 Identify and appraise possible strategy options for the implementation of policies.
5 Develop and implement an action plan that links policies and strategies to procedures and processes.
6 Develop an action plan that sets out a timescale and sequencing related to requirements, priorities, generation and availability of resources.

7 Develop an action plan that sets out how the plan will be implemented, and by whom.
8 Develop an action plan that implements procedures for monitoring and review.

The management plan must also address issues related to tensions and contra-dictions. Pearson and Sullivan (1995) suggest that the management plan should (among other things) do the following:

• Articulate the implications of the statement of significance.
• Be able to be implemented by the owner/authority that controls the asset.
• Pay due attention to the needs and desires of the community, and especially those with a special interest in the asset.
• Be financially feasible and economically viable.
• Be technically feasible and appropriate.
• Provide a long-term management framework.
• Be sufficiently flexible to allow review, improvement or alteration.

A conventional approach to developing a plan such as this might include asking:

• Where do we want to be?
• How are we going to get there?
• Where are we now?

And once the plan is implemented, asking:

• How are we doing?

Requirements, opportunities and barriers

Requirements, opportunities and barriers need to be considered before policies are developed. Some of the constraints would of course have been identified in the assessment of vulnerability. The issues to be addressed might include:

• Cultural and heritage values vs. other values on or around the asset (this may be an opportunity and a constraint, and of course may raise issues of trade-offs between heritage values and other (say, socio-economic) benefits);
• Requirements and aspirations of the owner (again, these may be an opportunity or a constraint);
• Resources – financial and skills and knowledge (a constraint perhaps, but also may be an opportunity as the production of the plan may provide access to grants/funds or identify development opportunities);
• Physical or environmental issues (difficulties in reducing vulnerability related to, say, poor condition, overuse, vandalism, pollution and natural risks such as flooding, erosion, etc.).

A SWOT (Strengths, Weaknesses, Opportunities, Threats) analysis or similar tool might be a useful way to approach this. Pearson and Sullivan (1995) suggest that such a process is beneficial in that it 'brings home to key people the real situation at the place and perhaps they can then provide vital support in its improvement'. We would also suggest that such an exercise can be a vehicle to involve a relatively wide constituency from inside and outside the organisation, and will highlight their perceptions of the asset and its value, which may itself be an opportunity and/or a barrier.

The question of the knock-on effect of certain actions not being achieved – or certain policies not being effective – should be addressed.

The client and organisational culture

As we have said, the management plan needs to be grounded in the reality of resources and organisational needs, particularly as the best theoretical plan will be no good in the face of organisational intransigence, apathy or antagonism. When developing a management plan, it is therefore extremely important, as we have stressed previously, that there is a thorough understanding of the nature and culture of the organisation that owns and occupies the asset and of its existing policies and procedures (generally, as well as those that are specifically related to 'property management'). This will be necessary to ensure the best fit between existing policies and procedures and those that it will be either desirable or necessary to introduce as a result of the assessment of significance.

As Pearson and Sullivan (1995) observe:

> *the ideal course of action based only on a consideration of the place is often in conflict with management constraints and limitations ... Alternatively assessment of the significance might point to a clear and unequivocal need to conserve the place in a certain way reducing options for use, interpretation and other aspects of management.*

It will also of course be necessary to consider owners' and occupiers' requirements for the asset. That is, the asset will have a functional value that it will be necessary to maintain. For non-heritage organisations, it will be a function that is probably unrelated to the cultural significance of the asset. Indeed, it may be in tension with it, although it may be that there is some kudos for the organisation in owning or occupying a building of cultural significance which they already set off against various issues, such as possible restrictions on development and use.

The management plan will also have to take into account the aspirations that the organisation has for the asset. Some of these issues may have already been identified as contributing to vulnerability – indeed, in some cases they are the main threat – but for other aspirations it may be more a matter of synchronising them to work with cultural values.

There needs to be an assessment that considers how, and the extent to which, the organisation's culture, management structure, policies, procedures and practices might do the following:

- Enhance and protect significance;
- Have little or no effect on significance;
- Have had, or might have in the future, a detrimental effect on significance.

Understanding the existing organisational culture as well as its policies and procedures should allow an assessment of the level of detail that needs to be provided in order to ensure the protection and, where possible, enhancement of significance. There is no point in having policies that are in conflict with procedures which are to be retained; for example, with maintenance management procedures that do not focus decision-making on an understanding of relative significance or which allow fabric and character to be lost in small increments (this is sometimes referred to as 'salami-slicing').

However, a perceived need to influence detail in processes has to be balanced against being seen to intervene with the professional judgement, and possibly the competing objectives, of the organisation and its managers. The key to addressing this dilemma is involving people from the organisation at an early stage, and ensuring that this involvement includes a range of people at different levels and from all the appropriate areas, such as visitor management, property management and maintenance management. Clearly this is important because they will be useful in identifying requirements, opportunities and barriers and then later helping to analyse the options for delivering the policies and ensuring the development, where necessary, of new practices and procedures. Conversely, if people throughout the organisation do not understand or accept the premise of the management plan, there is a danger that they may feel resentful and work against it either passively or actively. Put bluntly, the management plan will not work effectively, if the organisation at all levels is not committed to making it do so.

In addition, there will be a need to consider the resources that are or may be available for implementing the plan. This will obviously include financial resources (including how and when they are available), but it will also involve resources such as people, with appropriate skills and knowledge.

Other possible coverage of the management plan

This book is not about the production of management plans, but about the role of significance in management, and, as such, it is not necessary to continue to expound in detail about management plans and their content. However, before moving on, we should note that the *coverage* of a conservation plan and management plan for the same asset may overlap, although their content may differ. This is because the conservation plan explores and uses significance to define policies that will ensure that the asset's heritage value is properly considered, respected and, wherever possible, enhanced in decision-making, while the management plan looks to embed those policies into wider strategy and action for the plan period (typically perhaps, the next five years). In consequence, just as with the conservation plan, the management plan is likely to consider from its own perspective, for instance:

- *Conservation* – defining a clear strategic framework that shows how decisions about physical interventions with the asset's fabric will be made and the basis on which this should be done. In essence, this will dictate how conservation principles are to be interpreted and then integrated and applied within the significance-based management of the asset.
- *Management responsibilities and processes* – addressing issues such as the adequacy and efficiency of the management and decision-making structure as it relates to the organisation's heritage assets, and how this relates to management within the wider organisation.
- *Maintenance* – given its key role in protecting significance, it is important that maintenance management should be at the heart of proactive management rather than being a reactive provision. Maintenance management is discussed further in Chapter 6.
- *Interpretation and promotion of heritage values* – this will relate mainly to heritage management organisations that need to interpret their assets to visitors in a way that explains their value to society.
- *Property management strategies* – various strategies may be needed to cover the granting of leases, appropriate uses, acquisitions and disposals in the light of the asset's significance. There may be opportunities on larger sites to review the relationship between functional use and significance and to relocate functions to other buildings or spaces in order to achieve a better fit that protects and enhances significance (as discussed previously). The management plan is an opportunity to reflect on this.
- *New uses, new buildings* – the appropriateness of existing uses must be reconsidered in the light of the assessment of significance. This may demand that the management plan acts to herald the development of a comprehensive framework to guide decision-making about present and future uses. New uses may be part of the natural development of an asset or may be essential in securing its future, thereby safeguarding significance. Proposals for the adaption or removal of existing buildings or the development of the asset with one or more new buildings need to be based on a proper understanding of the relative significance of the main elements of the asset and of each of its component parts.
- *Setting* – just as with the conservation plan, the management plan will need to consider the setting of the asset and its relation to significance, in this instance, devising strategies and specific actions to maintain the contribution that it makes to the significance of the asset over the plan period and, where relevant and possible, addressing negative contributions made by elements within the setting in order to enhance significance.
- *Use of expert skills and advice* – the management plan should ensure that the necessary skills are available or else will be procured or developed in order that the organisation can undertake planning and management processes efficiently where they interact with the significance of the heritage. There should also be proper provision for ensuring that consultants and contractors – through their briefing, through contracts and specifications and their terms and conditions – understand the implications of their service delivery on the asset's significance.

Incorporating community perspectives and liaison with the community

Developing and delivering a common vision for the asset will obviously depend upon the aspirations and concerns of the organisation, but should also continue to involve other stakeholders.

The views of the local community and others associated with the asset should already have been taken into account in assessing significance. However, it is important, particularly with intangible aspects of significance, that it is clear how such individuals and groups will continue to be involved in decisions about protecting and enhancing significance and what management processes will be put in place to ensure this happens. It will be necessary to implement policies and a process for liaison with the community and other stakeholders in order to ensure that they understand the basis and the implications of management decisions and actions, and that they are given an opportunity for their views and insights to continue to be taken into account.

Although there may be constraints, depending on the asset and the management organisation, community involvement is essentially about an ethical approach. It is also of course concerned with minimising conflict.

Monitoring the plan

As we have observed elsewhere, there needs to be a process set in place to monitor how the plan is working. This will involve an assessment of how well the policies, strategies and planned actions are being applied (to the appropriate time-scale).

There will need to be targets in the plan and these will have to be monitored. These targets should be based on the policies and actions that are set out to enhance and protect significance and should therefore primarily be drawn from the assessment of significance and the assessment of vulnerability. This may mean that new performance indicators need to be developed or existing ones adjusted. These should fit into and complement the organisation's overall management and property management benchmarks, but they should be derived from a perspective which monitors issues of significance protection and enhancement (rather than concentrating on, for example, such things as financial expenditure).

Reviewing the plan

It is important to ensure that the policies, strategies and actions within the management plan are reviewed. As we have already observed, conservation plans and management plans should be dynamic. Not only does there need to be a robust method for ensuring that objectives are being met, but it will also be necessary to review whether they are the right objectives in the light of changing circumstances. Where both exist, it clearly makes sense to synchronise the review of the conservation plan and management plan with the strategic planning cycle of the organisation. Although three-year or five-year periods are quite common, there may be reasons why it should be shorter or longer, including perhaps where major changes are envisaged to the asset or to its management.

Management tools for historic areas

We observed in Chapter 2 that historic areas of cities, towns and villages tend to comprise numerous properties – many in the separate ownership of individuals, companies and other organisations – and public areas and spaces which in the UK are likely to be managed by the local authority on behalf of the wider community. The only statutory protection available for historic areas in the UK is as a designated conservation area, defined in law as an 'area of special architectural or historic interest, the character or appearance of which it is desirable to preserve or enhance' (Figures 5.2 (a) and (b)). The legislation requires local authorities to identify and designate such areas.

As Historic Scotland notes in the Introduction to its 2004 *Planning Advice Note 71: Conservation Area Management*: 'Effective management of conservation areas requires support and input from [all] stakeholders [in the area] … The management strategy for each conservation area should have shared ownership, involving all the stakeholders in an open and inclusive way.'

Indeed, this is true of any historic area whether designated or not, if its essential character makes a positive contribution to the life of the community. Pickard and de Thyse (2001) concluded that sustainable management of historic centres must:

- Respect community life;
- Improve the quality of life;
- Maintain identity, diversity and vitality;
- Minimise the depletion of non-renewable heritage assets;
- Change attitudes and perceptions – the process of managing change involves wider interests and should involve different actors from the public and private sectors; property owners, investors, residents, and other community and voluntary interests. In other words, the process should become part of everyone's conscience.
- Empower community action and responsibility through involvement;
- Provide a suitable policy framework for integrating conservation objectives with the aims of sustainable development;
- Define the capacity by which the historic centre can permit change.

Maintaining identity, minimising the depletion of non-renewable assets and defining the capacity by which a historic area can change, all presuppose that an accurate, detailed and up-to-date understanding exists of the character and interest of the area. Without this, sustainable management of the area is not possible.

(a)

(b)

Figure 5.2 (a),(b)   Historic areas take many forms. Here, views of university buildings within Tyndall's Park Conservation Area in Bristol (a), and along the High Street in the Dorset village of Sydling St Nicholas (b). Despite their considerable differences, some key issues, such as the management of street furniture, bollards, cables and the like, are often similar.

A number of tools are available that can be used to analyse the character and special interest of historic areas, but we intend to concentrate upon just three: the conservation plan; historic area appraisals; and characterisation.

The conservation plan discussed again

We examined the nature and use of conservation plans in some detail earlier in this chapter and much of that discussion centred around conservation plans for individual sites. However, the conservation plan approach and structure are equally suited for use on historic areas. The same logical process needs to be applied, whatever the asset. The evaluation of a historic area may of necessity involve extra layers of development history and will undoubtedly introduce different cultural values.

Nonetheless, as a platform for sustainable management of a historic area, the conservation plan offers the same ability to develop policy in a structured way built on an understanding of the locality, its significance and vulnerability to deleterious change. A conservation plan, prepared in 2005 for the St Katharine Docks area immediately to the east of the Tower of London, adopted the typical four-step structure of understanding, significance, vulnerability/issues and policies. Unusually, however, it contained a major focus on modern townscape character and strategic views into and out of the area, for these were recognised to be key values within the area and particularly susceptible to rapid compromise through development pressures. Thus, embedded within the conservation plan was a historic area appraisal (an analytical tool which we will discuss in more detail shortly). This illustrates usefully a general point that should be made about conservation planning and associated management tools. Such things should not be treated inflexibly. The best means of analysis needs to be fashioned to suit the particular circumstances and issues that are involved. One conservation professional, who was a consultee on the draft St Katharine Docks conservation plan, reacted negatively to the amalgamation of the historic area appraisal within the conservation plan. In our view, it was a fitting approach in the prevailing circumstances and considerably enhanced the analysis of significance and vulnerability and the development of appropriate conservation management policies for the area. In that instance, lateral thinking about values strengthened the output and impact of the conservation plan.

Historic area appraisals

There is no set structure for a historic area appraisal – indeed, a number of different approaches have been adopted in various circumstances within the UK and internationally. However, a certain degree of commonality exists to most appraisal methods. In our opinion, with more than a nod in the direction of significance-based conservation planning, it is possible to set out a representative appraisal structure that, with intelligent individual adaptation, will meet most needs. Just as with a conservation plan, we believe that the principal objectives of a historic area appraisal are to understand why the area is as it is, in order to do the following:

- Define what makes it special, what makes it 'tick'.
- Assess what is truly significant and of value about the area to society at large.
- Establish how the area has changed and fared positively or negatively in recent decades under the existing management regime.
- Surmise how it is likely to continue to develop, and to understand the prevailing driving forces for change and specific influences that together will shape its future.
- Generate management approaches that will protect what is of value yet is vulnerable.
- Target regenerative action or improvements on elements that do not work well in order to optimise the benefit gained to all from the area.

Almost inevitably, the area appraisal process involves input from three interrelated activities, which may commence in a self-contained way, but eventually must come together through an iterative dynamic process of analysis and synthesis. The three activities from which the appraisal will be built are: (1) desk and archival study; (2) site evaluation; and (3) public engagement and consultation. As with conservation plans, historic area appraisals require people to think laterally and 'outside the box'. Sticking rigidly to a set range of disciplines and approaches to analysis is an assured way of delivering a flawed appraisal. Compromises of this kind can only lead to poor management decision-making and subsequent action.

With appropriate adaptation to take account of particular circumstances, including whether the historic area is statutorily protected in any way, an area appraisal might comprise the following (Box 5.3).

Box 5.3   Area appraisal

Section 1: Introduction to background

- Background to appraisal
- Purpose and scope of study
- Key dates and milestones
- Methodology
- Contributions

Section 2: Context and overview of area today

- General identity including summary of the area's character and significance
- General context to wider settlement, landscape and historic environment
- Location and study area maps
- Climate
- Modern land use and ownership patterns

- Economic circumstances and key data
- Demography
- Management arrangements
- Planning context
- Nature and level of statutory protection/designations affecting area, including individual structures, landscapes, species, etc. within and close by

Section 3: Origins, historical development and archaeology

- Underlying natural factors and characteristics, including landscape setting, geology and soil types
- Origins of settlement
- Reasons for location
- Overview of history and principal events affecting area and wider context; growth, change and their causes
- Historic land use patterns and changes
- Early plan form and subsequent development
- Historical development of wider setting – the local historic environment
- Review of archaeological evidence for any or all of the above
- Assessment of archaeological potential within area and immediate setting

Section 4: Defining the place today

Area-wide overview:

- Modern plan form, street pattern, built density and urban grain, highlighting survivals of earlier forms
- Balance between and interrelationship of built form and spaces
- Overview of definable distinct character zones
- Building typology, typical architectural style(s) and detailing, materials
- General contribution of public and private spaces, and of vegetation
- Key vistas into, across and out from area

The area in use:

- Concentrations of activity and relationship to modern land use and other factors
- People and vehicular movement patterns
- Places of inactivity, seclusion, relaxation and privacy
- Variations (24/7/52)
  - over the day
  - by days of week
  - by months of year/seasons
- Accessibility
- The visitor experience

Character: zone-by-zone analysis:

- Distinctive characteristics of zone
- Sense of place and intangible qualities, including sounds and smells

- Planned streetscapes and landscapes
- Key protected buildings
- Key unprotected buildings
- Qualities of buildings in zone and their contribution
- Key spaces
- Qualities of all spaces in zone and their contribution
- Trees and planting
- Highways and byways
- Contribution of surface materials, signage, street furniture; the effect of night-time lighting
- Aspects of neutral contribution
- Damaging and negative contributions

Section 5: Significance of the historic area

- Values
- Relative significance of the area
- Significance of constituent parts, including character zones and key spaces and places

Section 6: Issues facing the area

Needs to be assessed for the area itself, but might cover:

- Effectiveness of current management regime
- Impact of negative contributions
- Condition of buildings, spatial elements, etc.
- Development and infrastructure pressures, including those in wider setting with capability of impacting on the historic area
- Manmade and environmental hazards
- Economic drivers and the changing needs of the community
- Tourism and other 'people pressures'
- Demographic change
- Political pressures
- Disaster management issues
- Capacity to absorb changes without damage to its special interest; specific 'pinch' points of concern

Section 7: Conservation strategy flowing from appraisal's findings

Again, this must be assessed and structured to suit the particular circumstances, but the strategy should look beyond the immediate future and might include:

- Cross-referral to relevant policies and their application to and within the historic area
- Identification of the various needs for change, for related guidance and development briefing
- Proposals for improved management performance to increase protection of vulnerable elements
- A strategy of planning enforcement
- Resource requirements, including manpower and funding

- Links to appropriate regeneration initiatives and other strategic aspirations of potential value to the area
- A methodology for monitoring and review, including key performance measures

Section 8: Recommendations

- Specific management improvements, including preparation/revision of management plan; need for adjustments to management strategy for area
- Requirement for specific policies to reflect conservation strategy (see Section 7) so as to influence future change
- Need for additional statutory protection for the area or constituent parts or changes to existing designations
- Opportunities for regeneration, beneficial development and improvement, and enhancement
- Need for imposition of protective controls on wider setting to area or for strategic views in, across or out of area
- Requirements for further study
- Monitoring and review mechanisms
- Need for preparations and dissemination of care and design or other guidance to individual property owners

Section 9: Record information

- Schedule of documentary and research sources
- Extensive photographic record for future comparative use to demonstrate ongoing change and effectiveness of management regime

Looking over the model framework for a historic area analysis as set out above, it can be seen how its structure shadows that of the typical conservation plan. Setting aside introductory material, Sections 2–4 equate to the development of an understanding of the asset in a conservation plan; Section 5 evaluates its significance; Section 6 explores the area's vulnerability to pressure and change; while Sections 7 and 8 use that platform to define essential and desirable management policies for effective, beneficial and benign future care.

The appraisal framework is as beneficial for establishing cultural value and guiding change in small rural settlements (irrespective of whether they are designated) as it is for historic market towns facing considerable development pressures and large or complex urban quarters as might be found in, say, Vienna or Amsterdam. It is also appropriate as a tool for use in multi-layered, historically rich sub-regions. An instance of this kind of application is to be found in a heritage and tourism master plan for Mtskheta in Georgia, produced in 2003 by UNESCO in association with the United Nation's Development Program (UNDP). Mtskheta, a World Heritage Site, was the ancient capital of Georgia and today, still its spiritual heart, is of enormous religious and cultural importance for Georgians. With the collapse of the Soviet Union and its influence over Eastern Europe in 1989, Mtskheta became profoundly at risk, first, from economic decline, and thereafter from the threat of ill-planned new developments targeted at stabilising and turning around the region's economy. The master plan was developed to help in the process of managing beneficial and benign change, thus acting as a catalyst to economic revitalisation. It was built on the platform provided by a sub-regional appraisal – covering both the city and its wider environmental and rural contexts and linkages – that, to all intents and purposes, mirrored our own outline framework above.

In developing historic area appraisals, the character and significance of an asset should not be confused. Significance is essentially a hierarchical concept assessed in ascending levels of value. It is a very different concept to character (although, clearly, there may be some overlap). Significance is about social and cultural value. Character is 'the combination of qualities or features that distinguishes one place from another'. The character of an asset may form part of its wider holistic value to society, but an assessment of significance is a far broader and deeper concept.

The development of a conservation management strategy (Section 7 in our framework above) and the implementation of recommendations such as those outlined in Section 8 of the framework (for instance, the need for additional statutory protection or the generation of bespoke design and care guidance for building owners, developers and architects) are crucial to effecting responsible and sustainable improvements in the management of a historic area. However, ensuring common ownership of strategies and policy direction is equally vital if management is to deliver its objectives successfully. Undoubtedly, this demands planned but transparent consultation and briefing on the appraisal's outcome, but, just as importantly, it requires real engagement by the community in the appraisal process itself. This is rarely attempted – let alone achieved – by those responsible for the planning and commissioning of appraisal projects.

As with conservation plans, the appraisal and the effectiveness of the management policies that are derived from it need to be monitored regularly and reviewed periodically.

Characterisation

The term 'historic environment' is used to represent 'all aspects of the environment resulting from the interaction between people and places through time, including all surviving physical remains of past human activity, whether visible or buried, and deliberately planted or managed flora' (English Heritage, 2008). The kinship between this definition and that for the cultural landscape – whether Sauer's (1925), 'The cultural landscape is fashioned from a natural landscape by a culture group. Culture is the agent, the natural area is the medium, the cultural landscape the result', or, as we have put it, '[the] vital interaction between mankind and the natural environment (or perhaps more accurately the pre-existing cultural environments) over time' – is obvious. Historic England (Clark *et al.*, 2004) has also stated that the historic environment:

- Knows no chronological limits;
- Knows no thematic limits, covering everything from an individual site or building to the whole historic landscape;
- Knows no geographic limits, being applicable in town and country alike;
- Knows no limits to its scale, the locally-distinctive now being recognised as equally worthy of consideration, in its own way, as the internationally significant;
- Knows no limits of culture or ethnicity.

Characterisation is an analytical tool that was developed initially for use on rural landscapes, but it is rapidly being promoted as invaluable in managing change throughout the historic environment. Indeed, in a review of the application of historic landscape characterisation, published by English Heritage and Lancashire County Council in 2004, it was emphasised that 'some of the most innovative [characterisation] work at present concerns the past – industrial towns of Cornwall and Lancashire, the great conurbations such as Merseyside, and the ambitious regeneration programmes of the London–Stanstead–Cambridge and Thames Gateway Growth Areas' (Clark *et al.*, 2004).

As that same review makes clear, the development of characterisation as a process was intimately linked to that of the historic area appraisal, for it was built from 'the concept of "character" articulated in 1967 Conservation Area legislation' (e.g. Civic Amenities Act 1967). As will become clear, the two approaches are closely related but they should not be confused. Characterisation incorporates a focus on mapping that makes it distinct from the usual historic area appraisal and, most specifically, it concentrates on landscapes (rural or urban) rather than sites (or as the English Heritage /Lancashire County Council review puts it, characterisation is 'concerned with area not point data' (Clark *et al.*, 2004)). This is consciously different from the standard historic area appraisal, which (while producing an assessment of the area as a coherent place) reads it, at least partially, as being built up of individual buildings and spaces which each make a positive, neutral or negative contribution to the character of the whole. Characterisation does not deny that contribution, but provides a tool for exploring an area, and demonstrating it as a landscape resulting from many years (often centuries) of enriching growth, development and change – the dynamic ebb and flow of life. From this vantage point, the problem, such as it is, with the historic area appraisal is the same conceptual shortcoming that has permeated thinking in the UK (as well as much of the rest of the western world) over the past century about heritage, and which, for the moment, continues to define the legislative approach towards its protection. Until recently, the notion of heritage in the western world has centred not on the all-encompassing holism that is the historic environment, but on individual 'jewels' of historic interest that are worthy of reverence and protection scattered in a 'sea of mediocrity' (that, by definition, does not warrant protection and can be repeatedly recycled for reuse). To a degree, an injudiciously prepared historic area appraisal risks replicating this attitude; for, in seeing the area as being built up of 'good' and 'bad' things, it risks drawing protective 'red lines' around the good while offering up the remainder for recycling. This is not what significance-based sustainable management should be about. At any one time, the local historic environment represents the present summation of accretive cultural change to the underlying natural landscape (and see here the immediate correlation and convergence with the concept of the cultural landscape). As the English Heritage and Lancashire County Council review of characterisation observes, 'if we celebrate the result of past changes, we must logically accept further change'. (Clark *et al.*, 2004). Once we have made that challenging philosophical leap of faith, we must then be prepared to sanction, and perhaps occasionally even encourage, planned change to the 'good' as well as the 'bad' in the interests of sustainable management of the whole. That is where reactionary protective 'red-lining' breaks down.

As an analytical process, characterisation 'helps to manage change in the historic environment by tracing the imprint of history ... It builds up area-based pictures of how places in town and country have developed over time. It shows how the past [survives] within today's world' (English Heritage, undated). Critically, however, characterisation studies the present-day world. It does not simply focus on areas of special architectural or historic interest; it does not ignore the modern as part of the landscape; it is just as much about the everyday ordinary places that predominate in the world as about the exceptional or the distinctive.

GIS (Geographic Information System)-based mapping usually lies at the heart of characterisation. However, despite the generally perceived exactitude of GIS-based data, characterisation is, in essence, a broad-brush interpretive approach to analysis. One of the principles laid down by Clark *et al.* (2004) is that characterisation 'is a matter of interpretation not record, perception not facts; understand "landscape" as an idea, not purely as an objective thing'. English Heritage's (2004) *Conservation Bulletin Issue 47*, dedicated to characterisation, described it as providing a dynamic and fluid yet provisional 'big picture' of a place (which might be a whole county as much as, say, a market town), a 'frame into which others can add their perceptions and views'. It went on to pinpoint the primary objective of characterisation as being:

> to understand better the complex intertwining roads of past decisions, actions and inactions that have led to the present day's historic environment, to our world, whether we like it or not. We can map the trajectory of a place's evolution and chart possible future directions ... This ability to set out choices – to preserve or manage, to create or leave well alone – is why characterisation is a tool for the future.
>
> (English Heritage, 2004)

In some ways, there is 'nothing new in the world' in respect of the evaluation of assets and places. Just as with other analytical management tools we have already examined, characterisation involves a combination of desk-based and archival study, field survey, community engagement and synthesis. Indeed, what separates one analytical tool from another might be regarded as being simply gradation and emphasis. However, circumstances and objectives vary, and each process has its strengths and best uses. Characterisation builds on systematic identification of prevailing characteristics within the 'landscape' or place that is under study. As has already been noted, it deals with areas, not with individual sites, it concentrates on mappable patterns and attributes. Maps are used extensively, both for the purposes of map regression analysis (the detailed comparison of chronologically sequential historic maps to develop an understanding of change) and as the primary medium for presenting findings and recommendations from the process.

Characterisation explores the 'time-depth' that gives character and sense of place to an area or landscape. It analyses past change and land usage. It establishes the survival and pattern of meaningful historic elements in the present-day environment through map regression and rapid field survey. A typical example in the town might be substantive traces of former burgage holdings within the urban grain; in the countryside, the continued presence of medieval field systems as part of the modern landscape.

Characterisation practitioners see their approach to study falling into two distinct sections, which might loosely be thought of as: creating the 'story' of the area, and consideration of its future, based on that interpretation of its present. Characterisation is seen as being a 'vital tool' for management planning rather than an intellectually fulfilling end in its own right. It is perhaps no coincidence then that, by seeing the process in two stages, its proponents place greater emphasis on consideration of the future as an integral component than in the typically four-step conservation plan where far too often, the final step feels to have been 'bolted on' as an afterthought rather than being the principal objective at the outset. Perhaps this is why, to date, over-emphasis has been placed upon the conservation plan process as a self-contained entity of value (in every respect!), instead of its use as a platform for day-to-day asset or area management.

In the characterisation process 'creating the story' involves data gathering, analysis, mapping and interpretation. It must be stressed that, in characterisation, much of the presentation of the 'story' of the area's character development takes place pictorially/diagrammatically with considerable emphasis on layered maps. As Clark *et al.* (2004) have observed, characterisation 'provides a context for existing data', demonstrating that 'the historic landscape has importance as a whole – the sum of all its parts'. By the end of its first stage, characterisation should paint a picture for area managers or those involved in planning change, interpreting the present-day environment in a way that reveals it to be the summation of the underlying natural world and subsequent change through its history. Again, this reinforces the notion that the historic environment is everything about us, and also connects back to the developing idea that urban and rural landscapes are different guises of the same entity – the cultural landscape.

The second stage in the characterisation process – consideration of the area's future based on the picture that has been painted of its present – involves making judgements about how to manage, even encourage, further change in a way that sustains character, local diversity and value.

Hopefully, the message from this brief analysis of three management tools for historic areas shines through with clarity. In most circumstances, conservation has moved away from seeking to inhibit or prevent change to heritage assets. Instead, it has taken on board what should have been self-evident all along. Urban or rural, the landscape is not made up of a small number of heritage jewels scattered in a sea of mediocrity. The world around us is the cumulative result of all historic change to the underlying natural environment. Some of that change has, and continues to, come about through the impact of the climate and other natural forces; much, though, is change – purposeful or incidental – brought about by mankind. To quote Clark *et al.* once more, 'If we celebrate the result of past changes, we must logically accept further change.' The task at hand, therefore, is not how to suppress ongoing change, but how to shape it so that we continue to derive precious benefit from the historic environment and its vital sense of place, whilst investing in its development in a way that optimises the cultural value of both the old and the new for society at large. That, for want of any better phrase, is conservation planning and management. Arguably, it is the only satisfactory way we have to manage our world and its cultural heritage resources sustainability.

Heritage impact assessments

As its name implies, this procedure looks in detail at the possible impact of a particular action or actions upon the significance of an asset. Essentially, it is the same concept as environmental impact assessments which are used routinely in the wider land planning context. Clark (2001) categorises them as being 'about risk assessments for historic buildings and their landscapes'. A heritage impact assessment (HIA) procedure will be appropriate for all heritage assets irrespective of their size or complexity.

It is hopefully obvious that a heritage impact assessment needs to be based upon a balanced, objective and reliable assessment of the nature and extent of the significance of the heritage asset. If one does not already exist, whether in the form of an assessment of significance or a fully developed and adopted conservation plan, this preparatory work must be the first step in the HIA process. For complex assets, where a conservation plan and a management plan are already in place, impact assessments should be a normal and integral part of the management processes that have been agreed and implemented to protect and enhance significance. For such assets, the framework for making a judgement on the likely impact should have been developed through the management plan and should be in place, as should, at least, the contextual information relating to significance. However, depending on the amount of detail on significance that is already available in a coherent form, and the particulars of the change proposal, it may still be necessary to seek more information about the significance of the items or elements that will be affected.

In a sense, HIAs are a test of the rigour and clarity of any preceding assessment of significance and its identification of relative significance and sensitivity to change. For a place without a conservation plan or a statement/assessment of significance, an HIA will necessitate an investigation and articulation of the significance of the element or item in question. It is important that all involved understand that proposals that will generate the need for an HIA are not just those that may have an effect on the physical fabric; indirect impacts on setting may well be just as important and potentially harmful. For example, interventions that have an effect on a 'sense of place' – perhaps on views in and out, or on character or 'atmosphere' – should be subject to an HIA.

Whether or not the HIA is generated within the context of an already established statement of significance, it is important to understand that a relatively small action or intervention can have a relatively large impact on the significance of an asset. The cumulative effect of a number of small interventions can be particularly harmful. Therefore, the trigger for an HIA cannot be based simply on notions of the size of the intervention.

The HIA system that is adopted will be dependent upon the nature and complexity of the development or other change proposal and should do the following:

- Clarify the nature, purpose, detail and timing of the proposal, the reasons for it, and the benefits to the organisation/individual owner, or indeed the wider community;
- Clarify which aspects of significance are possibly affected, directly or indirectly, now or in the future, and the ways in which those effects will be, or may be, manifested. Some impacts may be easily 'measured' or identified. However, others may be a possible problem and/or add to the potential vulnerability of the element, but it is difficult to determine the exact effect. In that case a detailed risk assessment will be required;
- Clarify what information is required to judge the impact of the proposal;
- Make a judgement about the effect on significance of the proposal;
- Make a decision on whether the proposal should be accepted, rejected or amended, and on how to mitigate further its potential impact on significance and on the historic integrity of the asset.

As with other management activities it should be clear what triggers the need for an HIA. But there should also be clarity and transparency about the information-collecting and decision-making process.

Clearly some proposals may not be a potential threat to the heritage value of an asset because they are neutral in their impact and effect on significance. Where amendments to the proposal are necessary or action needs to be taken to protect vulnerable aspects of the asset in order to mitigate harm to significance, this may involve, for example:

- *Technical issues* – for instance, in requiring a different approach to repair or the provision of site-specific protection to guard against impact or other damage during implementation of building works;

- *Architectural/aesthetic issues* – for instance, alterations to a design, or,
- *Use issues* – for instance, suggesting that the use driving the change should be integrated elsewhere where there will be a less negative impact on significance.

The emphasis should be not on preventing change, but on finding alternative ways of achieving change without harming significance, although the question of what will be the outcome if nothing is done will always be a useful one to consider and is a valid component of a heritage impact assessment.

In some cases, the impact of a development proposal may be positive, in that the intervention is intended to, or may contain the possibility to, further protect and enhance significance. It may well be that any amendments in these cases are intended to maximise potential heritage benefits or ensure that opportunities are not lost. Therefore, in some instances, the outcome of an HIA may be about increasing the scope of the work rather than restricting or redirecting it.

Impact assessments range from the simple to the complex. It is probably a fair observation that the past decade has seen an increasing move towards elaborateness, as the need for quantification/measurement of the relative magnitude of impact has been seen to be more important.

At its simplest, the heart of a heritage impact assessment may well comprise a tabular analysis of the asset, broken down into appropriate constituent parts: setting out relevant aspects of significance; the nature of the proposed works or changes to each part; their potential impact; and intended mitigation. This table is usually introduced by a commentary, dealing with the kinds of issues discussed above and supported by drawings and schedules specifying methods of providing physical protection or other ways of mitigating known risks.

Table 5.1 shows an extract from a tabular presentation of an HIA for a project involving the upgrading of building services and various repairs to the structure and fabric of a large historic house. Under 'Specific mitigation requirements', the impact assessment refers to a general mitigation statement ('General Mitigation Procedure 1') and to various scheduled mitigation arrangements (for example, 'Special Protection Procedure 3') that have been designed individually to suit particular circumstances. The general mitigation statement for this specific project might include the following:

> *The works have been designed specifically to mitigate, as far as reasonably and safely possible, the quantity and degree of intrusion into previously undisturbed historic fabric. Throughout implementation of the proposed scheme, emphasis will be placed on minimising the impact on historic fabric and decoration, whilst also minimising disturbance to previously disturbed areas.*
>
> *New power, lighting and fire alarm fittings and fixtures will be installed with the utmost care to avoid excessive damage to the building fabric. Any debris and dust created by the works will be carefully controlled to avoid damaging the contents of sensitive rooms and spaces, including those adjacent to the works and along access routes for delivery of materials to the working area.*

Table 5.1 Extract from a heritage impact assessment for a historic house.

Room number	History and significance	Proposed work	Potential impact	Specific mitigation requirements
FIRST FLOOR (Drawing References 1363/FF1 & 1363/FF2)				
FF01	Building phase: 1740s 2005 plan: **Dolls' House Room** (public area) 1954 plan: not named Previous works: not known Significance: (i) Rare survival of dolls' house belonging to elder daughter of first Earl; figures and artefacts within house include French pieces belonging to 'Revolutionary' period (1790–91); (ii) Family 'story' that Isobel, the third Earl's third daughter, was locked up in room for three years until her death as punishment for dropping Chinese vase beloved of her dead grandmother	New smoke detector in room and additional detector in Dolls' House display cabinet.	Fixing points in ceiling and wiring through ceiling void for smoke detectors.	See General Mitigation Procedure 1. Additional protective measures (Special Protection Procedure 11) for temporary relocation of Dolls' House once removed from display cabinet for duration of works in room to be agreed with curatorial section.
FF02	Building phase: 1740s 2005 plan: **Hall** (public area) 1954 plan: Housemaid's Closet Previous works: not known Significance: None beyond surviving historic fabric and as component part of second major post-medieval development phase of Hall.	Replacement of existing smoke detector and 'break glass' call point.	Negligible	See General Mitigation Procedure 1.

(continued)

Table 5.1 *(Continued)*

Room number	History and significance	Proposed work	Potential impact	Specific mitigation requirements
FF03	Building phase: 1620s **2005 plan: Leather Gallery (public area)** 1954 plan: The Gallery Previous works: Repairs to timber ceiling joists, truss ends, wall plates and lintels in 1980s due to long-term water ingress from flat lead roof above and consequential fungal decay; some poor resin repairs; moulded cornice to ceiling reinstated (untidily); other interventions suspected from uneven line of plaster but cannot be identified from documentary evidence Significance: (i) Part of first major expansion of medieval Hall (1620s) which reflected the growing political importance of the family and established the national significance of the Hall	(a) Removal of unsatisfactory 1980s work to cornice and ceiling to permit inspection and rectification of failed resin repairs to structural timbers; (b) Insertion of new aspirating smoke detection pipework through modern replacement ceiling plaster, routed through void above; (c) Replacement of 2no existing power sockets and 2no light switches. Replacement of existing light fitting.	**Generally** High risk of damage to leather hangings from all works from dust, impact from debris or accidental contact by site operatives. *NB These hangings will remain in place throughout as they are considered too fragile to demount and move.* **Additionally:** *Specific risks* (a) Destabilising/loosening, collapse or impact damage to seventeenth-century ceiling plaster;	(i) Special 'tool box' training at commencement of works for site operatives to emphasise sensitivity of working area and risks; daily reminder by site foreman (to be registered on daily log kept in site hut and initialled by foreman); (ii) Special Protection Procedure 3 to be implemented by curatorial section to erect/secure robust dustproof protective casing around leather hangings; (iii) Temporary ceiling propping with padding to be erected and kept in place during works (a) and (b); see drawing ref 1363/17 and Special Protection Procedure 4;

(continued)

Table 5.1 (Continued)

Room number	History and significance	Proposed work	Potential impact	Specific mitigation requirements
	(ii) Survival of part of original seventeenth-century ornate plaster ceiling (iii) Extremely rare seventeenth-century Spanish leather hangings mounted on walls; known to have been hung in this room since 1703 (and possibly before)		(b) as (a); also potential for weakening of undersized historic ceiling joists if notched or otherwise cut to facilitate routing of pipework for smoke detection installation; also note presence of protected species of bats in roof void over FF03 – see entry for Roof Void RV05 and its significance; risk from (c) as replacing existing units.	(iv) No access to roof void without prior approval of ecologist and without attendance of registered bat handler; timing of works within void and associated areas must be restricted as set out in Special Protection Procedure 10 and in accordance with ecological policy 02 of site management plan; (v) For all works, General Mitigation Procedure 1.
FF04	Building phase: 1620s and 1740s **2005 plan: 3rd Earl's Room** (showroom from barriers in door openings, but no public access) 1954 plan: Damask Room (then used as private living room) Previous works: *Mid-eighteenth century –* chimney piece and joinery *1896* – papered and painted *Post-1957*– damask removed, room furnished as a bedroom. Current wallpaper (1997) is a copy of the late-nineteenth-century paper, from a sample found during the room's renovation.	Lifting of all floor boards to provide access to void below as part of installation of aspirating pipework for very early smoke detection installation to main public rooms below.	(a) Damage to eighteenth-century floor boards and adjacent surfaces and joinery; (b) Impact damage to chimney piece; (c) Impact damage to wallpaper, decorations and furnishings;	(i) For all works, see General Mitigation Procedure 1, including numbering, etc. of lifted boards; (ii) Lifting of boards to be supervised by foreman. Temporary storage arrangements for boards to be agreed prior to commencement of work with contract administrator and curatorial section;

Where feasible, replacement fittings will re-use existing fixing points to avoid further loss of historic fabric. Any new fixing points will be selected with care and consideration for the building fabric and decoration. Where electrical fittings are to be rewired, existing cable and conduit routes will be re-used to avoid impacting upon undisturbed historic fabric. Where sections of new wiring are to be created for points/outlets in new locations, these will follow existing cable and conduit routes, so far as is possible, and make full use of existing access points to floor and ceiling voids.

Floorboards requiring temporary removal for access will be recorded and numbered where taken up in sufficient quantities; otherwise, they will be kept adjacent to their location for ease of refixing in their original position. All floorboards will be carefully removed to avoid damage and will be refixed through their original fixing points

The appointed Contractor will be provided with a 'tool box' talk prior to the commencement of the project and all the contractor's staff and any sub-contractors will be required to be briefed on the need for the utmost sensitivity and attention to detail in their work prior to commencing work on site.

The situation-specific special protection measures might include matters such as:

- Careful erection of temporary plywood casings to walls, balustrades, architraves and other vulnerable elements along access routes to and within working areas;
- Plywood boxing around vulnerable fire surrounds which must be left *in situ* during conduct of the works;
- Procedures for working in spaces known to be used by protected species such as bats; and
- Propping up of delicate plasterwork to ceilings.

It is stressed that the foregoing is a very simple kind of heritage impact assessment. Its great shortcoming is that it does not permit satisfactory measurement of the levels of likely impacts that might flow from implementation of proposals for change. A more detailed and refined process is required to achieve this, although it can be argued that the more elaborate the process the more subjectivity is introduced into the analysis. Thus, choosing a methodology for impact assessment must be regarded as being a 'horses for courses' activity.

Various published HIA methodologies exist; many of them are similar and even share terminology and text. If anything, this demonstrates that this is a field comparatively in its infancy, requiring further thought and development. In 2011, ICOMOS published its *Guidance on Heritage Impact Assessments for Cultural World Heritage Properties* (ICOMOS, 2011). Although expressly intended for use on inscribed World Heritage assets, with thought and adaptation, the guidance can be used appropriately for impact assessment on other heritage assets, too. Comparison shows that the ICOMOS guidance is closely related to the 2007 version of an impact assessment methodology for heritage assets generally published in the UK as part of the *Design Manual for Road and Bridges* (DMRB; HA208/13,) by the Highways Agency, Transport Scotland, the Welsh Assembly Government, and the Department for Regional Development Northern Ireland. This latter HIA methodology has been updated (in 2013) since the publication of the ICOMOS World Heritage guidance. It is again stressed that other methodologies have been published, but, in order to provide some comparison between such 'complex' impact assessment procedures and the more simplistic methodology described above, the DMRB will be used as an example.

In essence, the DMRB approach involves a three-step process:

1 The assessment of significance of the heritage asset(s) potentially experiencing impacts from a development or change proposal.
2 An assessment of the magnitude of impact(s) involved.
3 Quantification of the effect upon the asset's (or assets') significance.

Of course, there are hidden additional steps within this tri-partite approach. For instance, where a significant development proposal is being planned, especially in an urban context, a balanced and objective assessment needs to be made of the full range of heritage assets that may be affected by implementation of the proposal. Equally, the content of the proposals for change needs to be fully comprehended and their capacity to create impacts must be properly appreciated.

As we saw in Chapter 4, various hierarchies to 'quantify' or 'measure' the comparative significance of heritage values have been used in recent years (Table 5.2). They all have strengths and weaknesses, given the inevitability that such comparisons will always be somewhat subjective in their nature, especially when attempting to predict what future generations will find of value. For UK readers, it is worth noting that the 'value hierarchy' published in the *Design Manual for Roads and Bridges* has been subjected to scrutiny in the UK planning system, including Public Inquiries, and is the only one published by a government department. With minor adaptation made simply for the purposes of this explanation, the DMRB provides terminology and definitions for a cultural heritage hierarchy of significance, as set out in Table 5.2 below.

While, inevitably, some subjectivity is at times involved in making value judgements, this hierarchy of values has to be appreciated as a continuum. There will be shades of interpretation where, for instance, an asset lies close to the borderline between the descriptions of 'high' and 'very high' significance.

The first stage in the DMRB approach to impact assessment involves the allocation of one of these levels of significance to the asset(s) that are considered to be vulnerable to impact from the change proposal. The next key step is consideration of the likely magnitude of impacts that will be experienced by these 'receptor' asset(s). This assessment is made using a second table (Table 5.3).

Some brief explanation is required of the descriptions set against each possible magnitude of impact here. It can be seen that the impact assessment process needs to consider impacts on the setting of the asset(s) as much as impacts on the built fabric of each receptor asset. This is because, as we have discussed in

Table 5.2   Levels of significance.

Level of significance	Criteria
Very high	World Heritage Sites
	Assets of acknowledged international importance
	Assets that can contribute significantly to acknowledged international research objectives
	Historic landscapes of international value (designated or not) and extremely well-preserved historic landscapes with exceptional coherence, time depth, or other critical factor(s)
High	Scheduled Monuments and undesignated assets of Schedulable quality and importance
	Grade I and II* Listed buildings (Scotland category A)
	Other Listed buildings that can be shown to have exceptional qualities in their fabric or associations not adequately reflected in their Listing grade
	Conservation Areas containing very important buildings
	Undesignated structures of clear national importance
	Designated and undesignated historic landscapes of outstanding historic interest (including Grade I and Grade II* Registered Parks and Gardens); undesignated landscapes of high quality and importance of demonstrable national value; and well-preserved historic landscapes exhibiting considerable coherence, time depth or other critical factor(s)
	Assets that can contribute significantly to acknowledged national research objectives
Medium	Designated or undesignated assets that contribute to regional research objectives
	Grade II (Scotland category B) Listed buildings
	Historic (unlisted) buildings that can be shown to have exceptional qualities in their fabric or historical association;
	Conservation Areas containing important buildings that contribute significantly to their historic character
	Historic townscapes or built-up areas with important historic integrity in their buildings, or built settings (for example, including street furniture or other structures)
	Designated landscapes of special historic interest (including Grade II Registered Parks and Gardens); undesignated landscapes that would justify such a designation; averagely well-preserved historic landscapes with reasonable coherence, time depth or other critical factor(s); landscapes of regional value
Low	Designated and undesignated assets of local importance including those compromised by poor preservation and/or poor survival of contextual associations
	Assets of limited value, but with potential to contribute to local research objectives
	Locally Listed buildings (Scotland category C(S) Listed Buildings) and historic (unlisted) buildings of modest quality in their fabric or historical association
	Historic townscape or built-up areas of limited historic integrity in their buildings or built settings (for example, including street furniture or other structures)
	Robust undesignated historic landscapes; historic landscapes with importance to local interest groups; and historic landscapes whose value is limited by poor preservation and/or poor survival of contextual associations
Negligible	Assets with very little surviving archaeological interest
	Buildings of little architectural or historical note
	Landscapes with little significant historical interest

Table 5.3   Magnitude of impact.

	Magnitude of impact
Major	Change to key historic building elements, such that the asset is totally altered Comprehensive change to the setting.
Moderate	Change to many key historic building elements, such as the asset is significantly modified Changes to setting of an historic building, such that it is significantly modified
Minor	Changes to key historic building elements, such that the asset is slightly different Changes to setting of an historic building, such that it is noticeably changed
Negligible	Slight changes to historic building elements or setting that hardly affect it
No Change	No change to fabric or setting

Chapters 2 and 4, all built heritage assets are considered to have a setting. In general terms, heritage assets can experience impacts from implementation of development and other change proposals in two distinct ways: direct physical impacts on their fabric, and indirect impacts on the contribution that their setting makes to the assessed significance. The relationship and relative balance between these two different kinds of potential impact are discussed further below.

The final step in the DMRB impact assessment methodology is the quantification of the overall effect of the change proposal upon the asset's significance. This is undertaken using a matrix that brings together the assessments of significance and the likely magnitude of impact of change (Table 5.4).

Where two alternatives are given in this matrix, objective judgement has to be used to decide which best reflects the significance of the effect of the impact

Table 5.4   Matrix of significance of effects.

	Very High	Neutral	Slight	Moderate / large	Large or very large	Very large
	High	Neutral	Slight	Moderate / slight	Moderate / large	Large / very large
Heritage Value	*Medium*	Neutral	Neutral / slight	Slight	Moderate	Moderate / large
	Low	Neutral	Neutral / slight	Neutral / slight	Slight	Slight / moderate
	Negligible	Neutral	Neutral	Neutral / slight	Neutral / slight	Slight
		No Change	*Negligible*	*Minor*	*Moderate*	*Major*
		Magnitude of Impact				

identified. The significance of effects from impacts read from this matrix can be positive or negative. Thus, for example, where proposals affect the setting of a heritage asset of *high* value to the extent that that setting is significantly modified (a *moderate* magnitude of impact), the significance of the effect of the proposal on the setting of the heritage asset is deemed to be *moderate* or *large* (with precise determination being dependent upon application of objective judgement) and positive or negative depending upon circumstance.

It can be seen that this 'complex' approach to impact assessment is very different to the more simplistic tabular procedure explained earlier in this section. The outcome of such complex methodologies involve assessments of levels of impacts and the resulting effect upon significance. As has already been noted, arguably the more 'objective' judgements that are required, the greater the risk that subjectivity creeps in to the impact assessment process. In the end, it must be appreciated that all that can be done is to seek a balanced understanding of the foreseeable *likely* effect on significance of predicted impacts. There is nothing absolute about the process.

Moreover, two potential issues/anomalies are inherent within the DMRB and all similar impact assessment methodologies (for these comments are as pertinent to other methodologies allowing quantification of impacts as to DMRB). These must always be borne in mind when undertaking impact assessment.

The first potential anomaly involves the magnitude of impact as a direct function of the degree of change. It has been noted already that:

- In common with others, the DMRB impact assessment methodology uses significance as a sensitivity weighting to convert the magnitude of impact of a proposal into an overall significance of effect.
- A three-step process is involved: (1) the level of significance of the asset needs to be determined; (2) the proposals must be examined for impacts on the asset, so that the degree of change to the fabric and its setting can be gauged; and (3) finally, using a pre-defined matrix, the significance-weighted magnitude of impact can be read off as a cumulatively positive or negative effect of the development proposals on the asset's significance.

The crux of the problem – the cause of the first anomaly – is that the methodology gauges magnitude of impact as a measure of the degree of change that will occur to the fabric and/or setting of the asset. So far, so good, but the methodology then assumes that the degree of change in an asset's key historic elements or its setting will equate to a proportionately positive or negative effect on the asset. This does not necessarily follow. At the most extreme, a major change may occur to the key elements or setting of an asset that has very little or no positive or negative overall effect on the asset's significance. Sometimes, change does not bring any positive benefits or negative effects; in other cases of a complex nature, extensive change may bring a mix of some positive and some negative results, so that the overall positive or negative effect is nowhere near proportionate to the degree of change that has occurred in the setting of the asset. Neither the DMRB nor similar methodologies recognise these eventualities or permit such outcomes from the assessment process. At the very least, such issues need to be properly understood within the context of the asset and the development proposals under assessment. The measurement of the asset's sensitivity to change or its robustness may also prove invaluable.

This anomaly has to be recognised and understood for what it is. It does not render the use of the DMRB or similar methodologies invalid. But, where it does occur, judgement has to be applied to determine the true effect on the asset's significance from the change proposal. In reality, that adjudged effect on significance may be found to lie at one of the extremes or somewhere in between, once the matters discussed as part of the impact assessment have been taken into account.

The second potential anomaly involves the comparative weighting that should be applied within the process between direct physical impacts and indirect impacts on the setting of the heritage asset. As explained, the DMRB and other such methodologies are predicated on direct change to an asset's physical fabric and indirect impacts on its setting resulting in equal degrees of effect on its significance, that is, a direct impact on fabric or a comparable magnitude of impact on setting are assumed to be of equal 1:1 weight and effect. Thus, for instance, in Table 5.3, a *moderate* magnitude of change is defined as being either 'Change to many key historic building elements, such as the asset is significantly modified' or 'Changes to setting of an historic building, such that it is significantly modified'. That assumes that, in every instance, the setting of an asset contributes as much to significance as the physical fabric itself. If that were not the case and, say, the built fabric of an asset was deemed to be intrinsically more important to significance than the setting, the magnitude of change to the setting necessary to have the same end effect on significance as (to use the same example) significant modification of the built elements would have to be proportionately greater. Methodologies such as DMRB (which otherwise do have their strengths) cannot cope with this readily within a set tabular form and, accordingly, judgement once again must be applied openly and objectively to determine a correct weighting for the balance between direct impacts on fabric and indirect impacts on setting. The existence of a full and balanced evaluation of relative significance, importantly including the setting as well as the primary asset itself, is critical within this objective judgement.

There is one final critical shortcoming within such impact assessment methodologies that needs to be recognised. Consistently, they are better able to assess impacts on physical attributes and to quantify the effects on significance where tangible values are involved. To date, heritage impact assessment processes are poorly equipped to cope where intangible values are important. Failure to understand this risks building significant bias into the process and can lead to skewed management decision-making based on partial impact assessment.

We would stress that these anomalies affect all impact assessment methodologies of this kind. The ability to measure or quantify impacts and their effects on an asset's significance is very important, but the shortcomings in whatever HIA process is selected must always be understood and objective 'professional' judgement applied, accordingly.

Heritage statements within the development planning process

This section looks at the way a consideration of significance, and the management of its protection, may be built into the development planning process, using the present-day situation in England as an example.

In England, the National Planning Policy Framework (NPPF), was adopted as the UK Government's official planning policy framework in March 2012. It incorporates, among other things, national policy relating to the conservation of the historic environment, supplanting Planning Policy Statement 5 (PPS5), which had been in force since March 2010.

Due to constraints imposed by its underlying heritage legislation, which in some ways is now outmoded and out of line with current conservation thinking internationally, England's NPPF considers that significance can only comprise archaeological, architectural, artistic or historic values. It does, however, recognise that 'Significance derives not only from a heritage asset's physical presence, but also from its setting' (DCLG, 2012). Where a heritage asset or its setting may potentially be affected (whether directly or indirectly) by development proposals, the NPPF requires applicants who are seeking planning permission to provide an assessment of significance that is sufficiently detailed to understand the potential impact (whether positive or negative) of the proposal on both the heritage asset and, where applicable, any others in the vicinity. Expressly, in order to comply with paragraph 128 of the NPPF:

> *local planning authorities should require an applicant to describe the significance of any heritage assets affected, including any contribution made by their setting. The level of detail should be proportionate to the assets' importance and no more than is sufficient to understand the potential impact of the proposal on their significance.*
>
> (DCLG, 2012)

This policy is based on government acceptance that better development planning decisions are made when all parties properly understand the particular nature of each and every heritage asset's significance, including the extent of its fabric to which the significance relates and the level of importance of that significance.

In essence, the NPPF anticipates that applicants seeking consent for a development proposal will provide the regulatory authority with a heritage statement that:

1 Identifies each and every heritage asset, whether already designated/classified or not, which could conceivably be affected directly or indirectly by the development proposal.
2 Provides sufficient information to develop and substantiate in a convincing manner an objective assessment of the significance of each of those heritage assets, including establishing:
  (a) the extent of physical fabric to which that significance relates;

   (b) the level of significance that is involved;

   (c) the contribution that the setting of each heritage asset makes to its significance.

3 Establishes the contribution that the application site makes to the local historic environment (this contribution needs to be characterised and may contain positive, neutral and/or negative components).

4 Provides an assessment of impact of and mitigation for the development proposals on the totality of local historic environment, quantifying the level of harm that will be incurred by any of the heritage assets identified in (1).

5 Provides convincing justifications for such harm on grounds that are compliant with heritage and planning policy.

It can be seen that an assessment of significance (or, rather, assessments, where multiple heritage assets are involved) lies at the heart of this development planning policy. We have discussed assessments of significance in detail in Chapter 4 and will not repeat that discussion here. The Ministerial Foreword of the NPPF explains this focus on significance, noting that 'Sustainable development is about change for the better, and not only in our built environment..... Our historic environment – buildings, landscapes, towns and villages – can better be cherished if their spirit of place thrives, rather than withers.' The crucial underlying point is that, to be sustainable, development planning must consider and involve the protection and enhancement of our natural, built and historic environment. The NPPF concludes:

> *The purpose of the planning system is to contribute to the achievement of sustainable development. The policies in [the NPPF], taken as a whole, constitute the Government's view of what sustainable development in England means in practice for the planning system ... Pursuing sustainable development involves seeking positive improvements in the quality of the built, natural and historic environment, as well as in people's quality of life...*

As an example, a case study of the Royal Dart Hotel in Kingswear, Devon, is provided in Chapter 9. As that explains, the hotel was developed out of a pre-existing inn in the 1860s when England's railway network reached the previously remote village. The Italianate building dominates its immediate urban setting, which is designated as a conservation area, and it occupies a key waterfront site, making it a focal point and landmark structure. In 2014, a development proposal was advanced to convert the building into apartments, which would involve not only subdivision of its interior, but also construction of a glass enclosure at roof level overlooking the River Dart alongside. The proportionate heritage statement that was prepared for submission to the local planning authority established that the development proposals could directly affect the significance of the hotel (which was protected already as a listed building) by physical impacts on its fabric and plan form, while the change of use and construction of the glass enclosure extension on its roof might have the potential to affect indirectly the significance of the wider Conservation Area, the neighbouring railway station (which was both a listed building and, historically, intimately associated with the hotel), and several other heritage assets in the vicinity whose settings included the hotel building. Accordingly, the heritage statement *inter alia*:

- Included assessments of the significance of each of these assets;
- In respect to the hotel itself, identified the surviving physical attributes of its significance and established the relative importance of each such element within the building;
- In respect to the other heritage assets, identified the contribution made by the setting of each to its significance;
- Assessed the character of views into, across and out of the designated conservation area, the contribution of the hotel thereto;
- Provided heritage-based development guidelines for the hotel building, based on the foregoing and national and local heritage policy;
- Assessed and quantified the likely impacts that would flow from implementation of the development proposals and the effect on significance that these impacts might cause;
- Proposed appropriate mitigation measures for any significant adverse effects on the significance of heritage assets;
- Provided justification for any unresolved potential harm to significance based on the delivery of wider public benefits (since the NPPF requires that, where a proposed development will lead to substantial harm to or total loss of significance of a designated heritage asset, the local planning authority should refuse consent, unless it can be demonstrated that the substantial harm or loss is necessary to achieve substantial public benefits that outweigh that harm or loss).

The Royal Dart Hotel is a useful example of what can be involved in this kind of use of assessments of significance and this is explored in the case study. Without a balanced understanding, the surviving physical attributes of the asset's significance and the relative importance of each could not have been adequately assessed. In turn, that would have constrained the generation of relevant development guidance and prevented objective assessment of the likely impacts of the development proposals and their effects on significance.

Local management agreements

In Streamlining Listed Building Consent, a research report produced by the Paul Drury Partnership with the Environmental Project Consulting Group for English Heritage in 2003, management guidelines or agreements are described as: 'Informal memoranda of understanding between the owners and managers of listed buildings, the local planning authority and (usually) English Heritage' (English Heritage, 2003).

To make this applicable to the breadth of built heritage assets covered within this book, we need to expand this concept to cover situations that lie outside England and its legislative framework (where in fact, subsequently, local management agreements have been relabelled – perhaps with some loss of wider clarity of meaning – as 'heritage partnership agreements'). Management agreements are generally made between the party or parties that own or manage a heritage asset and those responsible for the administration of relevant statutory planning and protective powers. The asset may be a building, site, estate, historic area or cultural landscape. Often it may carry some form of designation or statutory protection, although this does not necessarily have to be the case. To be successful, it is probable that the various parties to the agreement will have the shared objective of ensuring, through the agreement, the adoption of an appropriate management regime for the asset that will lead to more effective, efficient and sustainable day-to-day decision-making.

The 2003 research report goes on to note that:

Management agreements or guidelines tend to be brief documents that provide a structured framework for decision-making by informed professionals, not (unlike a conservation management plan) an assessment of the significance and vulnerability of all elements of the building fabric at the outset.

(English Heritage, 2003)

Within the context and objectives of the report, this was a reasonable assertion to make about the form of the local management agreement. However, it is our contention that significance-based local management agreements have enormous potential to offer in ensuring that sustainable and effective management practices are adopted by local managers of heritage assets – be they individuals or organisations of one kind or another. Again, it is vital to recognise that, although often such agreements relate to a single building, the concept is appropriate for application to any definable coherent or integral entity within the historic environment. In England, local area agreements have been promoted as being 'of increasing importance in determining the future of a local area. The historic environment must be a part of this process, both as an asset in its own right and for the wider contributions it can make to community goals' (English Heritage, 2006).

In 1995, English Heritage introduced into England the concept of local management guidelines for historic or architecturally important listed buildings in its guidance note *Developing Guidelines for the Management of Listed Buildings* (English Heritage, 1995). This guidance was built upon experience gained in the development of a seminal one-off agreement three years earlier between English Heritage, Ipswich Borough Council and the owners of the Willis Faber building in Ipswich, which was designed by Foster Associates in 1970 and had been listed as Grade I in 1991. As with most subsequent local management agreements, the primary objective of the Willis Faber agreement was 'to provide clarification as to what proposals for the building may not require listed building consent and/or planning permission'. However, it should be stressed that this is not the only benefit to be gained from, or catalyst to the development of, local management guidelines for built heritage assets. Other agreements, as the 2003 report cites (English Heritage, 2003), have been aimed at agreeing management principles for the care of the asset and its significance, establishing a framework and positive environment for the resolution of differences of opinion on proposed management action, and optimising management efficiency and costs by creating a structure for informed decision-making.

The 1995 guidance note envisaged that local management agreements would be suitable and beneficial where large and complex assets were involved. Initially, the guidance was aimed at large commercial and industrial sites, shopping precincts, institutional complexes and housing schemes listed for their 'group value' (or contribution as an unified assemblage) to the local historic environment.

Prior to this development of the concept of local management agreements, a handful of one-off quasi local management agreements had been used to improve management effectiveness in specific situations – some far removed from the kind of context for which they later became known. One example will suffice. In 1991/1992, a form of local management agreement was negotiated between English Heritage (acting as agent for the then Department of National Heritage in its role as the administrator responsible for scheduled ancient monument matters) and Historic Royal Palaces. At the time, the latter was a government agency, established in 1989 to care for five English palaces, which, to all intents and purposes, were no longer occupied by members of the Royal Family. This estate included Hampton Court Palace (Figure 5.3) and the Tower of London.

Although little more than two years old at the time, Historic Royal Palaces had built up a strong and experienced conservation-aware staff. The Agency's brief was to manage and improve its nationally important estate with a strong commercial focus, while delivering uncompromised 'best practice' conservation. This meant that rapid and extensive change was being planned at the Palaces. In practical terms, neither English Heritage nor the Department of National Heritage had sufficient spare resources to administer and determine the enormous volume of applications that would be required under the relevant legislation, if it were to be applied strictly. It was recognised that the most effective management solution would be to negotiate and agree a list of works which could be carried out at the Palaces by Historic Royal Palaces without the need for further discussion and the submission of applications for consent. This agreed list then became the subject of an annual Scheduled Monument Consent and could be monitored retrospectively for compliance, allowing the Department of National Heritage to terminate the arrangement if it was advised by English Heritage that the letter or spirit of the local management agreement was being flouted or compromised. A system of quarterly review meetings agreement was also built into the agreement to allow for regular monitoring of the implementation and impact of the arrangement.

Figure 5.3   Hampton Court Palace. Historic Royal Palaces developed what was, in effect, a local management agreement with English Heritage which applied to all five of the palaces in its care.

This demonstrates that the concept of the local management agreement can be readily extended to address very specific needs and circumstances. Such flexibility can involve risk – particularly of harm being 'sanctioned' to the significance of the heritage asset. This risk can and must be managed through regular monitoring, review meetings and feedback. This and the consequential power to rescind the agreement and/or impose other penalties have to be active components of any successful local management agreement. Bluntly, if this risk management cannot be effectively delivered, the situation is not suitable for using a local management agreement.

It is worth exploring some other ways in which local management agreements can be applied to the benefit of all parties and to the care of the particular asset. The objective of the 2003 Historic England research report (English Heritage, 2003) was to learn the lessons from the use of management agreements and to apply those to 'streamlining listed building consent' (that is, statutory protection) arrangements. The report concluded: 'Management agreements have considerable potential to contribute to streamlining the listed building consent process by making it more transparent, consistent and therefore predictable ... and they can bring about a net saving of resources for all involved.' Since then, further consideration has been given to whether parts of a revised statutory designation process for England might be built around significance-based local management agreements. In effect, this approach might one day lead to the 'self-certification' of a range of pre-agreed work types by 'conservation-intelligent' heritage asset management organisations (a typical example in England being the National

Trust). This would simplify both sides of the application/consent process and, it has been suggested, make conservation management more efficient.

In a very different way, the local management agreement can be extended to assist in situations of varying kinds, where day-to-day management responsibility for one or more heritage assets is to be divorced temporarily from the ownership interest. In these circumstances, a significance-based local management agreement can help in bringing clarity to the tenancy or contractual responsibilities and establish a mutually agreed sound management platform. The potential of this approach can be illustrated by an example. In 2002, a charitable trust decided to let one of its estate properties (a large former yeoman's farmhouse) in England to an individual on a long lease. It was concerned to ensure that the significance and historic integrity of the asset were protected, such that, when it reverted to the organisation's direct management control on expiration of the lease term, it would be in sound condition and undiminished in its state and significance from when the leasehold interest had commenced. A conservation plan for the site was prepared, and, using this assessment of significance and vulnerability, essential and desirable conservation management policies were defined. These policies were developed into specific guidelines for the care of the property, including its future maintenance and the management of its use and change. This document then became the core of a significance-based local management agreement between the charitable trust and the prospective tenant, which was embedded within the legal leasehold contract itself.

By extension, local management agreements of this nature, based upon a conservation plan or other assessment of cultural value, have considerable potential for use wherever asset management functions are to be divided from property ownership. This might include subsequent sub-letting, as in the example above, or even contracting out of some management functions, for instance, where facilities' management or some elements of estate management are being purchased for a fixed period of years from a private sector contracting organisation. So far, this application for significance-based local management agreements remains largely unexplored, but it has much to offer in improving sound management of potentially vulnerable heritage assets.

A general framework for a local management agreement might include:

- Definition of the parties involved in the agreement and their roles.
- Identification of the asset(s) covered by the agreement and a brief description of each, including definition of the curtilage of the asset.
- Description of the management arrangements in place to care for the/each asset.
- Details of the nature of the agreement, including its duration and any limitations on its application.
- Establishment of a review mechanism of implementation or performance of the agreement, including a structure for regular meetings between the parties.
- A summary of the/each asset's significance, including emphasis on the range of cultural values that are present.

- A summary of the vulnerability of and issues that might affect the/each asset and its significance.
- Definition of the management approach to be adopted towards the/each asset.
- Identification of general and specific management policies to be set in place and implemented to care for the/each asset and the cultural values that are present.
- Definition of works, or categories of works, or other changes that can be undertaken without reference back to, or the need for, prior consent from the relevant statutory authority (who should be one of the parties to the agreement).
- Definition of works, or categories of works, or other changes that must not be commenced without reference back to, or granting of, prior consent by the relevant statutory authority.
- Practical guidelines for sustainable care of the asset(s), including management of use and change.
- Establishment of a framework for resolution of disagreements resulting from implementation of the local management agreement.

Care, design and quality standards guidance

A core part of the effective management of historic areas – urban or rural – has to be the dissemination of user-friendly guidance, setting out fundamental requirements for the responsible care of buildings and the design of appropriate alterations and additions to structures, streetscape and the like. The provision of good guidance can minimise conflict and inadvertent damage to the character and/or significance of individual properties, as well as the area at large. It can also reduce the burden of production of very detailed heritage impact assessments, by providing direct or indirect mitigation advice in advance of design development and more subtly influencing wants and expectations.

A myriad of design guidance has already been produced in recent decades – much by or through local planning authorities – encouraging appropriate design of extensions and alterations both to listed buildings and unprotected buildings in conservation areas. Some of this guidance has been sound and extremely focused; a large amount has been over-generalised, and has failed to deliver the anticipated improvements in the quality of applications for planning permission and listed building consent and in the final construction work. Recent work by national bodies in Scotland and England (and some local authorities) has focused on the particular issue of energy improvements in the historic environment where striking a balance between the twin sustainability issues of protecting significance while addressing climate change is an interesting and challenging concern.

Curiously, rather less care and quality standards' guidance has been produced – yet it is often through poor maintenance or the selection of unsuitable mortar mixes or surface coatings that the most marked piecemeal degradation of the character of historic areas occurs.

The development of the concept of significance-based management has provided a powerful platform for the production of targeted guidance of this kind. On the back of an assessment of significance and vulnerability the guidance can be developed to tackle the day-to-day issues that are likely to affect the area and to diminish its value and potential.

As has already been implied, typically, guidance of this sort can be divided into three distinct categories, although sometimes two or even all three may be amalgamated within a single published document, depending upon circumstance. The growth in the use of the internet has made web-based dissemination extremely popular, cost-efficient and effective. These three categories are:

- *Care guidance* – provides advice to building or landscape owners, occupiers or managers on the basics of good protective maintenance. Some of this advice will simply reflect common good practice (for instance, the need for regular inspection and cleaning of gutters and rainwater downpipes) and will thus be of a generalised nature. However, structured on sound assessments of significance and of character (and, again, these should not be confused), the opportunity exists to explain what is considered to be of particular value about the asset and its component parts and, specifically, how such value can be protected and enhanced by care and maintenance actions. (Note: The wider issue of maintenance management is addressed in Chapter 6.)
- *Design guidance* – can be targeted at the same owners, occupiers and managers of buildings or landscapes. Additionally, it can be directed towards: public sector employees who determine applications relating to development in the historic area/asset or who are responsible for the maintenance and upkeep of public spaces and streetscapes; professional practitioners who design and specify alterations or new elements or structures within the area/asset; and contractors who implement those designs and specifications. Within historic urban areas and rural settlements, it is often design issues in the public realm (especially, the selection of materials for the construction and repair of pavements and road surfaces and the design and positioning of street furniture, including signage) that cause the most damage to character and significance. Strangely, this type of damage is frequently only perceived subliminally and is therefore the most overlooked area requiring guidance. Design guidance can cover a wide range of matters, depending upon circumstance and need, including detailing, size, massing, proportion, use, density, location of change, availability and selection of materials, ease of maintenance, accessibility, character, craftsmanship, species of planting, distribution of elements, vistas, and so forth.
- *Quality standards guidance* – is related to both care and design advice. But it is being used increasingly to inform regeneration agencies, local authority administrators and professional practitioners about particular standards that need to be achieved in working in a historic area in order to safeguard both character and significance. An example of adoption of this approach in England was the joint commissioning in 2005 by English Heritage, the Heritage Lottery Fund (HLF) and the regional regeneration agency, Elevate, of quality standard guidance for group repair of nineteenth-century terraced

Figure 5.4   Nineteenth-century terraced housing in East Lancashire – unlisted but deserving of proper care steered by value-based quality standards guidance.

housing in every conservation area in East Lancashire where HLF grant funding was being provided (Figure 5.4). The guidance in that instance concentrated on the exteriors of the buildings and the wider streetscape and provided appropriate advice for care, maintenance, repair and renewal of roof coverings, chimneys, rainwater goods, external walling (including coatings and finishes), windows and doors, decorative detailing, boundary walls and railings, external yard areas, and the streets and pavements.

The content of care, design and quality standards guidance needs to be very carefully honed to each case's specific needs. This makes identification of suitable content impossible. However, in a very general sense, a framework for such guidance notes might cover:

- Explanation of the purpose of the guidance;
- Identification of the target audience(s);
- Identification of the asset(s) covered by the guidance;
- Description of the management arrangements, statutory protection and planning policies in place to care for the asset (be it an area, estate, landscape, or other multi-property asset);
- An explanation of the structure and content of the guidance;
- The date of production of the guidance and any limitations on its application;
- An outline of the history of the asset and its development to the present day;
- A summary of the character of the asset, where relevant;

- A summary of the significance of the asset, including emphasis on the range of cultural values that are present;
- A summary of the pressures for change in the area/asset and the vulnerability of and issues that might affect the asset and its significance;
- Definition of the management approach that it is proposed should be adopted towards the asset;
- Identification of general and specific management policies to be set in place and implemented to care for the asset and the cultural values that are present;
- General care, design or quality standards advice;
- Specific care, design or quality standards advice, perhaps structured element by element, if dealing with buildings, or component by component for landscapes, and, then, for design advice additionally by alteration type;
- Summary of the objectives of the guidance, the asset's value, the care, design and quality standards advice that has been given, and the intended impact of the advice;
- Bibliography/further reading for those whose interest in the asset has been awakened;
- Sources of further advice.

It is worth noting and reflecting in passing on the marked similarities between this general framework and that set out for use in the production of local management agreements. As has been observed in a number of different ways throughout this book, this is typical of significance-based management tools and stems from the fundamental logic of the conservation planning approach.

One example of care and design guidance will suffice to demonstrate the use of the foregoing general framework in practice. In 2005, the London Borough of Redbridge published care and design guidance for the Aldersbrook Estate, which, roughly two years before, had been newly designated as a conservation area. The Aldersbrook Estate (see Figure 5.5) lies within a triangular-shaped block of land and was largely built between 1899 and 1910. A small number of minor additions had occurred after that time, but since 1945 open land had been carefully protected and so new buildings in the second half of the twentieth century were limited to infill sites within the boundaries of the Estate. The essence of the character of the Aldersbrook Estate is its remarkable wealth and variation of external ornamentation to otherwise relatively similar dwellings which evolved within a short building period. It was this that the guidance sought to protect and enhance where it had become compromised or degraded. The guidance was structured into eight sections:

1 An introduction setting the scene for the guidance on the basis of the designation of the conservation area.
2 A chapter providing essential background, including the historic development of the estate, the legislative background and practical purpose behind

Figure 5.5   An example of the wealth of decorative detail to housing within the Aldersbrook Estate Conservation Area.

designation of conservation areas, and the conceptual thinking that drove development of the guidance and its content.

3 An illustrated explanation of what makes the estate special, both in terms of character and significance. After a general discussion, this was set out on an external building element-by-element basis, pointing out both typical and special characteristics and aspects of cultural value.

4 A brief assessment of why the estate and its significance should be protected.

5 A more detailed illustrated analysis of the pressures for change facing the estate and the damage that these could cause.

6 The illustrated core of the care and design guidance: this commenced with general observations about the basics of successful care and then was expanded first elementally looking at:
- chimneys and chimney pots;
- roofs;
- rainwater goods;
- fascias, eaves and bargeboarding;
- walls, gables, bays, rendering and pebbledashing;
- windows;
- porches;
- external doors;
- architectural ornamentation and decorative features;

- entrance lights, burglar alarms and other outside fittings;
- paintwork and colour;
- front boundaries and gardens;
- rear boundaries and gardens;
- signage;
- pavements;
- street lighting;
- interiors.

7 Thereafter, addressing design issues 'when making major changes', approaching these by alteration type, as relevant to the circumstances and issues facing the estate itself:
- sub-division of houses into multiple units;
- conversions;
- loft conversions, dormers and rooflights;
- extensions and conservatories;
- garages;
- car parking within front gardens and the design and impact of 'crossovers' of public pavements;
- aerials and satellite dishes;
- reinstatement of lost features;
- new build;
- temporary buildings.

8 Summary.
9 Further reading and sources of information.

Over and above the logical structure and development of the significance-based argument, experience shows that one of the most critical factors influencing the success, or otherwise, of guidance of this kind is being able to express significance and value in a way that appeals to the target audience and makes them want to take ownership of the principles espoused by the guidance.

References

Australia ICOMOS (2013) *The Burra Charter: The Australia ICOMOS Charter for Places of Cultural Significance*. Burwood, VIC, Australia: Australia ICOMOS Inc.

Blunstone, D. (2000) Challenges for heritage conservation and the role of research on values. In *Values and Heritage Conservation, Research Report* (eds E. Avrami, R. Mason and M. de la Torre). Los Angeles, The Getty Conservation Institute.

Clark, J., Darlington, J. and Fairclough, G. (2004) *Using Historic Landscape Characterisation*. London, English Heritage and Lancashire County Council.

Clark, K. (1999) Conservation plans in action. In *Proceedings of the Oxford Conference. Conservation Plans for Historic Places*, 27–28 March 1998, Oxford. English Heritage.

Clark, K. (2001) *Informed Conservation*. London, English Heritage.

DCLG (2012) *National Planning Policy Framework*. London, Department of Communities and Local Government.

DMRB; HA208/13 (2013), Volume 11 Section 3 Part 2) by the Highways Agency, Transport Scotland, the Welsh Assembly Government, and the Department for Regional Development Northern Ireland.

English Heritage (1995) *Developing Guidelines for the Management of Listed Buildings*. London, English Heritage.

English Heritage (1997) *Sustaining the Historic Environment*. London, English Heritage.

English Heritage (2003) *Streamlining Listed Building Consent: Lessons from the Use of Management Agreements*. London: English Heritage.

English Heritage (2004) *Conservation Bulletin Issue 47: Characterisation*. London, English Heritage.

English Heritage (2006) *Local Area Agreements and the Historic Environment*. London, English Heritage.

English Heritage (2008) *Conservation Principles, Policies and Guidance for the Sustainable Management of the Historic Environment*. London, English Heritage.

English Heritage (undated). *Characterisation*. Available at: www.english-heritage.org.uk/professional/research/landscapes-and-areas/characterisation/

Historic Scotland (2004) *Planning Advice Note 71: Conservation Area Management*. Edinburgh, Historic Scotland.

ICOMOS (1994) *The Nara Document on Authenticity*. Available at: www.international.icomos.org/charters.htm

ICOMOS (2011) *Guidance on Heritage Impact Assessments for Cultural World Heritage Properties*. Available at: www.international.icomos.org/world_heritage/HIA_20110201.pdf

Kerr, J.S. (2004) *The Conservation Plan* (6th edition). Sydney, J.S. Kerr on behalf of The National Trust of Australia.

Kerr, J.S. (2013) *The Conservation Plan* (7th ed.). J.S. Kerr on behalf of The National Trust of Australia, Sydney. Available as a download from Australia ICOMOS site.

Landorf, C. (2011) A future for the past: a new theoretical model for sustainable historic urban environments. *Planning Practice and Research* **26** (2).

Pearson, M. and Marshall, D. (2005) *National Library of Australia: Conservation Management Plan*. Canberra, National Library of Australia.

Pearson, M. and Sullivan, S. (1995) *Looking After Heritage Places*. Melbourne, Melbourne University Publishing.

Pickard, R. and de Thyse, M. (2001) The management of historic centres: towards a common goal. In *Management of Historic Centres* (ed. R. Pickard). London, Spon.

Sauer, C. (1925). *Morphology of Landscape*. Berkeley, CA: University of California Publications in Geography.

Stovel, H. (2007) Effective use of authenticity and integrity as World Heritage qualifying conditions. *City & Time* **2** (3): 3. Available at: www.ct.ceci-br.org

Chapter 6
Maintenance Management

Introduction

One particular area of activity that is essential to the care and protection of all assets is maintenance management and therefore, because effective maintenance of the fabric is such an important part of protecting significance (and because it is also a process which is often carried out badly), we have devoted this separate chapter to it.

The idea that effective maintenance of the built fabric is a fundamentally important activity goes back to the writings of John Ruskin and William Morris, along with other early pioneers of the conservation movement. Ruskin exhorted people to 'Take proper care of your monuments and you will not need to restore them' (Ruskin, 1989), and Morris (1877), in his *Manifesto*, which heralded the creation of the Society for the Protection of Ancient Buildings (SPAB), called upon those who deal with monuments to 'put Protection in the place of Restoration, to stave off decay by daily care'. This historic emphasis is reinforced in the current SPAB document 'SPAB's Purpose', which states that regular maintenance is 'the most practical and economical form of preservation'.

James Semple Kerr's observation that 'Maintenance is the single most important conservation process, whether the place is architectural, mechanical or botanical, prevention is better than cure' (Kerr, 1996) is echoed in many international guidelines, which emphasise the importance of an effective maintenance programme in protecting the significance embodied in and represented by the fabric of buildings. As the now replaced British Standard, BS 7913 (British Standards Institute, 1998), *Guide to the Principles for the Conservation of Historic Buildings* once advised, 'Systematic care based on good housekeeping is both cost effective and fundamental to good conservation.'

The British Standard on building maintenance, BS 8210 (British Standards Institute, 1986), describes maintenance as a 'combination of any actions carried

Managing Built Heritage: The Role of Cultural Values and Significance, Second Edition.
Stephen Bond and Derek Worthing.
© 2016 Stephen Bond and Derek Worthing. Published 2016 by John Wiley & Sons, Ltd.

out to retain an item in or restore it to an acceptable condition'. However, it is important to note that, while for the maintenance of the majority of buildings, the distinction between repair, restoration and improvement will not be conceptually important, for heritage assets, these definitions and the actions which are implied, are of fundamental importance. The phrase 'As much as necessary, but as little as possible' is a maxim in the Burra Charter (Australia ICOMOS, 2013) which encapsulates a key overarching theme for the care of heritage assets and echoes the conservation principle of minimum intervention (see Chapter 8). The Burra Charter refers to maintenance as 'the continuous protective care of the fabric', and goes on to say that it should be distinguished from repair. Obviously repair works will become necessary for heritage assets and, when carried out properly and judiciously, they will prolong the life of an element and the building. Good repairs are important for the long-term protection of significance, but it is important that it is understood that they are an intervention that will, in most cases, involve some level of damage or loss to the fabric – they are in a sense inevitably either restoration or reconstruction. Brereton (1991) makes the point that any unnecessary replacement of fabric is likely to diminish its authenticity and thus its historical/cultural value. The balance therefore between preventative maintenance and repair is important, not just in relation to the conservation of fabric, but also because of significance. As Clark (2001) points out, sensitive repair and management do not merely involve specifying appropriate materials and techniques, they also require an understanding of the asset's significance, how this is manifested in the fabric, and the effects that any repair action might have.

Feilden (1994) suggests a hierarchy of interventions, which implicitly puts some actions in order of least harm to the fabric:

- The prevention of deterioration;
- Protective measures;
- Consolidation;
- Repair.

This hierarchy reinforces the previous point about the need to distinguish between maintenance and repair when dealing with heritage assets, as repair can be seen as a 'point of failure' because, as mentioned, it will usually involve damage to or replacement of historic fabric. Feilden's explanation of a hierarchy of intervention is a useful way of considering maintenance activity from the perspective of emphasising the need to protect and enhance the significance represented by the fabric. In order to ensure this, he suggests that the degree of intervention should be informed by conservation principles. This should include, in particular, the notion that 'Conservation is based on a respect for the existing fabric and should involve the least possible intervention' (Australia ICOMOS, 2013).

Maintenance then can be seen as the primary activity supporting the key building conservation principles of retaining the maximum embodied significance through a process of minimal intervention in the fabric of heritage assets.

A strategic perspective

The notion of strategic maintenance management suggests that the overall medium to long-term aims of an organisation should inform policy, tactics and day-to-day activities. There should also be clarity about where the maintenance function resides in the organisational structure, what other functions and processes it interacts with, and how and why this occurs. This is important because maintenance management generally, and within corporate contexts particularly, often has a low status and is seen as non-strategic. Even within 'estates departments', maintenance management generally lacks kudos. This seems to be the case even in organisations whose *raison d'être* is the care of heritage assets (Feilden, 1982). One consequence of this is to produce a reactive maintenance provision, which, because it is not integrated into the property or wider organisational strategies, does not have a strategic perspective and does not think in terms of organisational goals.

Whether we are considering heritage or non-heritage organisations, the essential aim of maintenance should be related to the protection and use of the physical asset. In turn, this asset should be conceived as a resource that can be managed proactively in order to help deliver corporate goals via processes that focus on the needs and requirements of the users, customers and stakeholders. Effective maintenance will be one of the processes that can maximise the potential of the built resource by protecting and enhancing the asset, but to do so, the maintenance management culture and activities will need to be strategic, proactive and integrated in nature.

The objectives of most maintenance programmes will include retention of continuity of function, protection of the capital asset represented by the buildings, protection of the comfort and convenience of users, reinforcement of image and, increasingly, meeting statutory obligations (related to such matters as fire, health and safety, disabled access, etc.). For most organisations there will be specific drivers and emphases which might prioritise certain activities because of the nature of the corporate goals or the key activities. For example, for a health service, the possible impact of building condition on a range of issues, from infection control to the psychological impact on patients' feelings of well-being, should be taken into account.

With heritage assets, irrespective of both ownership and wider organisational goals, a key specific driver for maintenance should be that it is the fabric itself that is important because of its possible contribution to significance – and not just because of the asset's function. As the Burra Charter observes: 'Cultural significance is embodied in the place itself, its fabric, setting, use, associations, meanings, records, related places and related objects' (Australia ICOMOS, 2013). That is, the heritage asset itself is an artefact, and it is the value represented by and embodied in such assets that should be the focus for maintenance strategies and process. It follows that the maintenance management of heritage assets requires the development of a plan for maintenance which integrates it into the wider strategy for the management of the property portfolio, but all within the context of an assessment of significance and vulnerability that provides a framework and reference point for maintenance and drives its strategy, processes and actions.

For what we might term 'heritage management organisations', that is, those organisations for whom the protection of heritage assets is a significant component of their core business, such a focus is easily adoptable for their maintenance strategies/policies because the protection and enhancement of the physical estate, or rather the significance represented by it, are part of their 'core business'. However, for most organisations with a property portfolio, the length of interest in their property is usually determined by the length of tenure, which is, in turn, linked to organisational goals and other functional requirements (as discussed in Wordsworth, 2001). Hence, for non-heritage organisations, the emphasis tends to be on functional life (which could be very short for dynamic, fast-changing businesses), and the importance of the physical life of the fabric is related to the effect that it has on function. For organisations with 'mixed' estates (that is, organisations whose business is not 'heritage', but who nevertheless own or use some heritage assets among a wider portfolio), the justification for expenditure is likely to be in relation to functional life and a 'core business' which is separate from the assets. The problem in such organisations might be that the maintenance of their heritage assets may tend to be driven solely, or at least mainly, by a statutory compliance culture, not by a sense of obligation to protect a heritage asset. This may be particularly so in decision-making processes involving the reconciliation of a number of competing organisational priorities. There could also be an issue in situations where the organisation sees the primary value that ownership of a heritage asset contributes as being related mainly to the image they wish to project. In such cases, there is the danger that the priority for maintenance activity is focused more on retaining the aesthetic appearance of the building and less on protecting its significance, which could lead to inappropriate priorities and early interventions. It is important, therefore, that for all estates where heritage assets are part of the portfolio, a culture and system are created that acknowledge, understand and contextualise conservation principles, and which link these to an understanding and use of significance as a driver for strategic and operational activities. This should help to ensure that any decision on the protection of heritage assets is not (mainly) based on bureaucratic and pragmatic criteria – particularly in those organisations where such assets are seen as a burden – but on the development of an approach that protects and enhances significance.

As discussed above, in order to be effective, maintenance management must be related to the overall goals of the organisation and integrated with its corporate strategy. This should then inform policy, tactics and day-to-day activities. Property management generally and maintenance management in particular have long been criticised for lacking a strategic approach. Without strategic awareness and data (on significance and vulnerability), there is a danger that a non-integrated approach will develop between the maintenance activity, other property management functions and other organisational interests that interact with the fabric (for example, visitor interpretation in a heritage organisation). This can result in maintenance activity being undertaken and prioritised in isolation. There is the danger of the maintenance function adopting an inward-looking logic of its own, where efficiency of the process is measured rather than how effective it is in serving organisational objectives. This may work contrary to the principle of minimum intervention.

Rather than comprising a series of individual elements, the maintenance management operation should be a coherent, integrated system. This system should be driven fundamentally by the concepts of significance and minimal intervention through to an inception of the policies, programmes, management and practices derived from those concepts. It follows, therefore, that a strategy for maintenance cannot be truly effective unless the organisation has a clear understanding of the significance of the heritage assets within its care, and a commitment to protecting and enhancing it over and above that which is a requirement of statute. Such an understanding needs to permeate the organisation and this, along with minimum intervention, should be the focus and driver.

Given the importance of maintenance for buildings, an overarching strategic plan for heritage organisations should provide a clear indication of how maintenance is to be managed. In addition, the plan should explain where and how it integrates with the organisation's overall structure, as well as its asset management function.

By implication, this reinforces the need, in mixed estates, as well as heritage management organisations, for comprehensive and rigorous conservation planning in the form of a conservation plan and management plan (or other appropriate tool), which is based upon conservation principles and addresses issues of significance and vulnerability. This should then be followed up by integrated management plans that make the vertical and horizontal connections through all activities, including the operationalising of maintenance. As emphasised in Chapter 4, assessments of significance should identify which aspects of the fabric are important and why, and from this there should be some sense of recontextualisation and prioritisation by the maintenance organisation in order to operationalise this idea of relative significance for the functions/processes that it carries out.

The idea of maintenance management implies a context that involves notions of time, the gathering and use of data, and the generation, manipulation and allocation of resources (finance, expertise, materials). For all organisations, whether heritage or non-heritage, a balance will need to be struck between performance and resource inputs, which implies that maintenance management involves determining a series of relative priorities. This emphasises the requirement for setting standards appropriate to the needs of the asset, and also to the objectives of the organisations – something that must permeate through in both strategy and tactics. As we have observed, in some organisations, maintenance management tends to be driven by process, or rather optimising the efficiency of the process, rather than a clear articulation about what that process is serving. The tendency is for aspects of maintenance management orthodoxy to be imported from elsewhere without recontextualising them for the needs of heritage assets. For example, while planned maintenance programmes can provide cost savings, they may, without the proper focus, work against the principle of minimum intervention.

Maintenance programmes should therefore, as we have observed, be set within the context of rigorous policies focused on minimum intervention and the need to retain and enhance significance, and they must use these concepts as the context and drivers for management decisions and processes. Working within the context of a conservation plan or management plan, the maintenance plan will take this overview of the historic stock and must reflect the identification of significance, how, and the extent to which it is represented by and embodied in the fabric, along with the identification of the relative significance of different parts of the fabric. The maintenance plan should show how decisions based on significance and relative priority will affect the organisation of maintenance and how it is carried out. This will include reference to how conservation principles, such as minimum intervention, honest repairs, and the like (see Chapter 8), are to be interpreted by the organisation.

These issues and connections might be articulated through a maintenance manual containing:

- Extracts from the conservation plan and/or management plan showing how the identification of significance has been recontextualised and synthesised with conservation principles, and how these inform and direct maintenance objectives and processes;
- A breakdown of the elements of the asset, showing relative significance (of the various buildings and the elements and components of each building).

This should be supplemented by:

- Plans and elevations showing the site and buildings that together make up the asset;
- An architectural historical account;
- A description of the asset's construction materials;
- An identification of vulnerable points and areas of risk from a cultural and a functional perspective, and an analysis of the interaction between the two;
- Information on condition, at both a broad brush and a detailed level, which is updated by the surveys and inspection.

Both the Government Historic Buildings Advisory Unit (1998) and BS 7913 (British Standards Institute, 2013) also recommend the use of logbooks. The British Standard characterises these as current information on key persons and managers and concise instructions on maintenance and inspection routines, and recommends that completed logbooks should be kept as part of the permanent record of the asset.

Recording

Records are likely to be a combination of drawings and text and will both describe the fabric and record interventions (and the reasons for making them).

Good information and records are vital for the effective maintenance management of heritage assets. The recording of maintenance processes and actions is important in terms of developing management information and informing decisions (for example, on cost of works carried out). But for heritage assets, the keeping of proper records of decisions made, their context and the reasoning behind them is an important conservation principle, as the maintenance and repair of the fabric form part of the story of the historical development of the asset. Clearly, decisions made now, and the reasoning behind them, will also give future generations an insight into the conservation consciousness of current times.

There is some evidence of an interesting blind spot here, even among heritage management organisations. Although they will acknowledge the importance of records as management information documents, often they will not conceive modern records as important archival documents even though they treasure the equivalent documents of the past. Yet, these are part of the history and therefore the significance of the asset.

Programmes

Feilden and Jokilehto (1993) suggest that preventative maintenance is 'the highest form of conservation', and comment on maintenance programming:

> *The maintenance programme is aimed at keeping the cultural resources in a manner that will prevent loss of any part of them. It concerns all practical and technical measures that should be taken to maintain the site in proper order. This is a continuous process not a product.*

Clearly the maintenance strategy needs to be delivered through a coherent and cohesive set of processes and actions, which will operationalise maintenance in a way that reflects the aims of the strategy. As we have said, maintenance should be driven by an understanding of the significance of the fabric. However, this driver also needs to be related to the proper functioning of the asset and to be synthesised with insurance requirements, health and safety considerations and other statutory obligations. There also needs to be set in place a process which identifies what maintenance and repair work is to be carried out, and how and when it is to be done, particularly taking into consideration the continuing functionality of the asset (including, for heritage management organisations, the visitor experience). The questions of how work is to be prioritised and on what basis are also of fundamental importance.

Wordsworth (2001) defines programming as 'scheduling the manner in which maintenance work will be carried out'. He emphasises different time-scales for programmes: long-term (an expression of policy rather than a detailed scheduling of tasks); medium-term (on an annual basis); and short-term (daily, weekly and monthly tasks). Similarly, the importance of scheduled, but flexible, routines of daily, monthly, annual and quinquennial maintenance tasks is emphasised by Feilden (1982) and Feilden and Jokilehto (1993).

It is usual to make a distinction between two broad types of maintenance action:

- *Reactive* – day-to-day, or corrective. This is usually seen as a response to a problem or failure, and an intervention that is usually initiated by the building user.
- *Preventative* – this is a planned approach that maintains assets through a rationalised programme formulated through knowledge of condition, identified priorities and predictive assessments. It creates benefits associated with economies of scale and simpler management arrangements. Although a focus on economies of scale can work against the notion of minimum intervention, generally, problems identified and dealt with in the early stages can minimise the need for more intervention and costly repairs later on, and, therefore, this approach is seen as functionally and financially effective. Planned maintenance may also play a role in ensuring that the assets project the right image for the organisation, in protecting the visual impression that 'well-maintained' buildings give to occupiers and the public at large.

Holmes (1994) suggests that planned maintenance can be divided into 'condition independent' and 'condition dependent'. Condition-independent maintenance, which is often called 'cyclical maintenance', requires no pre-inspection and tends to be work that is undertaken at regular intervals – work such as external painting, annual safety checks, clearing gutters, lubricating moving parts, removing plant growth and bird droppings, painting and testing, etc. (some of which might relate to statutory or insurance requirements). Condition-dependent maintenance occurs when an element or component is assessed through an inspection or a condition survey and the action to repair or maintain it is subsequently prioritised. Where such intervention is carried out in time to avoid failure, it could be termed 'planned preventative' maintenance. In practice, however, intervention/condition surveys also identify immediate remedial work that is necessary as a result of deterioration/failure that has already occurred.

Clearly a management system based on condition-dependent maintenance is the more complicated and resource-dependent, as it requires monitoring of the condition of the fabric, effective information collection and management, and the development of an approach that involves decision-making informed by a system based on relative priorities.

Even with an efficient planned maintenance programme, some form of user-initiated reactive ('response' or 'day-to-day') maintenance is inevitable. This needs to be considered at both the strategic and operational stages, in terms of establishing response criteria, timing, procurement and recording. An over-reliance on response maintenance is costly, not just in terms of financial costs, but also with regard to the loss of function, the resultant disruption, and management efficiency. Good practice guidance in the public sector in the UK (see, for example, HEFCE, 1998; Audit Commission, 2002) advocates that – for reasons of equity, efficiency and effectiveness – the majority of the maintenance budget should be spent on planned maintenance, with a smaller amount on response maintenance. Criticism of this approach (Williams, 1994; Wood, 2003) contends that it may appear economic in the long term, but, if the wider organisational and political context is one of uncertainty, then the use of risk analysis and a focus on the short term (response maintenance) can reduce immediate costs, give greater flexibility and should have the additional advantage of immediate 'customer' (user) satisfaction (Wordsworth, 2001). For heritage assets, however, planned maintenance should be the overwhelmingly dominant approach, mainly because of the need for a minimal intervention ethos (rather than for budgetary control, as might be the reason in other building types) and the fact that reactive maintenance by definition allows a failure to occur – and therefore entails the possible loss of historic fabric. Clearly some reactive maintenance will be necessary to deal with emergencies and also in terms of 'customer service'. It should, however, be kept to an absolute minimum, because, as we have said, it allows failure to occur.

Prioritisation

Making decisions about relative and competing priorities is a fundamental maintenance management process. Prioritising work will be important from a functional perspective and a cost perspective in all organisations. But it should also take wider organisational issues into account, such as the impact that condition has on the overall performance of the particular asset (energy loss and consumption, for example) or the overarching property strategy of the organisation (corporate image, for example).

Of course, statutory concerns will drive priorities, particularly issues related to health and safety, fire, disabled access, etc., but problems exist where aspects of such legislation are in conflict with the statutory provision for heritage assets and/or conservation principles. As we have observed, there can be a tendency for aspects of the maintenance management process to be imported from elsewhere without re-contextualising them for the needs of heritage assets. It is important, therefore, to avoid a situation where the approach to maintenance management tends to be driven by process, especially one that emphasises optimising the efficiency of the process, rather than by a clear strategy about what that process is serving. In the case of heritage assets, therefore, it will be important to prioritise by using significance and, importantly, relative significance as a driver for decision-making. Prioritisation should take the assessment of significance of the elements/components and their vulnerability as a starting point and link this to functional performance and cost issues and to the practicalities of carrying out the work. Planned maintenance programmes can provide cost savings, but they may work against the principle of minimal intervention where they develop a logic and momentum of their own, For example:

- By its nature, repair and maintenance work consists of a number of small jobs. Batching them for economic reasons or other management priorities may result in repair work being undertaken too early or maintenance work being undertaken too late.

(a)

(b)

Figure 6.1 (a),(b)   The cost of items, such as scaffolding, which are necessary to gain access and work effectively on roofs, spires and walls, etc. may have an effect on decisions about such issues as 'minimum intervention'.

- Where access costs (such as for scaffolding) are high, both financially and also in terms of loss of function or even image (or, for heritage management organisations a reduction, say, in the quality of the visitor experience). This may lead to work that will involve unnecessary damage to the original fabric, through repairs undertaken early just because the scaffolding is in place (Figures 6.1 (a) and (b)).

In addition to being possibly at odds with cost and programming concerns, minimum intervention can also be in tension with a 'let's do something' attitude, a culture of spending fixed budgets and, in some circumstances, issues of health and safety.

Another aspect of prioritisation comes more directly from the issue of relative priorities. The logic of an assessment of significance is that relative significance is attributed to the physical elements of the asset. It follows that repair decisions should not only take into account functional and technical issues, but also a consideration of where one element might be sacrificed in order to ensure the protection of another of greater heritage value. For example, a lead roof covering might be replaced or repaired earlier than might be absolutely necessary because its functional role includes the protection of a stone exterior wall or a plaster ceiling which is considered more significant. This (rather obvious) notion raises interesting questions that need to be addressed in both the conservation plan and the management plan. For example, the question of whether in a traditional timber-framed building the infill panels are as significant as the frame may not need to be considered until a situation arises where the presence of one is damaging to the other, perhaps through damp retention and/or expansion problems related to a brick panel. A proper repair will involve an understanding of the technical and functional issues related to the cause and effect of the processes of deterioration occurring here (water penetration, timber pest, and distortion of the frame and panel, for example) and the physical interaction between the frame and the panel. But a solution should also be based on notions of relative significance of the elements. A similar issue arises around the question of whether to improve technical performance by altering details. For example, altering the detail around, say, a window on a sleek modernist building in order to improve the shedding of rainwater and therefore protect the fabric, judged against the detrimental effect on the significance of the architectural integrity of the building.

Prioritisation should also be linked, particularly in heritage management organisations, to policies regarding such activities as visitor management and interpretation. This connection raises various issues – for example, access, timing of repairs, presentation of the building/site – as all of these interactions will be affected by the implementation of conservation principles, such as minimum intervention and honest repair, as well as the carrying out of a maintenance regime.

Condition surveys

An exhaustive guide to the art and science of carrying out condition surveys of heritage assets will not be presented here. Instead, we will examine the conservation planning and management issues that impact or interface with the condition survey as a management tool.

An essential element in any management process is the collection, analysis and use of information. Effective management can only develop from a basis of knowledge of the asset, its problems, needs and life expectancy. In a maintenance management system, the important information is the state of the fabric, and the collection of such data is normally carried out through condition surveys. A condition survey is a snapshot that will provide information on the physical condition of the building. Such surveys involve the systematic inspection of the fabric of a building in order to produce accurate information on its condition and an assessment of the extent and timing of future work. A condition survey is the foundation for decisions on future planned maintenance programmes, as well as the opportunity to consider the effectiveness of previous programmes. A good condition survey informs the asset manager about the materials that are present in the built fabric; about their condition, rate of degradation and remaining serviceable life; about the asset's vulnerability (whether, for instance, to the elements, vandalism, mismanagement or to other causal factors of decline); and about its critical needs in the foreseeable future in terms of maintenance, protection, repair, adaptation and investment. Condition surveys thus lie at the heart of the proper management of use and change in historic assets (as indeed they do for every kind of asset).

All this may seem perfectly obvious to us today, but it must be recognised that it has only been in very recent decades that the desirability of conducting regular detailed condition audits has been recognised for even the most culturally significant assets. In 2000, English Heritage published *Power of Place*, in which it was still deemed necessary to urge that, 'There should be a shift from cure to prevention, by encouraging regular condition surveys and planned maintenance' (English Heritage, 2000). What we think seems obvious is not always what transpires on the ground in practice. Even today in the UK, in professional heritage management organisations that look after some of our most major heritage assets and which have adopted policies that promise to conduct or commission regular condition surveys on all their principal assets, there remains the strong possibility that reliable up-to-date condition data is not available for many assets. Programming, funding and organising condition audits on a cyclical basis form a fundamental management task, yet this is easily overlooked and, like maintenance management generally, readily put off until another time when funds are less tight. This is bad economics and poor management.

It is important that the organisation is clear about what information it wants to obtain from a condition survey. There is a common tendency to collect too much information without being clear about purpose and this can be a waste of resources, but more importantly it can disturb clarity and inhibit decision-making. In addition, the organisation also needs to be clear about:

- The level of detail required;
- The format in which the information is to be collected and expressed;
- The uses to which the information is to be put;

- The manner in which it is to be stored, retrieved and analysed;
- The nature and detail of the other management information that informs, and is informed by, the surveys.

These issues will be discussed further in due course.

Experience has shown that, for assets of any substance, condition surveys should be conducted every four or five years (respectively, quadrennial and quinquennial inspections). Best practice would undoubtedly be to programme detailed surveys at these intervals, with annual updates being undertaken in between. Indeed, a five-yearly survey is recommended in BS 7913 (British Standards Institute, 2013), and the British Standard BS 8210 on building maintenance (British Standards Institute, 2012) refers to full inspection of the building fabric at no more than a five-year interval. The quinquennial model is nearly 60 years old, originating in the *Inspection of Churches Measures 1955*, which was the first statutory recognition in the UK of the need to inspect heritage assets. Its successor remains the only statutory requirement to inspect heritage assets. However, in practice, it seems that few organisations have the luxury of the availability of resources and funding to make such cycles work satisfactorily. Most, if not all, heritage management organisations in the UK have been unable to strictly maintain five-yearly periodic condition survey programmes across their complete estate. Instead, they have resorted either to prioritising which assets will be resurveyed to comply with their intended cycles or have allowed the whole programme to slip – sometimes in effect tacitly tolerating decennial or even more extended survey cycles. Survey programmes that are unrealistic, whether because of restricted availability of resources or the prevailing management culture of the organisation, are extremely dangerous. They bring the process into disrepute; they fail to deliver to operational managers' expectations and needs; and they form a millstone around the maintenance manager's neck. In short, an ill-judged, over-optimistic programme of cyclical survey may well undermine sound decision-making instead of providing the fundamentals for informed management. Within reason, it is better to establish a longer cycle for survey inspections that suits the management organisation than to adopt a short cycle that cannot be delivered reliably. However, this has particular problems for heritage assets, since it leaves fabric, which contributes to or forms the mainstay of significance, exposed to perhaps unknown levels of risk. This places greater emphasis and importance on the need for annual update inspections. Unfortunately, the record of implementation of these across estates is woefully poor. This is a problem to which management organisations need to give consideration – it remains the case that performance generally across the sector has to be improved dramatically.

Outside of the condition survey cycle, the presence of non-technical staff and other users and visitors on a daily basis can provide the maintenance management function with vital information regarding condition, which would otherwise wait until a subsequent inspection cycle (or until failure becomes impossible to ignore). While users will doubtless report those defects that are causing a functional breakdown which directly affects them, their presence could also be used in a more proactive way to highlight factors that might lead to failure. A number of maintenance management texts refer to the value of enlisting building users as an informal source of information on building condition. Feilden (1982) and Feilden and Jokilehto (1993) emphasise the importance of making use of staff (for example, cleaners) and building users' informal observations of building condition, although they recognise the need for a co-ordinated strategy to collect, process and store these observations so that they may inform action. Anecdotal evidence would suggest that this aspect of information gathering is either ignored or not carried out very effectively, with little thought being given to collecting and integrating users' observations in a way that can actually inform decision-making and action. It should be considered, however, that listening to and reacting to occupiers' observations have a value over and above the effect that this might have on the condition of the built fabric because of the way it includes people, values their experience, and invites them to make a positive contribution to the protection of 'their' heritage asset. This is an important way of helping to develop widespread ownership of heritage assets and their significance. Conversely, the management organisation needs to develop ways of assessing and managing this input. In one case, a heritage management organisation was potentially over-relying on the observations and interpretation of potential defects to significant high-level fabric on a historic building by a steeplejack/mason, who, though skilled at his own job, was less sound on defect analysis and building pathology. The encouragement of user participation in defect/failure reporting must not be allowed to dilute professional interpretation and management decision-making.

We said in the introduction that the condition survey is a snapshot in time, providing vital information on the physical condition of the built stock. If designed, conducted and written up properly, cyclical condition survey reports can build up a history of snapshot images of the state and vulnerability of an asset that can often prove extremely valuable. The National Trust's guidance on quinquennial inspections requires the building surveyor to report on significant changes in the condition of built elements since the last survey, and also upon the success in implementing the principal recommendations made in the preceding inspection report over the intervening years. This provides a useful check both on the increasing or changing vulnerability of parts of the asset and on the organisation's own asset management and work planning performance.

Frequently, in-house asset managers express reservations about disclosing previous survey material to surveyors who are about to conduct a new condition survey. (Hereafter, the terms 'surveyor' and 'building surveyor' will be used generically to include any qualified practitioner undertaking condition surveys whatever his/her professional background.) This fallacious notion presumably reflects concern that the findings of the inspection process may be coloured or skewed by the existence of the previous survey report. If it does, the fault lies in the choice of building surveyor whose task must always be to provide an independent professional assessment of condition at the time of inspection. However, the surveyor's understanding may well be greatly enriched by the provision of data from one or more earlier surveys. This highlights the need for condition audits to be carefully planned. Often, a limited investment in background research to inform the survey process pays dividends.

Figure 6.2   A 'cherry picker' being used to inspect the Wellington Monument.

A condition survey of the Wellington Monument in Somerset for the National Trust in 2005, provides a suitable example. The survey inspection, conducted using a 62-metre-high, mobile access platform ('cherry picker' in common parlance) revealed, among other things, long but narrow vertical fractures close to the blades of the triangular sectioned shaft of the obelisk (Figure 6.2). It also revealed newly bulging panels of ashlar, where courses of individual stones had seemingly been drilled for dowelled repairs and refilled at some time in the past. Whatever interpretation might have been reached in isolation about these apparently relatively modest defects, the surveyor's comprehension was significantly improved by background research, which revealed that identical failures had iteratively been seen and subsequently repaired approximately every 10–15 years over the preceding 60 years. Clearly, the reappearance of these striking defects was a matter of some considerable importance and meaning – a fundamental point that would not and could not have been appreciated if access to previous survey material had been restricted by the National Trust.

The foregoing demonstrates the importance of providing copies of previous survey reports and associated data to the building surveyor. The heritage manager should also provide other information as part of the condition survey briefing process (it should be remembered that this is as critical for in-house building surveyors as for consultants). Ideally, material provided as part of the survey brief should include:

- Previous survey data;
- History of major repairs for the preceding 10+ years;
- Maintenance history since last condition survey was undertaken;
- Maintenance plan;
- Site plan;
- Accurate floor and roof plans;
- Elevational drawings and sections, if available;
- A conservation plan, a conservation statement, a statement of significance or other assessment of the cultural value and special interest of the asset (and the wider area, if applicable);
- The current management plan, or, if this does not exist, the specific conservation policies that the management organisation or building manager applies to the asset;
- A health and safety plan, identifying known or perceived risks relating to the asset of which the building surveyor should be aware;
- Copies of access, fire safety or any other current assessments of the asset in use;
- Ecological data on the known presence of protected or otherwise vulnerable species that may be disturbed or damaged during the conduct of the survey inspection.

As has already been said, this is not a comprehensive guide to condition surveys of heritage assets, but a number of the preceding items do need explanation or expansion.

The provision and use of maintenance and repair data require little further comment. Such information can prove critical if the building surveyor is to interpret signs of failure correctly and with appropriate balance in respect of severity, urgency of action and long-term ramifications. Provision of the maintenance plan enables the surveyor to appreciate the asset's current condition within the context of the manager's wider intentions for care. Responsible managers will wish the building surveyor to comment, for better or worse, on the appropriateness and success of the maintenance plan, given his/her findings about the state of the asset, as well as evidence which highlights the level of adherence to the maintenance plan that is being achieved by the management regime.

Equally, the provision of drawn records of the asset and individual structures to the surveyor should need no detailed explanation. At the most basic level, the surveyor must understand without ambiguity precisely what is in ownership and who has responsibility for the maintenance of elements such as boundaries. Floor and roof plans are essential for planning the survey work, let alone as a means of helping to identify and record survey findings. All the drawn record data identified in the list of documentation above is integral to developing an understanding of the asset before and during the inspection process. As we note elsewhere, the availability of accurate record information of this kind is often woefully poor, even where major heritage management organisations and/or nationally significant heritage assets are concerned. This is a problem that the conservation sector needs to address urgently.

The inclusion of the conservation plan, statement of significance or other assessment of cultural value on the list brings us to the heart of the matter. Regrettably, many will find it peculiar that it is there. Why does the building surveyor need to understand the values enshrined within an asset and the relative significance of its elements and fabric merely to assess its condition? Hopefully, within the context of our argument, the answer is obvious. The building surveyor cannot advise on priorities for action unless he or she has an intimate grasp of these matters. To be effective, a condition survey report needs to dovetail into the management organisation's policies and wider priorities for action. These should be built around some form of evaluation of the asset's significance. Equally, a good survey report must be able to challenge such aspects of the prevailing management culture, if it has been built upon weak or partial analysis. These are necessary checks and balances in striving to achieve proper management and care. As has already been seen, a key component of the conservation plan is an assessment of the vulnerability of the place and its significance to causal factors of potentially deleterious effect. Many such factors will fall within the ambit of the detailed condition survey. The building surveyor needs to understand how the built fabric and the wider site are perceived to be vulnerable in order to produce a balanced interpretation of survey findings. Conversely, the building surveyor, in undertaking a detailed assessment of condition, should be well placed to advise on how the exposition of vulnerability could be finessed. The surveyor can contribute, accordingly, to the essential ongoing review of the conservation plan or assessment of significance and the conservation management policies that flow from these.

The most pressing yet simplest reason why the building surveyor needs sight of the conservation plan or equivalent has been left to last. Such documents, if well prepared, are likely to give the best oversight available of the history of development of the heritage asset. Once again, the building surveyor cannot hope to interpret properly unless he or she understands this history and, where relevant, places observed issues and defects into this context. The Wellington Monument once more can be used to illustrate this point. When conceived in 1817/18, the Monument was not intended to be the 53.6m (175 feet) high obelisk we see today, but a 36m (118 feet) triangular column surmounted by a 10m (32 feet) cast-iron statue of the Iron Duke. That was how it was constructed. The triangular column was completed in the 1820s to its full height, but finance dried up and the statue of Wellington was never cast. The incomplete Monument, in a severely dilapidated state, was only extended and transformed into obelisk form after the Duke's death in 1852. Remarkably, externally this is simply not apparent, the monument appears to be of a single build (although admittedly some evidence is to be found in the tight unlit internal spiral staircase at the junction between the two phases some 36 metres above ground level). Crucially for the building surveyor, many of the most significant external defects up the shaft that were identified in the 2005 condition survey were concentrated immediately above the join between the repaired head of the original column and the 1850s upwards extension. The reasons for this do not need to detain us here; the fundamental point is that satisfactory interpretation of the cluster of defects two-thirds the way up the obelisk was entirely reliant upon the building surveyor comprehending the development and repair histories of the structure. This is another area where the conservation plan or equivalent has so much to offer the surveyor. For all these reasons, the provision of an assessment of significance, should be a key component of every condition survey briefing on heritage assets of any substance. Unfortunately, at the present time, many assets in the UK are lacking this crucial documentation.

We referred in Chapter 5 to the need to assess the condition of the asset in outline as part of the process of understanding the asset as it is now, and to understand whether its present condition makes its vulnerable to harm. Unfortunately, some conservation plan commissions incorporate the preparation of a detailed condition survey as an integral task. Admittedly, the availability of an up-to-date condition survey is so important to sound asset care that, in the event that this is absent, it is desirable to have one prepared as soon as it can be funded and undertaken. An understanding of condition is also essential to appreciating certain aspects of an asset's vulnerability to harm. Nonetheless, in an ideal world, the conservation plan should come first to aid interpretation of the survey findings and the setting of priorities for repair. English Heritage's 2012 Standard for Periodic Condition Surveys and Reports (of its own properties) puts this simply and succinctly: 'Conservation Statements or Plans shall identify significance and are a prerequisite for all condition surveys' (English Heritage, 2012).

Experience shows that inadequate attention is paid by most heritage asset managers to the preferred format for their condition surveys and to the level of data that their reports should contain. These matters can be of considerable consequence to the usefulness of condition survey reports, to their cost and hence to the value for money that they provide.

Survey report formats tend to fall into three groups:

- Free text description and reporting on an elemental basis;
- Spreadsheet or database summaries;
- Hybrids of the two, based on or tending towards either free text or spreadsheet formats.

The implications of these differing formats need to be understood before a sound decision can be made on the appropriate one to be adopted to suit the asset and the management organisation or individual concerned.

Free text formats tend to be preferred by 'lay' readers, since they permit a full 'story' of the asset and each principal element to be told, describing what is there, the problems that exist, their cause and effect and any pertinent issues regarding remedial action, ongoing performance of the structure and fabric, and so forth. Illustrative photographs can be incorporated within the text or as an appendix at the end of the report (depending upon numbers and ease of use) to improve the narrative and the general reader's comprehension. However, for assets of some size or complexity, free text reports tend to become unwieldy, repetitive, lacking in balance and depressing to read, consisting of a litany of problems, failures and hazards. Although they may tell the 'story' well and in a logical fashion, with so many words rapid extraction of relevant information in the future by the manager is extremely difficult. Equally, the free text format does not facilitate reliable interrogation by computer or creation of a forward maintenance plan from the survey data. Thus, it is not particularly user-friendly for the maintenance or management professional.

In many ways, the use of a spreadsheet or database format represents the antithesis of the free text approach to reporting. These are excellent for recording the identification and location of different materials around the site; for summarising the condition of principal elements (or even of each individual component); flagging up priorities for remedial action and further inspection needs; and for ready comprehension of long-term repair and maintenance expenditure profiles. This data can be interrogated readily (if sufficient preparatory time is spent in structuring the report properly) and can be used to sort information electronically by, say, priority, condition or material. On the other hand, lay users generally find it more difficult to understand and interpret information presented in this way. Proper use of the data requires a certain level of aptitude in IT generally, and with spreadsheets or databases in particular. This format is unsatisfactory for telling the full story about a problem; and, practically, photographs can only be incorporated as an appendix or, more usefully perhaps, in a separate volume of the report. Offsetting these disadvantages, for the maintenance manager, the spreadsheet/database format makes production of a forward maintenance plan from the data a considerably easier task than when attempting to transcribe free text for this purpose.

So, free text and spreadsheet/database formats both have particular strengths and weaknesses as a reporting medium. To a degree, some inherent weaknesses of each can be ameliorated, as described, by creating a customised hybrid of the two approaches. An example of a well-tested successful hybrid is the quinquennial inspection format used by the National Trust in England. This supplements a free text-based report (which is often written in note form to reduce the word count, while retaining sense) with tabular presentation of forward maintenance and repair needs. This overcomes some weaknesses of free text condition reports, but inevitably has particular shortcomings of its own. Reading numerous pages of text in note form can be unrewarding and irritating. The tabular summary of future expenditure needs is very generalised and does not allow for sorting or interrogating data by material, element, condition, repair type or the like. In terms of facilitating the production of a long-term maintenance plan, this kind of hybrid is slightly better than a textual report, but far inferior to the full spreadsheet format. Hybrids can also be created to make the spreadsheet report approach more appealing to the general reader. Free text explanations of particular problems and issues can be inserted in an appendix, or as a subsection within a text-based introduction to the survey report and cross-referenced at appropriate places in the 'comments' field/column of the spreadsheet against the relevant entries. This is slightly cumbersome, but does help to tell the 'story' of the condition of the asset in a better way than is possible within individual cells of a spreadsheet.

There are a couple of additional matters that need to be considered when selecting an appropriate format for the condition survey report, if it is to constitute an effective management tool for the heritage asset. A number of heritage and large property management organisations have used condition surveys to feed data directly into asset management registers or plans. To be comprehensive – and there is little point taking this route, if the coverage is not total – this approach requires the building surveyor to record and report upon the location and nature of every element and each and every occurrence of different materials. Instead of reporting, by exception, on items that are defective or at risk of failure, the condition – good or bad – of every element or material occurrence needs to be recorded. Significant management benefits can flow from creating and maintaining this database of record information on the nature and condition of the asset, for instance, it is possible to flag up the presence of inappropriate materials used in past repair which can then be tackled in programmed packages of work. However, data collection is a labour-intensive and hence expensive process that tends to skew or overwhelm the conduct of the condition survey. Almost without exception, the future use of the data dictates that a spreadsheet or database format is adopted for reporting purposes. This approach can work well when dealing with relatively simple modern structures. It is more complicated in application on major heritage assets, primarily because efficient data collection and handling require the asset record to be based around a predetermined hierarchy of simple elemental descriptions (for example, elevation/window/casement/glazing) to strengthen consistency. Devising a meaningful hierarchy of this type for complex heritage assets is problematic, as extension of the example to encompass varieties of historic glass, lead cames, ferramenta, and so forth, as well as the condition of each and every material readily demonstrates. Heritage assets are often valued specifically for their individuality and idiosyncrasies. Fitting these into a simple, intelligible hierarchy for this use is bound to be challenging. Allow free text to define the unusual and the manager's ability to interrogate the asset register or condition survey is compromised immediately. This does not mean that the holistic asset management approach has no place in managing portfolios containing or consisting solely of heritage assets. Far from it, but, to be manageable, the approach almost certainly must be adapted and the compromises and weaknesses that this introduces must be appreciated by managers and kept in check. In the nightmare scenario, the manager wanting detailed asset data is frustrated by the dilution of a clear and simple interrogative elemental hierarchy through innumerable free text special entries, while the building/maintenance specialist regards the value and clarity of essential condition data as being degraded as a result of the process being 'hijacked' for a wider purpose. Equally, we have seen several instances where complex elemental hier-archies and reporting formats have been developed and adopted for condition surveys to fulfil the needs of global approaches to asset management, only for the condition survey record to be restricted to 'by exception' defect reporting so as to make the survey process less cumbersome and more affordable. This serves neither purpose particularly well.

The question is often asked as to whether condition surveys of heritage assets differ substantively from the process applied to their non-heritage counterparts. Intellectually and practically, however it is viewed, the answer must be a resound-ing 'yes'. Indirectly, some of the reasons have already been mentioned. Appro-priate repairs and the prioritisation of remedial action cannot be determined in isolation when dealing with heritage assets, such decisions have to be taken within the context established by an asset's wider significance and its vulnerabil-ity to harm. Correct interpretation of the evidence of failure in the fabric is often dependent upon an appreciation of the developmental history of the asset in a way that is rarely the case with non-heritage structures and estates. As we have noted already, heritage assets are frequently individual and idiosyncratic. Con-servation philosophy seeks to retain historic fabric that can be repaired, some-times irrespective of cost. That often demands inventiveness and flexibility of approach, fundamentally influencing recommendations for care and repair in the condition survey.

Traditionally, condition surveys tend to result in the need for repairs being identified based, broadly speaking, on concerns about functional performance, aesthetic considerations and cost (including the cost efficiencies to be made by packaging works together). Therefore, they often identify repairs as being urgent or specify a period within which they should ideally be carried out based on esti-mates of remaining life. The danger with this approach to the survey of heritage assets is that it may well operate contrary to the philosophical concept of mini-mum intervention, as it aims to set up a near-automatic process where a rate of deterioration is predicted, a prioritisation for action is set accordingly (in other words, the task of future repair is allocated to a particular year in the mainte-nance plan) and then acted upon at that future date, whether or not it is strictly necessary at that time. Put another way, the 'normal' conceptual approach to surveys is that, once a defect has been identified by inspection, repair will be carried out involving some kind of intervention into the built fabric. Such an 'automatic' approach does not necessarily make economic sense for any kind of building, but, when dealing with heritage assets, it increases the risk of historic fabric being removed or 'lost' unnecessarily. For historic stock, the concept of 'just in time' or 'little and often' maintenance is frequently determined to be the most appropriate way to manage this risk of premature degradation of the sig-nificance encapsulated within the built fabric. In its best application, this concept minimises intervention by initiating a second tier of survey through focused re-inspection of non-critically defective or deteriorating fabric that has been identi-fied in the previous periodic condition survey. By this process, it is intended that essential repairs or replacements are deferred until unavoidable, while ensuring that consequential damage to surrounding fabric and elements is not allowed to occur. The incorporation of second-tier survey work helps target precious (and often limited resources) and, in our view, should be a prominent planned feature of recommendations made in condition surveys of heritage assets.

Undoubtedly, this list of the differences between the survey of heritage and other built stock could be extended further. However, in essence, condition surveys of built heritage assets require a different skill set and attitude of mind from those on non-heritage assets. If the building surveyor does not realise this, the survey findings will be seriously compromised.

In considering the conduct of condition surveys, experience shows that there are three characteristics of historic structures that more frequently than any other baffle or are undervalued by surveyors more versed in inspecting 'simple' non-heritage buildings. These are:

- The identification and functional properties of both natural and traditionally used materials;
- Decorative ornament and features;
- The form and material properties of fixings used with the above.

It is true that, indirectly, the surveyor of, say, a rectangular, steel-framed light industrial 'shed' needs to give consideration to the material properties of its elements, such as its external profiled metal sheet cladding and concrete block walls. However, it is unlikely that analysis of these materials and their fixings is going to dominate the thinking behind and findings of the condition survey report in a way that is all too possible with a heritage asset. Again, the example that we have considered throughout this section, the Wellington Monument, can be used to illustrate this point simply. There, the iterative appearance of long vertical fractures close to the blades of the obelisk's shaft and repeated bulging of large panels of ashlar on its faces were found to be intimately linked to the nature, thickness and properties of the selected stone (extremely thin, local calcareous grit ashlar) and, given the innate characteristics of this ashlar facing, over-reliance on bedding mortar to hold stone to stone and each stone to the solid mortar and stone core behind (Figure 6.3).

This is not the place to wax lyrically about the importance of the notion of the 'breathability' of traditionally used materials such as lime, soft brick and stone to the durability and longevity of heritage assets, grand and modest. There is now a wealth of readily available material on this subject on various websites, as well as in recent publications. The point for us here is that the building surveyor analysing the performance of the built asset and the manager taking on the surveyor's findings and reaching decisions about how and when to repair need to understand that historic and modern structures tend to function in different, almost mutually exclusive, ways. Traditional buildings the world over depend upon the breathability of materials – or put another way, the absorption and subsequent evaporation of moisture – to work and survive, while most structures built in the last 100 years keep dry and sound through the use of impervious barriers – damp-proof courses and membranes and cementitious renders. Mix one approach with the other and, for traditional buildings at least,

Figure 6.3   Evidence of extensive past repair of varying kinds and ongoing fracturing and opening of stonework joints immediately above the junction between different construction phases roughly 37 metres above ground level on the Wellington Monument in Somerset.

disaster is just around the corner. Arguably, more damage has been occasioned to heritage assets in the UK by ill-judged attempts at care and repair by the insertion or use of impervious materials to form a barrier to damp ingress than by any single other factor. This places a massive responsibility upon building surveyors carrying out condition surveys of heritage assets.

The presence of decorative ornament or features – such as pinnacles, finials and crockets – is another pitfall for the unwary surveyor. With justification, good inspection practice tends to focus the surveyor's mind from the very start of his or her training on certain principal issues, especially the stability, integrity and adequacy of the structural elements of the building and the soundness and weather-tightness of its external envelope. Modern structures are generally barren of applied decorative ornament; larger or more complex heritage assets are sometimes extremely rich in it. Ornament frequently forms a significant part of the defining character of historic building exteriors. Often, especially with Gothic architecture, much of the external ornament is at high level and the adage 'out of sight, out of mind' may permeate the incautious surveyor's approach to the condition survey inspection. Experience highlights that ornament barely impinges upon a mindset that concentrates heavily upon structural elements and the external envelope. Yet, such ornament holds particular dangers for the building surveyor and the asset manager. Small, three-dimensional, and at high level, it is almost impossible to assess the condition of such ornamental elements from ground level, even using binoculars. Applied to the face of turrets, towers and walls, carved ornament is extremely vulnerable to degradation by the elements;

Figure 6.4 Ongoing fragmentation of previously repaired stone ornament on the tower of a nineteenth-century mansion roughly 48 metres above ground level. Almost every similar feature on the tower (of which there were many) exhibited similar defects, in each case caused by corrosion of concealed iron rods and cramps.

iron and other fixings employed to attach it to the main building fabric are especially liable to corrode or fail (Figure 6.4). Concentrated for effect around the visible perimeter of historic structures, debris from failed ornament represents a particular health and safety risk to building users and passers-by. On many larger buildings, similar ornamental components – such as pinnacles and finials – are used repeatedly and, typically, close inspection will reveal multiple failures of the same kind affecting these elements. Lastly, in terms of repair, access and labour costs to ornament tend to be very high and, where renewal is necessary, carving of replacement sections is expensive. One example will suffice to make the point. In a repair programme to the external stone fabric of the former Public Record Office in London – a Gothic building of 1855–1901 with a mixture of limestone and sandstone ashlar elevations and extensive, often replicated, Portland stone

Figure 6.5 Taylor's 1890s wing of the former Public Record Office (also known as the Rolls Estate) in Chancery Lane, London.

carved ornament above parapet level and to turrets and towers – the access and essential repair costs to the high-level ornament were some ten times higher than expenditure required to the principal structural elevations (Figure 6.5). This is not atypical. So why does ornament receive disproportionately little attention in so many condition surveys of buildings where it is present, and why are such survey inspections so often conducted without the use of appropriate means of achieving close access to the ornament (for instance, by 'cherry picker')?

One final issue remains to be mentioned in this discussion of the condition survey as a fundamental management tool in sustainable conservation of our built heritage. This is the problem of ensuring consistency of approach in multiple surveys across a historic estate, or from one cycle of periodic survey to the next, or where one survey of a single asset or site is undertaken by a team of several surveyors. Issues of consistency permeate and bedevil the condition survey process from beginning to end. Different individuals do not necessarily see the same thing as being a 'defect'. They may not interpret the cause and severity of a defect in the same way. They may use different terminology to describe or define the element they are looking at and its state of defectiveness. They may interpret the impact of the asset's assessment of significance and the management organisation's conservation policies on the condition survey process and recommendations in starkly different ways. They may hold diametrically opposed views on the appropriate remedial action for a particular defect, as well as the relative

priorities for action across the asset as a whole. It is the involvement of individuals that makes condition surveying an art not a precise science. Yet lack of
consistency puts at risk all subsequent management decision-making and action
that are based upon the findings and recommendations of a condition survey.

In the end, improving consistency, rather than achieving it as an absolute, is
probably a more realistic goal. This demands good, carefully co-ordinated briefing, training, planning and team management. It must involve the asset manager
as much as the survey team manager.

As a conduit to improved consistency, the best condition survey briefs set out
definitions for key terminology that may be used. Historic England's standard
brief (English Heritage, 2012) refers the surveyor generally to 'national norms
and standards', including two relevant British Standards (BS 8210:2012) *Guide
to Building Maintenance Management* and (BS 7913:1998) *Guide to the Principles of the Conservation of Historic Buildings* (it is worth noting that the latter
has subsequently been substantively revised in 2013), and sets out in a detailed
way definitions of 'alteration', 'asset', 'backlog', 'benchmark', 'breakdown maintenance', 'conservation', 'fabric', 'intervention', 'maintenance', 'planned maintenance', 'preservation', 'repair', 'restoration' and last, but by no means least, the
meaning of 'surveyor' itself. Either within the survey brief or within the pre-
inspection team planning and briefing process (or even better, as part of both),
it is essential that the definitions of all elemental descriptors and the elemental
hierarchy that is to be used are established unambiguously.

It is perhaps worth reviewing what has been said and implied about consistency in the survey and reporting processes and the ramifications of its absence
in order to emphasise the key part that it plays:

- Regular accurate cyclical condition surveys are crucial to the proper management of use and change in and around heritage assets.
- Effective management decision-making has to be based upon sound and reliable knowledge of the asset, its problems, needs and life expectancy.
- Inconsistency in condition survey data, findings and recommendations will
  undermine the asset manager's confidence in the process and in the survey
  output.
- Consistency needs to be achieved:
  - across multiple surveys where an estate or a dispersed portfolio of separate
    assets is involved;
  - through time, between successive cyclical surveys of the same asset;
  - within a single survey where two or more surveyors undertake the inspec-
    tion and prepare the report as a team.
- Among other things, inconsistency may occur in the use of terminology, in
  the identification of what is a defect, in its interpretation, in assessment of
  its severity and consequence, and in formulating recommended action and its
  relative priority.
- Management based on patchy data and analysis is likely to result in bad
  decision-making.

- Improved levels of consistency will only be achieved by a concerted and co-ordinated approach being taken to briefing, training, planning and team management by the client and service provider throughout the process. At the present time, this is rarely attempted and almost never delivered.

Financial management of maintenance management

Planned maintenance programmes allow for greater financial control and accountability. In such systems, money tends to be allocated to work identified as belonging to a number of categories such as:

- Cyclical maintenance;
- Maintenance and repair work identified through inspections;
- Unforeseen work – that is, reactive maintenance.

Although budgeting for maintenance works needs to take account of the likely resources available, it should be established on the basis of an assessment of the maintenance need and should reflect and be informed by the maintenance policy. Some sense of certainty about budgets over at least the medium term is important for effective management.

There are a number of factors in the way that budgets are often set, divided up and spent, which can work against the idea of minimum intervention and the protection and enhancement of significance. One of these, which can have negative effects irrespective of whether heritage assets are involved or not, is the tendency for budgets to be set and finalised on an annual basis – a situation which will work against the idea of a strategic approach to maintenance. A situation where an organisation has developed, say, a five-year programme but only has budget certainty of 12 months or less, produces an uncertainty which leads to inappropriate decisions being made. Ideally, at the least, there should be medium-term budgets for maintenance, which allow for some certainty in planning work based on clear priorities. In addition, and perhaps just as importantly, particularly for heritage assets, a medium-term budget may prevent unnecessary work being carried out, or necessary work being carried out too soon. Such problems may occur with an annual budget cycle, particularly when there is uncertainty about the level of maintenance funding for the next year (or a regime where next year's budget is reduced, if this year's is not spent). This situation will tend to encourage managers to ensure that the budget is spent. For heritage assets, a decision to spend money on repairs because it will be lost in the future can have a negative impact, if the intervention is not necessary at that time. Of course, one might suggest that the frequent re-prioritisation of planned maintenance may have the effect of producing a minimal intervention approach by default, but this is unlikely – and certainly does not constitute good stewardship of a cultural artefact.

For heritage assets, it is important that the budget for cyclical maintenance is 'ring fenced'.

Information management in maintenance management

The most important point about management information is to ensure that the right sort of information at the right level of detail is collected, that it is sufficient to allow clear judgements to be made – but that information is not collected just because it can be. In addition, there needs to be a system for analysing and disseminating information which will inform the decision-making process. Systems that manage such information should also make provision for feedback and monitoring.

Potentially huge quantities of information can be produced by the operation of a maintenance function (condition surveys, user feedback, the execution of the maintenance programme, building and service records, etc.), but the information, by its very nature, tends to be unstructured. That is, it is drawn from many different sources and in practice there is often no agreement about a common structure or levels of detail. Because the nature and form of information produced and required by maintenance activity are extremely diverse, maintenance information should be stored on an integrated database. The information stored should be easily retrievable and should be in a format, and at a level of detail, to enable it to be easily manipulated so as to inform both tactical and strategic decision-making. Information also needs to be in a form and a level of detail that allows it to be integrated into the wider property management role, both at a tactical and strategic level. In other words, there needs to be coherence between business strategy, maintenance strategy/policy, financial management and maintenance implementation.

Some traditional formats for condition surveys highlight a number of the problems with information management. In some heritage management organisations, for example, and as has been discussed already, condition surveys tend towards a lengthy textual format. To some extent, this is partly a cultural 'affectation', but it is also a valuable approach as it can provide detailed assessment of historical development to be interposed with data on condition and repair needs. It can, however, produce information which is relatively inaccessible and inflexible and therefore difficult to analyse and use in terms of management; for example, it often cannot deal with 'what if?' enquiries or, perhaps more basically, does not easily inform the development of work programmes.

Performance indicators

In the public sector, in particular, key performance indicators have become a common tool for monitoring past performance and for allocating future budgets. These performance indicators have certain characteristics in common: in particular, they are relatively easy to measure and they tend to be mainly associated with financial and budgetary information. Hence, indicators for maintenance that are often used are: the amount of backlog repairs; costs per metre squared (or per user); and the speed of response (for reactive maintenance). There is also commonly an indicator for the amount of stock in a particular condition. The problem with this is that important, more qualitative issues are potentially overlooked if politically the maintenance organisation is driven to work towards quantitative targets rather than seeing such benchmarks as (partial) management information. There have been some attempts to measure more qualitative issues, but the overwhelming majority of indicators tend to the quantitative. Whatever the arguments regarding the usefulness and relative importance of such performance measures, some feedback mechanism for management and other interested parties should be regarded as an essential part of a review process which considers whether maintenance strategies and policies are being successfully implemented.

References

Audit Commission (2002) *Briefing: Learning from Inspections, Housing Repairs and Maintenance*. London, Audit Commission.

Australia ICOMOS (2013) *The Burra Charter: The Australia ICOMOS Charter for Places of Cultural Significance*. Burwood, VIC, Australia, Australia ICOMOS Inc.

Brereton, C. (1991) *The Repair of Historic Buildings*. London, English Heritage.

British Standards Institute (1986) *BS 8210:1986, Guide to Building Maintenance Management*. London, BSI.

British Standards Institute (1998) *BS 7913:1998, Guide to the Principles of the Conservation of Historic Buildings*. London, BSI.

British Standards Institute (2012) *BS 8210:2012, Guide to Facilities Maintenance Management*. London, BSI.

British Standards Institute (2013) *BS 7913:2013, Guide to the Principles of the Conservation of Historic Buildings*. London, BSI.

Clark, K. (2001) *Informed Conservation*. London, English Heritage.

English Heritage (2000) *Power of Place: The Future of the Historic Environment*. London, English Heritage.

English Heritage (2012) *English Heritage Standard EHS 0004/2: Periodic Condition Surveys and Reports*. London, English Heritage. [Internal publication only.]

Feilden, B. (1982) *Conservation of Historic Buildings*. London, Architectural Press.

Feilden, B. (1994) *Conservation of Historic Buildings*. London, Architectural Press.

Feilden, B. and Jokilehto, J. (1993) *Management Guidelines for World Cultural Heritage Sites*. Rome, International Centre for the Study of the Preservation and Restoration of Cultural Property (ICCROM).

Government Historic Buildings Advisory Unit (1998) *The Care of Historic Buildings and Ancient Monument: Guidelines for Government Departments and Agencies*. London, English Heritage and the Department of National Heritage.

HEFCE (1998) *Building Repairs and Maintenance Study in Higher Education Sector: National Report and Management Review Guide*. Bristol, Higher Education Funding Council for England (HEFCE).

Holmes, R. (1994) Built asset management practice. In *The CIOB Handbook of Facilities Management* (ed. A. Spedding). Ascot, Chartered Institute of Building (CIOB).

Kerr, J.S. (1996) *Conservation Plans for Places of European Significance*. Auckland, National Trust of New South Wales.

Morris, W. (1877) *The Principles of the Society (for the Protection of Ancient Buildings) As Set Forth upon its Foundation.* Available on SPAB website: www.spab.org.uk/html/what-is-spab/the-manifesto/

Ruskin, J. (1989) The lamp of memory. In *The Seven Lamps of Architecture.* New York, Dover Publications, Chapter 6.

Williams, B. (1994) *Facilities Economics*, Bromley, BEB Press.

Wood, B. (2003) *Building Care.* London, Blackwell Science.

Wordsworth, P. (2001) *Lee's Building Maintenance Management* (4th edn). London, Blackwell Science.

Chapter 7

Sustainability, Built Heritage and Conservation Values: Some Observations

Introduction

*Each generation should therefore shape and sustain the historic environ-
ment in ways that allow people to use, enjoy and benefit from it, without
compromising the ability of future generations to do the same.*

(English Heritage, 2008)

*the places that are likely to be of significance are those which help an
understanding of the past or enrich the present, and which we believe
will be of value to future generations.*

(Australia ICOMOS, 1999)

The link between conserving the built heritage and sustainable development is an
interesting one, particularly as it has not been explored, at least philosophically,
in as much detail as one might expect. This interaction is too complex a subject
for this book and would, anyway, distract from its purpose. However, we would
suggest that the main theme that we have set out – the idea that significance-based
decision-making is vital to the effective protection of the historic environment –
encourages, and indeed requires, processes and outcomes that can be seen to
have the characteristics of a sustainable management approach to the protection
of built heritage.

Sustainable development

The idea of sustainable development, that is, to achieve sustainable outcomes
from human activity, has been around for some considerable time. Sustainability
can be seen as a rather complex notion that, in detail, if not in concept, has

Managing Built Heritage: The Role of Cultural Values and Significance, Second Edition.
Stephen Bond and Derek Worthing.

become so all-encompassing, and can include so many factors, that it is difficult to articulate it, never mind measure it. One of the consequences is that it is often easier to prove a negative, that is, that something is *not* sustainable, rather than a positive (that something is sustainable).

In 1983, the United Nations established a World Commission on Environment and Development under the leadership of the former Norwegian Prime Minister, Gro Harlem Brundtland. Their task was to prepare strategies on sustainable development. In 1987, this Commission published its report called *Our Common Future,* which is more generally known as 'The Brundtland Report' (United Nations, 1987). The Commission adopted the concept that sustainable development is '[development that] meets the needs of the present without compromising the ability of future generations to meet their own needs', and it is this phrase that has become the focal point of discussions on the concept. Although vague and open to interpretation, it is at the same time clearly aspirational, and, importantly, it refers to needs rather than wants.

Current (and real) concerns about climate change have, rightly, re-emphasised environmental issues. However, it is important to appreciate that, although the idea of sustainable development can be seen to have emerged from environmental concerns in the 1960s and 1970s, it is much wider in scope than just the interaction between development and the environment. Sustainability also encompasses social and economic issues and activities. Sustainable development then can be seen to be that which achieves the best fit between social, economic and environmental concerns. It aims to maximise all of these three benefit categories as far as possible, but there is also an implication that there may be a trade-off between them. That is, there may be a case, for example, where realising social benefits is justifiable, even where there may be some negative effects on the environment. Alternatively, the necessity to protect the environment in a particular instance may be at a cost to social and economic benefits. So although, as observed, a sustainable approach would be to seek solutions that maximise all three benefits, it may be that some aspects of sustainability are considered, in particular cases, to be more important than others. It is worth noting here that the idea of trade-offs and relative importance have become important issues in the management of built heritage. There is generally, however, an implication that economic benefits should be long-term rather than short-term, and should not be sought at the cost of social and environmental benefits. It can be seen that a key aspect of sustainability is social sustainability – and that environmental benefits and (some) economic benefits can also be social benefits. Cultural heritage is itself a social benefit (which may also produce environmental and economic benefits).

Sustainable development, and hence the notion of sustainability, then, are concerned with the synthesis and integration of social, economic and environmental benefits. It is also strongly associated with ideas of social justice, quality of life and the participation of citizens in decision-making. 'To be sustainable, investment in the conservation of the historic environment should bring social and economic benefits. On the other hand, investment in social and economic programmes should bring environmental benefits' (Cadw, 2011).

The notion of social capital is the most abstract of the four capital stocks and the most difficult to quantify yet perhaps the most important ... the sense of social cohesion based around shared ethical values is a capital stock of tremendous potency ... Harnessed properly, it leads to sustainability and the highest achievements of civilized capacity.

(Bransford *et al.*, 1997)

Sustainability and the built heritage

Our awareness of the fragility of old materials mirrors society's concerns with the fragility of the air, land and water, and with fossil fuels as a finite resource.

(Cassar, 2009)

As observed, the idea of sustainable development was initially grounded in concerns about environmental sustainability, but it has developed to consider the interaction between environmental, economic and social values. In the context of the conservation of the built heritage, it is interesting to note that the basic 'sustainability' concept of the stewardship of valuable resources was espoused by early conservationists. Writing in 1849 about buildings from the past, John Ruskin suggested: 'They are not ours. They belong partly to those who built them and partly to all the generations of mankind who are to follow us' and he emphasised that this inter-generational consideration referred to a responsibility to those from the past as well as the future when he observed (about buildings) that 'The dead still have their right in them' (Ruskin, 2011). William Morris, in stating the purpose of protecting buildings, wrote that it was to 'hand them down instructive and venerable to those that come after us' (Morris, 1996) and, in the early twentieth century, Riegl observed that 'a monument is a work of man erected for the specific purpose of keeping particular human deeds or destinies (or a complex accumulation thereof) alive and present in the consciousness of future generations ' (Riegl, 1902). The sense that we might conceive of a responsibility to past generations, as well as future ones, while rather esoteric, is perhaps an aspect of 'sustainability' which is sometimes overlooked.

The protection of the built heritage does potentially interact with all three aspects of the sustainability matrix:

- *Social value* – for instance, because of the sociological and psychological value to individuals, groups and nations of the physical connection to the past (and, through this, to notions of continuity, connectivity and identity). The educational potential of built heritage also has social value.
- *Environmental value* – for instance, in respect of embodied energy in the use and reuse of these existing buildings (and land), as the focus and driver for regeneration schemes, and for their aesthetic and amenity value, including diversity and a sense of place.
- *Economic value* – for instance, in tourist income, specifically and generally.

Trade-offs

The idea of trade-offs is a key concept in the notion of sustainability. We could use this sustainability idea of 'tradeability' to decide whether or not to protect/designate an asset by reference to the trade-off between its social or cultural value, as against the economic costs and perhaps environmental costs of protecting it. An example of this might be where a building is in such a poor physical condition, making repair and maintenance costs so high that, irrespective of whether or not the building still retains its heritage values, it would not be designated for protection. The same argument would apply where it was not possible to find a viable and appropriate new use (at present, neither of these factors are material considerations in the decision to list in the UK).

This idea of a trade-off between benefits could be applied to a decision not to (fully) upgrade the energy performance of a building because the available options would be likely to damage its cultural value. The relationship between energy and heritage is obviously pertinent to the wider issue of sustainability and heritage, particularly as addressing the problem of climate change is clearly one of the challenges, if not *the* most important challenge facing humankind.

Addressing the energy performance of buildings is a very important part of attempts to mitigate climate change because of the amount of carbon dioxide that can be attributed to them. Until relatively recently much of the emphasis on reducing energy consumption in buildings was focused on achieving zero carbon in new buildings. However, now a greater amount of attention is being paid to the existing stock, which, of course, includes heritage assets.

In European countries, this refocusing on the existing stock of buildings is being driven by, among other things, European Union directives. This push to upgrade the energy performance of the existing building stock clearly has implications for the historic environment. There is a danger that ill-considered energy improvements may, as with any intervention, potentially damage the cultural significance of an asset. Because of this potential conflict, the Energy Performance in Buildings Directive (European Union, 2010) states that 'buildings officially protected as part of a designated environment or because of their special architectural or historical merit', are exempt from the directive 'in so far as compliance with certain minimum energy performance requirements would unacceptably alter their character or appearance'.

In England, Part L of the Building Regulations deals with energy and buildings and the guidance to this section (the Approved Document) states that designated buildings (listed buildings, unlisted buildings in conservation areas and scheduled monuments) are exempt from the energy requirements. The use of the term 'exempt' is misleading because the 'exemption' applies only to the extent that compliance would unacceptably alter the character or appearance of the building. The guidance then goes on to say that, in addition, special consideration should be given to three further classes of buildings; those of architectural and historic interest and which are referred to as a material consideration in a local authority's development plan, buildings of architectural and historical interest within national parks, etc, and buildings of traditional construction with permeable fabric that both absorbs and readily allows the evaporation of moisture. According to English Heritage, this latter category includes the 20% (about 4 million) of existing domestic buildings that were constructed before 1919 and another 20% that were constructed between 1920 and 1939 (English Heritage, 2012). For all of these three further classes, the guidance says that the aim should be to improve energy efficiency as far as is reasonably practicable and that 'the work should not prejudice the character of the host building'.

Clearly this is a situation where the challenge is to decide how to achieve a 'best fit' between the maximisng of effective energy performance and the protection of cultural heritage. This then brings in the notion of a trade-off between the two and raises the question of the evidence base which is used to measure a quantitative social gain (improved energy use) against a qualitative social gain (protection of cultural heritage) and how the trade-off decision is made. This is not always a straightforward process, but in order to make a coherent decision, it is necessary to understand not only how much energy is used in a particular building, but also how it is used (including importantly how the occupiers behave and what their expectations are), and how energy proposals may affect significance. As we have said, the heritage values that contribute to the significance of the asset, and the elements of the asset that embody and represent those values, need to be understood rather than assumed. But unless there is some identification of significance and relative significance, there is a danger that the opportunity to maximise energy improvements while retaining significance will not be realised.

Charters and guidance documents

In *Heritage and Sustainability* (Coleman, 2004), a discussion paper produced by the New South Wales Heritage Office, Coleman observes that 'the social environment is important in considering political and cultural influences of decision making, which impact upon all aspects of sustainability' and she goes on to quote UNESCO thus:

> *sustainable development is widely understood to involve the natural sciences and economics, but it is more fundamentally concerned with culture: with the values people hold and how they perceive their relationship with others. It responds to an imperative need to imagine a new basis for relationships amongst peoples and with the habitats that sustain human life.*
>
> (UNESCO, 1997)

References to sustainability and built cultural heritage have been implicit in international charters going back to the Venice Charter in the 1960s (ICOMOS, 1964) but the connection is made more explicit in later charters, presumably in response to growing environmental concerns. For example:

> *The architectural heritage is a capital of irreplaceable spiritual, cultural, social and economic value … Our society now has to husband its resources. Far from being a luxury this heritage is an economic asset which can be used to save community resources.*
>
> (Council of Europe, 1975)

The 'Framework Convention on the Value of Cultural Heritage for Society' – sometimes referred to as the Faro Convention (Council of Europe, 2005) – places emphasis on 'the value and potential of cultural heritage wisely used as a resource for sustainable development and quality of life in a constantly evolving society' and the need to 'put people and human values at the centre of an enlarged and cross-disciplinary concept of cultural heritage'. The Convention also picks up on sustainability ideas of equity and inclusiveness when it refers to 'the need to involve everyone in society in the ongoing process of defining and managing cultural heritage' and 'the soundness of the principle of heritage policies and educational initiatives which treat all cultural heritages equitably'.

Although there is a clear link between conservation of built heritage and sustainability, some of the statements made by heritage bodies have been over-generalised. Such an example is the following from English Heritage:

> *Sustaining heritage values is likely to contribute to environmental sustainability, not least because much of the historic environment was designed for a comparatively low-energy economy. Many historic settlements and neighbourhoods, tending towards high density and mixed use, provide a model of sustainable development. Traditional landscape management patterns have been sustained over centuries. Many traditional buildings and building materials are durable, and perform well in terms of the energy needed to make and use them.*
>
> (English Heritage, 2008)

Another example is from a UK government department:

> *The historic environment has an important role to play in addressing climate change. The retention and reuse of heritage assets avoid the material and energy costs of new development. Many older settlements reflect good practice in sustainable urban design. They have compact layouts; co-locate employment, residential, retail and leisure uses; and are usually near to transport nodes. The historic environment can inform and inspire the best modern, sustainable development.*
>
> (DCLG, 2010)

This is not to suggest that there are not coherent arguments to be made in suggesting that heritage equates directly to sustainable activity, it is to suggest that such assertions as those quoted above need to be demonstrably substantiated. It has already been observed that the term and the actions associated with the notion of sustainability can sometimes be so vague – and sometimes so insubstantial – as to be meaningless in reality (the term 'greenwash' is often used in this context rather cynically to describe when organisations try to gain credibility by superficial actions). There is also the danger that the term is so misused that it becomes meaningless. Sustainability now often seems to be used to mean a reinforcement of the need to protect the historic environment, as distinct from using the idea of sustainability to engage with the basic ideas of conservation or at least consider the interaction between the two concepts and processes. Also Historic England has used the term 'sustain' to mean 'Maintain, nurture and affirm validity' (English Heritage, 2008) and so sustainability is often used just to mean 'to sustain something', 'to keep it going'. More problematically, it is sometimes used by others to describe an action that is sustainable because it has qualities such as logic, coherence and effectiveness. The term is also sometimes (mis)used to simply imply that something is effective or robust.

Sustaining the Historic Environment: New Perspectives on the Future was produced by English Heritage in the late 1990s (English Heritage, 1997). It was heavily influenced by the approach taken by management plans used in the natural environment (as was the Burra Charter), particularly in its use of the idea of ' environmental capital' and 'environmental capacity'. It is clear in fact that much of the thinking by built heritage organisations at this time was drawing upon and recontextualising ideas from the management of the natural world. This was partly because management plans had been in existence for some time in this sector, but also because there was a recognition of some synergy between the problems and issues being faced in the two areas, and that 'As with natural heritage, the cultural heritage specialist has to ensure continuity between past, present and future' (Historic Scotland, 2002).

However, although it makes perhaps only limited references to the social value of individual heritage assets (as against the overarching social value of heritage *per se*), the English Heritage publication did observe and acknowledge a need to encourage a move towards a more holistic and less elitist view of what might constitute the historic environment (English Heritage, 1997). The study suggested that there needed to be more emphasis given to the voices of the wider community in decision-making, including involving 'non-experts' in decisions about what was considered culturally valuable – and why. It also signalled a change of approach in its recognition that 'involving people' had to be more than just experts explaining the value of the historic environment, and that it was important to understand that a major part of the role of English Heritage was 'about helping people to develop an understanding of the whole of their historic environment so they can contribute their own perspectives to the debate about what is important and what should be conserved or changed' (English Heritage, 1997). Coleman makes a similar point in *Heritage and Sustainability* when she states that 'Participatory decision making in political processes is seen as the key to sustainability' (Coleman, 2004).

Although *Sustaining the Historic Environment* did not appear to raise much in the way of debate about the nature of heritage conservation, it did set out what it referred to as 'Key principles of sustainability', which it suggested were:

- Developing a stronger understanding of the historic environment, and promoting wide awareness of its role in modern life;
- Taking a long-term view of our actions;
- Looking at the environment as a whole;
- Achieving greater public involvement in making decisions about society's needs and the environment;
- Keeping our activities to levels which do not permanently damage the historic environment;
- Ensuring that decisions about the historic environment are made on the basis of the best possible information.

These ideas were later reflected in the English Heritage publication, *Conservation Principles* (English Heritage, 2008) which suggested six 'high level principles':

1 *The historic environment is a shared resource.*
2 *Everyone should be able to participate in sustaining the historic environment.*
3 *Understanding the significance of places is vital.*
4 *Significant places should be managed to sustain their values.*
5 *Decisions about change must be reasonable, transparent and consistent.*
6 *Documenting and learning from decisions are essential.*

Sustaining the Historic Environment (English Heritage, 1997) also introduced ideas borrowed, as observed earlier, from the natural environment and sustainability generally, by reflecting on the applicability of concepts such as environmental capital and environmental capacity. We can suggest that these ideas can be recontextualised for built heritage as the requirement to keep within thresholds of change and loss through the identification of the following:

- *Environmental capital*: what have we got and what is its value? That is, what is its significance?
- *Environmental capacity*: to what extent can built heritage accept change, and/or how much stress can it take before it is damaged to an extent that it suffers loss to its significance? That is, what is its sensitivity to change?

The same document also reflected on the applicability of the sustainability notion of trade-offs of one benefit in return for another, and doing so by deciding/categorising which elements of the (historic) environment are:

- *To be conserved at all costs (critical assets).*
- *Subject to limited change provided that the overall character of the resource is maintained (constant assets).*

- *Suitable for exchange in return for other benefits (tradeable assets).*

(English Heritage, 1997)

It can be seen that, in essence, this recognises the need to attribute relative signif-icance in order to manage (change) effectively, and that this needs to be carried out in order to reconcile the past and present.

Sustaining the Historic Environment also raised a discussion about the need to have a 'typology of values' in order to stimulate discussion about what people might value about a place in recognition of the fact that 'different elements of the historic environment are valued in different ways, for different reasons, and by different people'.

It also suggested steps that, though not expressed in the same manner, can be seen as informing the thinking behind processes based on significance-based planning and management in the way that it set out the need to do the following:

- Understand the resource and the values that it represented;
- Identify what might degrade or damage the resource now and in the future (its vulnerability);
- Use environmental indicators linked to an understanding of the extent to which the resource could accept change without its significance being damaged;
- Use the above information to formulate policies and plans;
- Implement effective policies and processes for monitoring the condition of the historic environment.

Sustainable management of historic buildings

> *The sustainable management of cultural heritage at the service of devel-opment bears at least two important dimensions, that of longevity and that of economic, environmental and social viability. Thus, in the first instance, the physical aspects of cultural heritage (the brick and mortar of historical buildings, the objects of material culture, etc.) are valued and their continued existence in good condition represents a form of sustain-ability of heritage management at the service of development ... social via-bility of cultural heritage – in addition to its economic and environmental viability – obtained through participation of local populations in its man-agement, is essential to ensure collective and individual pride in heritage, interest and involvement in its protection.*

(UNESCO, undated)

It could be suggested that, within the context of conservation management plan-ning, we can say that sustainable conservation is the proper management of use and change in and around historic places and spaces, so as to respect and enhance their value to society and that any management framework, planning and action should address the following issues:

- How, and under what circumstances, there can be a trade-off of conservation values against other benefits.
- Acknowledging, and incorporating in decision-making, a range of values that are broader and more holistic than are presently commonly used.
- The extent to which stakeholders are involved in deciding what is valuable and why (and involving a wider constituency in the identification of stakeholders).
- Realising the possible benefits for the wider constituency. As Throsby (2002) observes: 'It may be suggested that equity of access to cultural capital should be regarded as just as important as equity in the intergenerational distribution of benefits from any other sort of capital.'

It can be seen that within the conservation community there has been an increasing move towards a more holistic, integrative and inclusive view of how conservation should be conceived and therefore what qualities ought to be protected, and how this might be managed. To a large extent, this thinking has been driven explicitly and implicitly by the sustainablility agenda and notions of integrated management.

It is clear that the various significance-based management tools that we have discussed and advocated in the previous chapters have emerged as credible vehicles for the sustainable management of built heritage in that they emphasise the need for, and provide a framework for the following:

- Taking a long-term view, including a consideration of threats in the future and encouraging plans and processes which mitigate against vulnerability;
- Being holistic in nature and content, in that it sets the heritage asset in its wider context and integrates issues and concerns;
- Understanding an asset and articulating and debating its values as a precursor to making decisions on its future;
- Involving stakeholders not only in how the asset is managed, but also in deciding how important it is and why.
- Managing change, while protecting that which is valued by society;
- Adopting a 'precautionary principle' approach;
- Being rigorous and methodical in obtaining information and analysing it;
- Demonstrating transparency in decision-making;
- Allowing decision-makers to be held accountable for decisions.

As the document Conservation Principles states:

> Sustainable management of a place begins with understanding and defining how, why, and to what extent it has cultural and natural heritage values: in sum, its significance. Communicating that significance to everyone concerned with a place, particularly those whose actions may affect it, is then essential if all are to act in awareness of its heritage values. Only through understanding the significance of a place is it possible to assess how the qualities that people value are vulnerable to harm or loss. That understanding should then provide the basis for developing and

implementing management strategies (including maintenance, cyclical renewal and repair) that will best sustain the heritage values of the place in its setting. Every conservation decision should be based on an understanding of its likely impact on the significance of the fabric and other aspects of the place concerned.

(English Heritage, 2008)

References

Australia ICOMOS (1999) *The Burra Charter: The Australia ICOMOS Charter for Places of Cultural Significance*. Burwood, VIC, Australia, Australia ICOMOS Inc.

Bransford, P., Krause, T., Ottavino, K. and Sasson, D. (eds) (1997) *Sustainable Urban Preservation*. New York, World Monument Fund.

Cadw (2011) *Conservation Principles for the Sustainable Management of the Historic Environment in Wales*. Cardiff, Welsh Assembly Government.

Cassar, M. (2009) *Sustainable Heritage: Challenges and Strategies for the Twenty-First Century*. Springfield, IL, Journal of Preservation Technology.

Coleman, V. (2004) *Heritage and Sustainability: A Discussion Paper*. Parramatta, NSW, New South Wales Heritage Office.

Council of Europe (1975) *The European Charter of the Architectural Heritage*. Paris, ICOMOS.

Council of Europe (2005) *Framework Convention on the Value of Cultural Heritage for Society*. Strasbourg, Council of Europe.

DCLG (2010) *Planning Policy Statement 5: Planning for the Historic Environment*. London, Department of Communities and Local Government/HMSO. (Note: Now superseded by National Planning Policy Framework – PPS5 practice guide is still in force.)

English Heritage (1997) *Sustaining the Historic Environment: New Perspectives on the Future*. London, English Heritage.

English Heritage (2008) *Conservation Principles: Policies and Guidance for the Sustainable Management of the Historic Environment*. London, English Heritage.

English Heritage (2012) *Energy Efficiency and Historic Buildings*. London, English Heritage.

European Union (2010) Directive 2010/31/EU of the European Parliament and of the Council of 19 May 2010 on the Energy Performance of Buildings. *Official Journal of the European Union* L 153/13.

Historic Scotland (2002) *Passed to the Future: Historic Scotland's Policy for the Sustainable Management of the Historic Environment*. Edinburgh, Historic Scotland.

ICOMOS (1964) *International Charter for the Conservation and Restoration of Monuments and Sites* (The Venice Charter). Paris, ICOMOS.

Morris, W. (1996) *Manifesto of the Society for the Protection of Ancient Buildings*. In *Historical and Philosophical Issues in the Conservation of Cultural Heritage*. Los Angeles, The Getty Conservation Institute. (Originally published in *The Builder* in 1877.) Note: Also available at: www.spab.org.uk/html/what-is-spab/the-manifesto/ (as 'The Principles of the Society (for the Protection of Ancient Buildings) As Set Forth upon its Foundation'.

Riegl, A. (1902) The modern cult of monuments: its essence and its development (trans. Karin Bruckner with Karen Williams of *Der moderne Denkmalkultus*). In *Historical and Philosophical Issues in the Conservation of Cultural Heritage* (eds N.R. Price, K. Talley Jr and A.M. Vaccaro). Los Angeles. The Getty Conservation Institute.

Ruskin, J. (2011) *The Seven Lamps of Architecture.* Project Gutenberg ebook. (Note: Originally published in 1888 and reprinted in 1989 by Dover Publications, New York.)

Throsby, D. (2002) Cultural capital and sustainability concepts in the economics of cultural heritage. In *Assessing the Values of Cultural Heritage* (eds E. Avrami, R. Mason and M. de la Torre). Los Angeles, The Getty Conservation Institute

UNESCO (1997) *Educating for a Sustainable Future: A Transdisciplinary Vision for Concerted Action.* Paris, UNESCO.

UNESCO (undated) *Towards a UNESCO Culture and Development Indicators Suite. Working Document Dimension No. 3: Sustainable Management of Cultural Heritage for Development.* Paris, UNESCO.

United Nations (1987) *Report of the World Commission on Environment and Development.* New York, UN. [Also published as *Our Common Future* by Oxford University Press, 1987.]

Chapter 8
Conservation Principles

Introduction

We have written this penultimate chapter to serve as a reminder. While, with good reason, the heritage world has now moved to consider conservation as being the management of use and change affecting heritage assets and their settings, the internationally respected conservation principles that previously served as a management framework for many decades – especially for monuments and major assets – still underpin our consideration of potential solutions to physical conservation challenges. They will endure and are an important part of our approach to managing heritage assets. It is valuable therefore to reflect on those principles and their inter-relationship with the significance-based approach to management that we have been exploring.

Development of conservation principles

In Western cultures the concern for preserving certain physical artefacts has been around for many centuries, although perhaps the first stirrings of what we might discern as a conservation consciousness only really began to develop in the eighteenth century. However, in the UK, it was not really until the formation of the Society for the Protection of Ancient Buildings (SPAB) in 1877 that a coherent philosophy was articulated and developed. The driving force behind this early conservation movement was William Morris, who was much inspired by the thoughts and writing of John Ruskin. It is interesting to note the extent to which the ideas formulated during this period still inform much current thinking about approaches to the care of the built heritage. However, some of the rather dogmatic assertions about the 'evil' of restoration have been contextualised by the idea of the overriding importance of establishing and protecting significance.

Managing Built Heritage: The Role of Cultural Values and Significance, Second Edition.
Stephen Bond and Derek Worthing.
© 2016 Stephen Bond and Derek Worthing. Published 2016 by John Wiley & Sons, Ltd.

As we have observed previously, we can see in the development of this early movement the identification of the value of stewardship of existing resources (William Morris, writing in 1877, said: 'we are only trustees for those who come after us' (Morris, 1996)), as well as an emphasis on the spiritual and educational value of the built heritage and a concern for the dignity and pleasure to be gained from skilled creative work. John Ruskin, writing in 1849, expressed his feeling that old buildings were to be revered because they were the results of a living popular art (Ruskin, 2011).

Morris developed a manifesto for SPAB that implicitly and explicitly set down a number of principles, which still have relevance and resonance and can be seen as the basis of ideas in a number of charters and guidelines. Among the key ideas were:

- The uniqueness and therefore the importance of the fabric of buildings as a physical expression of the cultural values of the place as well as a source of education and understanding;
- The importance and significance of all the developments contained within these buildings and respect for all historic materials found there;
- The importance of maintenance.

In the early days of the conservation movement, there was a very strong emphasis, often to the exclusion of any other considerations, on the need to protect the original or authentic fabric of the structure, based on the idea that it represented the skill and art of the originator and, as mentioned previously, that age in itself conveyed cultural worth. This 'archaeological' perspective is still a strong theme today, and appropriately so – at least for certain buildings and certain situations. The 'archaeological' perspective, with its reverence for the work of the 'original hand' and the emphasis on respecting that art by not falsifying/copying or damaging it, was reinforced by the concerns of the art historian who would unequivocally be antagonistic to attempts to 'repair', say, a work of art painted by a great artist. The same concept would be applied to the buildings that were protected, based on the idea that they were also examples of great artistic achievement (and, indeed, those that were chosen were to a large extent singled out for that reason). This situation reinforced the anti-restoration rhetoric of SPAB and others, and underlined the basic tenets or principles of conservation philosophy, especially those of minimum intervention and honesty. As we have observed, the ideas developed by Morris and Ruskin and the early pioneers of the conservation movement – particularly, minimum intervention and honesty – though they have been developed and built upon, still form the core of conservation principles that are commonly referred to today.

Core conservation principles

Authenticity

The idea of authenticity is fundamental to conservation principles. Bell (1997) suggests: 'Authenticity is not an easy concept. Each part of a site's development is authentic in its own right, as a reflection of its time', and Feilden and Jokilehto (1993) state: 'Authenticity is ascribed to a heritage resource that is materially original or genuine and as it has aged and changed in time' and that 'The contributions of all periods to the place must be respected.' In practice, determining authenticity is closely linked to assessments of value and can cause problems when, for instance, the idea of age value influences decisions about the relative value of more recent developments to the asset.

The importance of the fabric

As the Burra Charter observes: 'Conservation is based on respect for existing fabric, use, associations and meanings.' The Charter also emphasises the importance of the fabric in understanding the asset when it suggests that 'the traces of additions, alterations and earlier treatments to the fabric of a place are evidence of its history and uses which may be part of its significance' (Australia ICOMOS, 2013) (Figure 8.1).

The importance of maintenance

This is emphasised in many charters and other guidance as a key activity in protecting the significance which is represented by fabric, and in reducing the need for inappropriate interventions. The Venice Charter, for instance, states: 'Protection must involve a continuing programme of maintenance' (ICOMOS, 1964).

Minimum intervention

This can be interpreted at two levels. The notion emphasises the importance of the fabric as evidence in understanding the development of the asset, as reference is often made to being able to 'read' the building and to allowing the building to tell its own story:

> Conservation should show the greatest respect for, and involve the least possible loss of, material of cultural heritage value.
>
> (ICOMOS New Zealand, 1992)

> The unnecessary replacement of historic fabric, no matter how carefully the work is carried out, will have an adverse effect on the appearance of a building or monument, will seriously diminish its authenticity, and will significantly reduce its value as a source of historical information.
>
> (Brereton, 1991)

But minimum intervention does not just refer to the fabric, it refers to all actions affecting the asset, including additions, new buildings and changes in use. The idea is not to stifle change, but to ensure that any changes protect and enhance significance. The Burra Charter emphasises a cautious approach to change and says: 'Do as much as necessary to care for the place and to make it useable, but otherwise change it as little as possible so that its cultural significance is retained' (Australia ICOMOS, 2013).

Figure 8.1   The story that the fabric of a building can tell is illustrated by the town walls of Spoleto. It is important that all the significant developments of a place are respected. Photograph courtesy of Tony Bryan.

Truth and honesty

The idea of truthfulness or honesty was a key idea for certain architectural movements. The neo-Gothic architect A.W.N. Pugin referred to the idea, as did John Ruskin in his discourses on architecture, for example, in *The Seven Lamps of Architecture* (Ruskin, 2011). It was also one of the central themes, for instance, in the Arts and Crafts Movement and the Modern Movement. The concern in such architectural movements was that, with such concepts, you would not disguise, but rather you would celebrate the materials that have been used in constructing a building. Furthermore, you should be able to understand by observing the building how it was put together and how its structure works, and also that its function should be decipherable by its design, and, indeed, that its form should be derived from its function. The idea of truthfulness and honesty has also long been a key conservation principle. One of the catalysts for the formation of the Society for the Protection of Ancient Buildings (SPAB) was the concern of Morris and others about the implications of the restoration of churches back to some previous state of Gothic purity – mostly a state that was imagined or based on conjecture. Ruskin, for example, suggested that 'Restoration … means the most total destruction which a building can suffer … The thing is a lie from beginning to end' (Ruskin, 2011). This anti-restoration stance has implicitly and explicitly driven much of the thinking on conservation actions, particularly in the UK, for some time. For example, a current document from SPAB states:

> *although no building can withstand decay, neglect and depredation entirely, neither can aesthetic judgment nor archaeological proof justify the reproduction of worn or missing parts. Only as a practical expedient on a small scale can a case for restoration be argued.*
>
> (SPAB undated)

However, other guidance, particularly where it uses significance as a reference point, has put this anti-restoration idea into perspective while still showing a cautionary stance about it. So, for example, in the English Heritage document, *The Repair of Historic Buildings* (Brereton, 1991), Brereton acknowledges that the restoration of lost features may be justified as long as there is no loss of historic fabric and that sufficient evidence exists for accurate replacement. But restoration can involve both adding something or taking it away, and on this latter point Brereton states that 'Additions or alterations including earlier repairs are of importance for the part they play in the cumulative history of a building or monument. There should always be a strong presumption in favour of their retention.' He goes on to state that any potential and architectural gains must be balanced against any likely loss of historic integrity. The Burra Charter (Australia ICOMOS, 2013) defines conservation as being 'all the processes of looking after a place so as to retain its cultural significance'. It goes on to expand on this by observing that:

> *Conservation may, according to circumstance, include the processes of: retention or reintroduction of a use; retention of associations and mean-ings; maintenance, preservation, restoration, reconstruction, adaptation and interpretation; and will commonly include a combination of more than one of these.*

The Charter qualifies this by stressing that restoration (and reconstruction) should only happen where it will reveal culturally significant aspects of the asset, and only if there is sufficient evidence of an earlier state of the fabric. The Charter reinforces this by stating that 'Changes to a place should not distort the physical or other evidence it provides nor be based on conjecture.'

The issue with restoration, particularly of, say, major parts of the asset, is not just an issue of truthfulness, it is also a process that, unless it is handled sensitively, negates the development of the place by suggesting that one era is more important than another. Also of course it may go against the principle of minimum intervention. Nevertheless, it is generally accepted that – with the provisos stated above – restoration may be an appropriate action, but this should only be carried out after the significance of the asset has been established.

The UK document, PPS5, *Planning for the Historic Environment: Historic Environment, Planning Practice Guide* (DCLG, 2010) states the conditions under which restoration is likely to be acceptable:

1 *The significance of the elements that would be restored decisively out-weigh the significance of those that would be lost.*
2 *The work proposed is justified by compelling evidence of the evolution of the heritage asset, and is executed in accordance with that evidence.*
3 *The form in which the heritage asset currently exists is not the result of a historically-significant event.*
4 *The work proposed respects previous forms of the heritage asset.*
5 *No archaeological interest is lost if the restoration work could later be confused with the original fabric.*
6 *The maintenance implications of the proposed restoration are considered to be sustainable.*

But the idea of truth and honesty is not just related to the issue of restoration. A basic principle of conservation is that all interventions in the fabric should be handled 'truthfully' to make clear what is 'original' and what has changed, in order to avoid producing a parody or facsimile of the past or pretending that something is what it is not. The Venice Charter (ICOMOS, 1964) states: 'Replacements of missing parts must … be distinguishable from the original so that restoration does not falsify the artistic or historic evidence.' In part, this is harking back to a Ruskin/Morris concept of respecting the work of previous generations, but it is also concerned with not obscuring the 'reading' of the building and the understanding that all developments of the place have value. Brereton (1991) makes the point that 'The authenticity of an historic building depends most crucially on the integrity of its fabric and on its design, which may be original or may incorporate different periods of addition and alteration'.

As with the concept of minimum intervention, the idea of honesty is most often perhaps used in reference to repairs to the fabric (Figures 8.2 (a) and (b)). However, as a principle, it should be applied to all intervention in the historic environment, including alterations, additions and indeed new buildings, which generally should respect the historic context and certainly not detract from its significance, but should also be clearly distinguishable as new work. The issue is one of truthfulness, but it also acknowledges that changes made now are part of the continuing history and development of the asset.

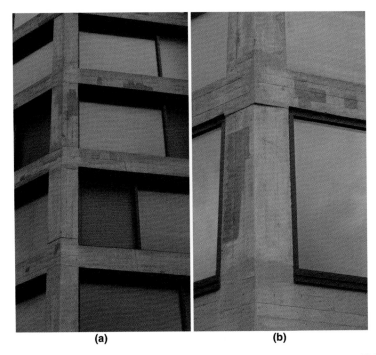

(a) **(b)**

Figure 8.2 (a), (b)   An example of an 'honest repair' to concrete on the Grade 2 star Parkhill estate in Sheffield, South Yorkshire, England.

Reversibility

To some extent, reversibility is a relatively pragmatic principle, in that it allows current actions to be substituted for future, possibly more appropriate, options – perhaps where a repair, for instance, is not functioning properly or where it is causing unforeseen damage to adjacent material. But something that is reversible also has an implied subservient quality in reference to the 'original' material, and could be taken to imply a hierarchy mainly based on age and the perceived (un)worthiness of modern intervention – that what we do now has less value than that done in the past. However, new interventions are often an important part of the 'story' of an asset. As with other principles, reversibility could equally apply to actions other than repairs, for example, with the physical aspects of the introduction of a new use where the design might allow for the removal of the new structure in the future without adverse impact on the 'original' fabric.

Fit the new to the old

This again works at a number of levels and covers 'moulding' the new to the old because this will usually reduce the amount of original material lost in repair work, and may, for example, reinforce the value of 'plastic' repairs in stonework. Equally, as with reversibility, it should also relate to how new uses, additions and new buildings are 'fitted in' with the existing environment.

Figure 8.3   These late nineteenth-century metal buttresses (or *stötta* in Swedish), which are used as props on a section of the medieval town wall in Visby, Gotland, are a good example of honesty, reversibility and minimum intervention.

The importance of the relationship of a site with its surroundings

The sense that the context of a building was important and that its loss would detract from its cultural significance led to the creation of Conservation Areas in the UK. The Venice Charter (ICOMOS, 1964) was emphatic in stating: 'A monument is inseparable from the history to which it bears witness and from the setting in which it occurs.' The Burra Charter (Australia ICOMOS, 2013) states: 'Conservation requires the retention of an appropriate setting. This includes retention of the visual and sensory setting, as well as the retention of spiritual and other cultural relationships that contribute to the cultural significance of the place.'

This principle also extends to the idea that buildings should not be moved. Again, as the Burra Charter states: 'The physical location of a place is part of its cultural significance. A building, work or other component of a place should remain in its historical location' (Australia ICOMOS, 2013). The SPAB document, *SPAB's Purpose*, confirms: 'As good buildings age, the bond with their site strengthens. A beautiful, interesting, or simply ancient building still belongs where it stands, however corrupted that place may have become' (SPAB undated).

The importance of records

Creating a record of the built heritage is part of the process of establishing its significance and also of managing the care and protection of an asset. The need to record all actions in order to help others to understand 'the story' of the place is also an important conservation principle. The Burra Charter states: 'Existing fabric, use, associations and meanings should be adequately recorded before any changes are made to the place' (Australia ICOMOS, 2013).

The maintenance and development of an accurate record are a key process in managing the care and protection of heritage assets. As the ICOMOS Charter (1990) on recording states:

> *[historic buildings] must be treated responsibly, and the understanding that is essential to their proper treatment can only be reached by making the best possible use of information about them and by ensuring too that future generations understand what the present generation has done for their care.*

Recording and interpretation of the built heritage are prerequisites for processes related to its effective management, for example, defect analysis, maintenance and visitor management, as well of course as part of the understanding of significance.

Reasons for recording historic assets include:

- To collect information in order to aid in the understanding of cultural significance. As Cooper (1991) observes, 'We record buildings because we want to discover certain things about them.' This may be primarily related to identifying the changes that have occurred over a period of time.
- To provide information for interpretation and public understanding of the building.
- To enable the reconstruction of part or the whole of the asset in the event of its damage or destruction. An accurate record is required for any reconstruction, necessitated, for example, by fire, flood or perhaps even theft (of course, whether or not such a reconstruction has value in cultural heritage terms is a matter of debate and context).
- As part of the process of proper management of the asset in relation to maintenance, repair or conversion projects where:
  - the information is used to inform decision-making about the effect that proposed changes will have on the historic fabric;

- an archival record of that which is inevitably lost or changed (even routine maintenance work can involve loss or change) is established. As Rosier (1996) points out, 'Prior recording can ensure that the removal or obstruction of historical evidence can be "preserved by record" while the agreed alterations allow the buildings a new lease of life.'
- hidden features revealed during the works can be recorded before they are re-concealed.

Given the above requirements and uses, we can see that the recording of a heritage asset is not a 'one-off' event but a continuous process that is a prerequisite of many conservation management activities. The ICOMOS (1990) guidelines state: 'The record of a building should be seen as cumulative with each stage adding both to the comprehensiveness of the record and the comprehension of the building that the record makes possible.'

It is important to recognise that recording is not value-free. It is, as stated, part of the process of understanding and interpreting the asset – of establishing significance – and therefore attributing value to the structure. 'The essence of the record lies in coming to an understanding of the building and of its development and structure, and that all recording should have as its objective the elucidation and illustration of this understanding' (ICOMOS, 1990). Similarly, Molyneux (1991) observes: 'The purpose of analytical recording is not merely to ascertain the initial form of the building but rather how the use of the structure has responded to and reflects social, cultural and economic change through time.' Recording should, therefore, so far as possible, not only illustrate and describe a building but also demonstrate significance.

Clearly, as mentioned before, decisions on how and what to record will involve varying measures of subjective judgement of the relative values embodied in, or represented by, the asset. However, it is also clear that the process used to communicate or disseminate the analytical record may in itself influence the interpretation of the asset and therefore the understanding of its significance.

New uses

A general principle is that the original use of an asset is the most appropriate use, and certainly where the use of an asset is of cultural significance, it should be retained. But from an economic perspective, finding a new use may be the only effective way of retaining the building or asset.

It needs to be borne in mind, however, that because of operating requirements, some uses that are the same as the original may be more intrusive now than if the asset were put to a different use, for example, hospitals with changing perspectives on service delivery, and requirements for security, based on sight lines, in many buildings.

New uses that reduce a building to nothing more than a façade are rarely justifiable in conservation terms. (The visual amenity that is kept is almost always a poor reason/substitute for the loss of the asset and encourages the sense that appearance is the main value.)

If an asset is to have a new use, it should be a compatible use (Australia ICOMOS, 2013). The basis of judging compatibility could be related to reducing interference with the fabric, and therefore any use that can fulfil its function without damaging the fabric may be compatible. However, the idea of compatibility may also relate to considering whether the proposed new use might be deemed, by some at least, as being more, or less, appropriate (the reuse of churches for some social good being preferable, maybe, for instance, to something with a purely commercial purpose or as a gambling casino perhaps). A new use that retains the same sort of 'spirit of place' associated with level of noise, atmosphere, etc. of the original use, as well as with its meanings and associations, would also be an important consideration.

While finding a new use may be absolutely necessary to the upkeep of the asset from an economic perspective, if the main, or a major aspect, of cultural significance is related to the type of use, then clearly this may be problematic.

Some reuses have been achieved by inserting a whole new structure within an original space in such a way that it does not damage the fabric (minimum intervention), it is constructed of modern material with a modern design (honesty), and it can be dismantled and removed (reversibility, even though, if successful, it will became part of the story of the asset).

The relationship between significance-based management and traditional conservation principles

As we noted in the Introduction to this chapter, the traditional conservation principles mentioned above have not disappeared and should not be dismissed as being irrelevant. Admittedly, significance-based management represents a very different perspective on heritage assets and their use and change, but the concepts of minimum intervention, honesty of repair, and so forth remain relevant and, in many circumstances, have much to offer when applied alongside a broader appreciation of heritage values.

The key point to remember about the traditional principles is that they are heavily biased towards the fabric-centric. Dearly held concepts such as:

- Minimum intervention;
- Repair to be undertaken 'little and often';
- Honesty in repair;
- Repair in preference to restoration or renewal;
- Avoidance of conjectural restoration;
- New works to be reversible, where practicable

are all about the primacy and sanctity of historic fabric. There are good reasons why the conservation world developed in that direction, for as we have seen earlier, traditionally, the focus of conservation was on monuments and 'high-society' assets. Today, we would see part of the significance of most such assets as being their rich architectural and early associative value, hence the interest in their historic fabric and the importance of its survival. It would seem fair to suggest that traditional conservation principles still have a particular relevance today in defining a management approach where an asset's significance is heavily inclined towards and dominated by some permutation of architectural, technological and early associative values. Conversely, the fabric-centric principles are likely to hold less sway where, for example, the asset's significance is heavily focused on intangible heritage values. Of course, these should be seen as being tendencies and not hard and fast rules. Arguably, the townscape contribution of serried ranks of nineteenth-century residential terraces in historic industrial mill towns is not particularly dependent upon the survival of individual historic bricks in their roadside elevations, while, equally, the commemorative and inspirational value of twentieth-century war cemeteries is regarded by many as being harmed by even minor deterioration in individual grave markers and pitted stone in memorials, for the powerful emotive value of such assets is invested in uniformity and fastidious attention to precluding any suggestion of decay and neglect, in order to fulfil the promise of perpetual homage and honour to the dead that was made in the dictum 'Their name liveth for evermore' (see Case Study 4 in Chapter 9).

This brings us neatly back to significance and its role in the management of heritage assets. Understanding both the essence and the underlying context of the values that society derives from a heritage asset are fundamental to good management. Getting significance-based management right requires careful investment in exploring and developing such understanding.

References

Australia ICOMOS (2013) *The Burra Charter*. Burwood, VIC, Australia, Australia ICOMOS Inc.

Bell, D. (1997) *The Historic Scotland Guide to International Conservation Charters*. Edinburgh, Historic Scotland

Brereton, C. (1991) *The Repair of Historic Buildings*. London, English Heritage.

Cooper, N. (1991) *Architectural Records: Recording Evidence and Recording Facts in Recording Historic Buildings*. London, RCHME.

DCLG (2010) *PPS5 Planning for the Historic Environment: Historic Environment, Planning Practice Guide*. London, Department of Communities and Local Government. (Note: this is a joint publication with English Heritage and the Department of Culture Media and Sport and Culture Media and Sport as well as the Department of Communities and Local Government, London.)

Feilden, B. and Jokilehto, J. (1993) *Management Guidelines for World Cultural Heritage Sites*. Rome, ICCROM.

ICOMOS(1964) *International Charter for the Conservation and Restoration of Monuments and Sites* (The Venice Charter). Available at: www.international.icomos.org/charters.htm

ICOMOS (1990) *Guide to Recording Historic Buildings*. London, Butterworth.

ICOMOS, New Zealand (1992) *Charter for the Conservation of Places of Cultural Heritage Value*. Parramatta, ICOMOS, New Zealand.

Molyneux, N. (1991) English Heritage and recording: policy and practice. In *Recording Historic Buildings*. London, RCHME.

Morris, W. (1996) *Manifesto of the Society for the Protection of Ancient Buildings*. In *Historical and Philosophical Issues in the Conservation of Cultural Heritage*. Los Angeles, The Getty Conservation Institute. (Originally published in *The Builder* in 1877. Note: Also available at: www.spab.org.uk/html/what-is-spab/the-manifesto/ (as 'The Principles of the Society (for the Protection of Ancient Buildings) As Set Forth upon its Foundation'.)

Rosier, C. (1996) *PPG and Recording: The Oxfordshire Experience. Context*, No. 52.

Ruskin, J. (2011) *The Seven Lamps of Architecture*. Project Gutenberg ebook. (Note: Originally published in 1849 and reprinted in 1989 by Dover Publications, New York.)

SPAB (undated) *SPAB's Purpose*. Available at: www.spab.org.uk/html/what-is-spab/spabs-purpose/

Chapter 9
Case Studies

We end this book with four wide-ranging case studies which involve the assessment of significance of very different heritage assets and the manner in which significance can thereby be used to influence management decision-making. We have not tried to draw together lessons or morals from these case studies; rather they are presented in an open-ended way for consideration and reflection.

Case Study 1: Royal Dart Hotel, Kingswear, Devon, England

Kingswear is a reasonably sized village of around 1500 inhabitants in the South Hams district of the county of Devon in England. It sits on the eastern side of the tidal River Dart, near to its mouth and facing the historic town of Dartmouth, home to the Royal Navy's officer training college since 1863, directly across the river.

The Italianate Royal Dart Hotel occupies a central waterfront site in Kingswear, 'sandwiched' between the slipway of the historic Lower Ferry, which linked the settlement with Dartmouth, and the village's now-closed railway terminus, which formerly connected with the mainline running from London's Paddington Station to the south-western counties of England (Figures 9.1 and 9.2). The hotel, once – along with the parish church – the communal heart of Kingswear, experienced hard times in the late twentieth century and closed in 2010. It was designated a Grade II listed building in 1985 and it lies within the designated Kingswear Conservation Area.

The local authority, South Hams District Council, noted in its 2013 Conservation Area Appraisal, that, although having distinct and separate origins, Kingswear's history is largely associated with the port of Dartmouth across the River Dart. Documentary evidence proves that a ferry operated to Dartmouth from the westernmost tip of the village south of the Royal Dart Hotel from

Managing Built Heritage: The Role of Cultural Values and Significance, Second Edition.
Stephen Bond and Derek Worthing.
© 2016 Stephen Bond and Derek Worthing. Published 2016 by John Wiley & Sons, Ltd.

Figure 9.1   The Royal Dart Hotel beside Kingswear Station, with the upper part of the town of Dartmouth behind on the hill across the River Dart.

Figure 9.2   The Royal Dart Hotel forms the focal point of the view down Fore Street towards the river.

around 1365. Kingswear's position near the mouth of the creek, where access could be gained by ships whatever the state of the tide, was extremely valuable and this led to a castle being built late in the fifteenth century to defend its harbour from attack. The village was actively involved in the Atlantic and other maritime trade from the mid-sixteenth century onwards, so that much of its economy came to be based on fishing, wool and, much later, the trading of coal. The post-medieval settlement grew around and below the church down to the waterfront in a tightly packed 'huddle of merchant houses, warehouses and wharves'. Victorian photographs of older houses and courts in the tight core of the village reveal that many of the earlier buildings were timber-framed or a mix of timber framing and stone. Very little remains of these houses, however, as the coming of the railway in the 1860s and the expansion and rebuilding that followed have significantly changed the built character of the village. A second village ferry, the Lower Ferry from the slipway immediately beside the site of the Royal Dart Hotel, began to operate around 1700. Yet, from around the same time, Kingswear's importance as a trading port started to wane and it became instead an increasingly desirable location for residences for the wealthy. As noted already, the character of the village was transformed by the coming of the railway in 1864. Kingswear functioned as the railway station for the much larger and more important Dartmouth across the river, so the Lower Ferry came to be an integral component of the railway and its station from that time. Kingswear's wharf behind the station was a stopping point for steamers between London and, variously, India, Barbados and Demerara, West Africa and Cape Town during much of the second half of the nineteenth century.

Even the foregoing introductory description suggests that the Royal Dart Hotel occupies a site of some local significance within the village. The owner, a local business, commissioned a statement of significance for the redundant asset to inform the design of proposals for its subdivision and conversion into five high-quality residential apartments and also to form the basis of a heritage statement which would accompany the planning submission to the local planning authority for consent to carry out the proposed development. The principal task of the statement of significance was to explore and eventually define the hotel's significance to the level of detail necessary to understand the extent of the present-day physical fabric holding heritage interest. Without that, it would be impossible to assess the effects of physical subdivision and other alterations on the asset's significance.

Initial analysis of the setting of the asset showed that, due to local topography, it occupies a prominent position in most key and informal views into and out from the core of the village. It is also the focal point of the view down Kingswear's Fore Street towards the Square – the principal approach of visitors to the core of the village and to the ferry to Dartmouth.

The process of assessing significance involved among other things:

• Extensive, but with one exception, non-intrusive examination of the built fabric of the hotel. This task was complicated by subdivision of many of its grander spaces in two or more phases after c.1914 and further later twentieth-century alterations for fire safety purposes. One of the major issues experienced in making the assessment was that no floor plans of the building appear to survive from earlier than 1982. This made comprehension of its 'original' layout exceedingly difficult.

- The use of a series of maps and plans from c.1802 onwards to 'deconstruct' the development of the area and the asset in particular.
- Searches for historical illustrations and photographs of the locality. These searches provided:
  - important information on a predecessor to the Royal Dart Hotel on the site – a public house known as the Plume of Feathers – in a meticulously detailed topographical drawing and a sketch from the 1790s, which were found in the online catalogue of a national museum.
  - critical information from several original photographs and a single engraved illustration about the development of the immediate setting of the asset during the construction of the railway station in 1864 and the associated timing of the 'disappearance' of the Plume of Feathers and the 'appearance' of the Dart Yacht Club Hotel (the first name for the Royal Dart Hotel), which was built by the Railway Company as its terminus hotel in 1866.
- The use of historical local newspaper articles, which supplied additional vital information on the everyday history of both the Plume of Feathers Inn and the Royal Dart Hotel and changes in their ownership and/or tenancy, the coming of the railway to the village and its impact on social life, and otherwise unobtainable detail of important guests who stayed at or visited the hotel, including Queen Victoria's youngest daughter, Princess Beatrice, and her own daughter, Princess Ena, and the exiled Napoleon III. These newspapers also revealed the importance of Kingswear's railway terminus. Local topography meant that it was not economically viable to build a railway overland to Dartmouth. In effect, the branch line to and terminus at Kingswear, across the river, were built as Dartmouth's railway station. The Railway Company took over the Lower Ferry and incorporated it as part of the railway service from London and Bristol to Dartmouth. The hotel was there to accommodate visitors arriving on the late train, who would travel on by ferry across the river to their destination the next morning after a night's stay.
- Searches of nineteenth- and early twentieth-century decennial census entries and annual commercial directories to understand and fill in missing detail about the owners and managers/tenants of the hotel and their servants and staff.
- In the absence of definitive nineteenth-century floor plans, examination of comparable hotel advertisements in commercial directories and the monthly railway timetables published as *Bradshaw's General Railway and Steam Navigation Guide* in order to understand the typical facilities that the Royal Dart Hotel would have needed to offer travellers in order to have been attractive and competitive. This in turn informed analysis and interpretation of the probable 'original' spaces that could be identified within the building and assessment of their relative significance.

- Consideration of the processes involved in arriving at, and the visitor experience of staying in, a nineteenth-century provincial hotel, informed by the surprisingly limited amount of material that has been written on the subject. Understanding that process and experience – the basic functional context of the nineteenth-century railway hotel – was again fundamental to determining the significance of spaces and of surviving fabric within the asset.
- Use of oral and published local histories and conversations with local historians and other residents to gather further information about the asset and its significance.

On top of this, as has already been described in Chapter 5, it proved necessary to build up a reasonably detailed understanding of topics such as:

- *The development of hotels in England from c.1760 as a building type*, including the facilities that they offered to their visitors;
- *The history of development of the interiors of hotels and inns in the nineteenth and early twentieth centuries*: this informed interpretation of the dating and use of various spaces within the hotel and a deeper understanding of the importance (or otherwise) of built fabric inside the building today;
- *The history of development of gas and electrical lighting in rural England*: this was important to an understanding of the hotel's decline as a business from c.1907, by which time the more urbane travellers were used to the comforts afforded by electric lighting. Since Kingswear had no piped gas supply and electricity did not arrive until 1914/1915, the hotel was lit merely by candles and oil lamps until that time, inevitably making it seem an old-fashioned and uninviting prospect for many of its potential guests.
- *The history of the railway branch line to Kingswear*: an understanding of the history of development, use and decline of the railway must be seen as being fundamental to consideration of the significance of a railway hotel;
- *Nineteenth- and twentieth-century tourism in the county of Devon*: and the railway's part in that development;
- *The fluctuating history of Kingswear's wharf as a stopping off location for passengers using mail steamer ships between London and South Africa, India and the Caribbean*: again, this was critical to developing an understanding of the profile of visitors wishing to stay at the hotel through time;
- *The Second World War history of Royal Navy's Coastal Forces and the role played by the hotel*: as HMS Cicala, a very active local headquarters for both the Coastal Forces and the Free French Navy.

At the end of the assessment process, the statement of significance was able to conclude that the significance of the Royal Dart Hotel as a heritage asset was as follows:

- It occupies a key central position within both the historical and modern settlement of Kingswear and, almost certainly, its site has been in continuous use since the early medieval period.

- It is a landmark and focal point structure within the Kingswear Conservation Area and within many local views. Indeed, it is one of the significant landmarks and focal point buildings along this shore of the River Dart.
- It is the most highly visible element of an interlinked historical economic group that comprised the station, wharf, passenger ferry, Lower Ferry and the railway's hotel. From c.1864–1866 onwards, this group was the life blood of Kingswear's community and to a lesser, but still important degree, that of Dartmouth, too.
- The Dart Yacht Club Hotel most probably absorbed the pre-existing Plume of Feathers Inn rather than physically replacing it. Fragments of that earlier structure and fabric may survive, hidden within the Victorian structure, although that is far from certain. Irrespective of that, comparison of historical and modern photographs and the detailed 1790s topographical drawing show that today's hotel retains an identical rhythm of built elements (chimney stacks, windows, blank sections of walls or bays, and changes of building line) along its long south elevation as the Plume of Feathers and therefore its plan form was and is inherently influenced by the historical layout of the Plume of Feathers, representing at the very least continuity of the 'shadow' of an earlier building on the site.
- The hotel is an integral part of the history of the coming of the railway to Kingswear and Dartmouth, arguably the most momentous time in the village's history.
- The architecture of the hotel directly influenced the transformation of the built character of the core of the Kingswear in the last 30 years of the nineteenth century.
- Coherent elements of the hotel's accommodation and architectural features still survive, meaning that some glimmer of an understanding of its functioning in its heyday (essentially, the 40 years from 1866 to 1906) can be read from those areas of legibility, despite the marked blurring that has occurred to legibility elsewhere in the building. It is right that the hotel's significance should be linked to its 'heyday', but caution is needed in this. Arguably, the hotel was never truly a viable concern and it had no 'glory days'. Its operators were faced perpetually by an irreconcilable dilemma. Kingswear was literally the end of the line, but it was barely ever considered a destination in itself. To the great majority of Victorian and Edwardian travellers, Kingswear was a place for passing through on the way to bigger, better or more beautiful places. The significance of the hotel in its heyday must be appreciated for what it was and was not.
- The hotel played an important role in the Second World War as a shore headquarters for the Coastal Forces and the Free French Navy up to the D-Day invasion of Normandy in June 1944. Contemporary German propaganda revealed a clear appreciation of the military importance of the hotel (as *HMS Cicala*) in the Allied war effort at a pivotal time.
- The hotel in its heyday could boast of its association with royalty and nobility, numbering Napoleon III and Princesses Beatrice and Ena among its guests or visitors. In its role as *HMS Cicala*, it was the working base for Philippe de

Gaulle, son of General Charles de Gaulle, and was most probably visited by François Mitterand, among other high-profile British and Free French officers.

In summary, the statement found that the Royal Dart Hotel has historical, associational, architectural and townscape value and, on this basis should be considered as a designated heritage asset of medium significance.

The case study is useful for illustrating the breadth of research and analysis that may be required, even on an everyday building such as the Royal Dart Hotel, if significance is to be understood to the extent and depth necessary to allow the effects of development proposals to be properly considered.

Various restrictions on the availability of research data have been mentioned as examples in this case study. The process of assessing significance is rarely 'pure' and unconstrained in its outcome. In this instance, it proved impossible to allocate past uses to every key space and to identify with complete certainty the layout and hence the functional dynamics of the 1866 hotel building. This, in turn, left 'grey areas' in the assessment of impact of the development proposals for the asset's conversion to residential apartments. In these circumstances, if development is to go ahead, greater emphasis has to be placed on the importance of creating a detailed record of the asset before, during and after implementation of the changes so that, wherever possible, late mitigation of the effects of the development can be considered and attempted and, in any case, the significance of permanently lost or harmed elements can be recorded and understood.

Case Study 2: Baixa, Maputo, Mozambique

Downtown Maputo is known as the 'Baixa' (Portuguese for 'low'), referring to the low flat land around the city's port and harbour. Baixa is the historic core of Mozambique's capital, Maputo. In the eighteenth and nineteenth centuries, it was the site of a Portuguese trading station and fort on a small island in Delagoa (now Maputo) Bay, which was separated from the mainland by a narrow, marshy channel. The swamp was drained by the Portuguese administration in the 1870s and Maputo, formerly known as Lourenço Marques, has developed northwards from the island since then to cover an area of almost 134 square miles (approximately 350 km^2). Perhaps inevitably, Baixa has the highest density of historic buildings and spaces in the city and these provide testament to the involvement and interests of Mozambicans and the colonial Portuguese in the historic settlement, as well as the Afrikaans, Dutch and British. After 50 years of little physical change, Baixa has come under considerable redevelopment pressure in the past 7–10 years. Much of this new high-rise development has been nondescript, failing to reflect Baixa's distinctiveness, shaped by the culture and traditions of Maputo and Mozambique, and its potential to be one of Africa's most remarkable urban districts.

Recognising the urgency of this situation, the city authority, the Conselho Municipal de Maputo, supported by the World Bank, commissioned the preparation of a partial urbanisation plan from consultants in 2013 to establish a new development vision and implementation strategy for the district. The objective was to create an integrated master plan that would deliver the protection and sustainable utilisation of Baixa's distinctive heritage and at the same time would improve the 'liveability' and economic competitiveness of the wider city, both regionally and globally.

Preparation of the plan involved many professional disciplines, with local and international specialists working together in each discipline to increase the objectivity and robustness of analysis and understanding. Assessment of Baixa's historic environment and the potential of its heritage involved extensive community engagement, which included the use of facilitated focus groups to explore the ways in which the local residential and business communities valued the area's heritage assets. Detailed characterisation and mapping of all Baixa's heritage assets were undertaken by the team's local and international heritage specialists across the complete 2.5 sq km district. Building on existing legislation and the work of Mozambican and Italian heritage experts in the preceding few years, the plan developed a proposal for the classification of heritage assets and an in-depth catalogue of the area's surviving 323 built/designed heritage assets, including monuments and public spaces with heritage value. Understanding the nature and spatial distribution of different asset types was regarded as being a key step in delivery of the master plan's heritage-focused objectives. It was found that Baixa's heritage could be considered as comprising a series of important 'collections' of heritage assets, which the plan defined as follows:

- *Pre-colonial town planning*: A handful of buildings survive from the period before the commencement of colonial town planning in 1877–1887. This collection of assets are architecturally simple, generally being single-storey, but historically these buildings are very important. It is possible that further survivals exist within the old historic core of Baixa, concealed by more modern façades or other construction.
- *Colonnaded buildings*: The presence of colonnades characterises many of Baixa's streets and street corners. These buildings, all dating from after the commencement of colonial town planning in 1877–1887 (but some considerably later) have colonnades overarching the public pavement. These are variously formed as a simple or multi-storey canopy attached to the principal façade of the building or by the projection of upper storey accommodation over the pavement. Some colonnades incorporate attractive and important cast iron detailing; others are built in concrete. The collection demonstrates the long-running importance of this form within Baixa, with examples ranging in date from the late nineteenth century to perhaps as late as the 1960s.
- *Individual Art Deco-inspired structures*: Baixa has an excellent collection of individual Art Deco-inspired architecture (Figure 9.3). This collection dates primarily from the 1930s to perhaps the early 1950s and must be regarded as being of considerable importance to Mozambique. It rivals the survival of such heritage assets in many key European capital cities and is believed to be among the better collections – if not, indeed, being the best – in Africa.

Figure 9.3   An Art Deco structure in front of Maputo's main railway station.

- *Planned industrial/warehousing zone*: Baixa's warehouse zone to the west of the old historic core of the area contains an unrivalled collection of largely low rise industrial buildings of great character (Figures 9.4 (a) and (b)). Essentially contemporaneous with the individual Art Deco-inspired structures, this was a carefully planned development. It is hard to identify any similar survival of a zone of Art Deco- and Modernist-inspired yet modest 'everyday' industrial/warehousing buildings with the completeness and integrity found in Baixa elsewhere in Africa, or, indeed, Europe. That makes the continued survival and use of these structures important for Mozambique, even though the character value of many of the units is essentially as a group, rather than as individual set piece/landmark architectural works.
- *Modernist tall buildings*: Among its many high buildings, Baixa has a good collection of important tall Modernist architecture dating from the 1930s to the late 1960s. A number of more widely influential and highly talented architects were resident in Maputo during this period or were commissioned, mainly from Portugal, to design commercial or residential tall buildings within Baixa. Most renowned and celebrated among these was Pancho Guedes (Figure 9.5). These tall buildings represent another key aspect of the character of Baixa's historic urban landscape. As with its individual Art Deco-inspired architecture, this collection offers considerable potential for important research, for the identity of many contributing architects is currently unknown.
- *Local neighbourhood character groups*: Local neighbourhood character groups by their very nature are made up of buildings of little individual architectural or historical merit, but which together make an underlying contribution to the distinctiveness and interest of the immediate area. Baixa's collection of these contains small groupings of buildings of similar age and style, other groupings of characterful buildings of different age and style but similar height and mass, and some unified composite streetscape components made up of two or more buildings essentially of repeated design, form or style.

(a)

(b)

Figure 9.4 (a), (b)   Buildings within Baixa's planned industrial zone.

- *Memorials and statues*: Memorials and statues commemorate significant national or local events and people, serving as an everyday reminder to people of their inheritance from the past. Mainly, but not entirely, associated with important public spaces in Baixa, such key commemorative artwork can be overlooked. However, focus group sessions with members of the local residential and business communities during the master plan study revealed that they place strong historical and associational value on this heritage collection.
- *Key views*: Set-piece and more informal snatched views between important public spaces and landmarks and across open spaces were found to be vital to the community for orientation, linkage and movement, and cultural memory.

Figure 9.5 Buildings by architect Pancho Guedes near to the main railway station.

They also provide an understanding of aspects of Baixa's historical development and the underlying original coastal escarpment and topography.

The detailed characterisation and assessment of the area's significance formed a key continuous thread underlying the urbanisation plan's proposals for the future of the area and supported by an economic valuation of Baixa's heritage and its potential, which adopted a Total Economic Valuation methodology similar to that used in environmental economics. This methodology calculates the value society gains from a heritage asset (or, within the wider environment, a natural resource or ecosystem), as compared to not having it. It takes into account both use value and non-use value, including existence value (the benefit of knowing that a heritage asset simply exists), bequest value (the benefit attained from ensuring that a heritage asset will be preserved for future generations), and option value (the willingness of individuals and communities to pay to preserve a heritage asset for the future, even if the likelihood of its future use is low).

Case Study 3: The Site of the Former Taunton Gaol, Taunton, Somerset, England

Taunton is the county town (that is, the principal administrative centre) of Somerset in the south-west of England. In 2013, in advance of planned relocation of its main police station, the police authority and the local authorities (who had differing responsibilities for, and interests in, the site) jointly sought advice on its cultural significance and the effect that this might hold for its redevelopment potential.

Set on a main road in the suburbs to the south-west of the town centre, the site occupies a position that once would have been recognised as being immediately

Figure 9.6   The 1942 police station frontage building on the site of the former Taunton Gaol.

extramural to the line of Taunton's medieval town walls, although these have long since disappeared at this point in their circuit. Almost inevitably in these circumstances, therefore, the police station site had already been in use for many years – perhaps from the late medieval period (say, from 1450) – for housing, gardens and orchards, when it came to be partially redeveloped as the site of Taunton's prison in the mid-eighteenth century.

The asset has two very different personas. Most local people would characterise the site by its dominant early-1940s institutional frontage building, positioned on a marked curve in a main road running around the town centre (Figure 9.6). Although this is not designated as a heritage asset, it is a focal point and landmark building of some note in the local urban landscape. However, the site is deep and, largely hidden from view behind this frontage building, stands a robust three-storied, once 'X'-shaped nineteenth-century prison, which, along with an adjacent former prison hospital, is designated as a Grade II listed building. These designated buildings dominate a scattering of smaller, individually undesignated, structures and large open-air car parks that are concealed by the frontage police station.

The key issue that needed to be addressed by the assessment of significance for this multi-faceted asset was the relative importance of the different phases and built elements of the site and the potential for archaeology – whether below ground or within the standing structures – to affect its redevelopment. Given the nature of the secured institutional use of the site for more than 250 years, it was evident from the outset that much information, including floor plans of the current police station, would be restricted in terms of access and essentially unavailable for use in the assessment process. Research for the assessment of significance was limited to a single cursory and accompanied visit to the secure buildings and such records as were freely available in the public domain – primarily, a good series of historical maps and plans, conveyances of land resulting from several phases of expansion of the gaol, nineteenth-century census information, articles in nineteenth-century local newspapers (although use of this source was made unusually difficult by the subject matter, since online search engine queries using terms such as 'Taunton prison' or 'Taunton gaol' produced multiple thousands of hits from every article ever printed on local court cases), and two reports from the time of the construction of the main prison building in the transactions of a learned scientific society. Historical photographic and other imagery proved abnormally limited. Clearly, restrictions on physical access and inspection and on the availability of research data were of concern in achieving an objective assessment of significance and this issue needed to be considered in the final report. In such circumstances, it is always possible that key material, which might influence the assessment of significance, is unavailable or otherwise missing. Nonetheless, despite these limitations, in this case, it was concluded that the available sources of information were sufficient in coverage and definitive enough in content to be able to place some considerable reliance on the findings of the assessment.

In summary, the final statement of significance was able to determine in some reasonable detail the history of development of the composite asset from the construction of the first 'House of Correction' or bridewell, as it was colloquially known, on the site in 1754, through to the demolition of one wing of the later 'X'-shaped gaol at its core in 1974 and consequent designation of the remaining parts of the same building in 1975. The available series of historical maps and plans and contemporary local newspaper articles on alterations made to the prison at various times in the nineteenth century were key to developing this understanding. The assessment demonstrated in particular that the significance of the site as a heritage asset was not primarily focused on the two individual previously-designated mid-nineteenth-century gaol buildings that lie at its centre, but (irrespective of the absence of official recognition and designation), that the surviving elements of the old Taunton Gaol taken together comprise an equally, if not more, important composite heritage asset. The assessment revealed that the extant above-ground remains are surprisingly – indeed, unusually – extensive, given that the gaol function ceased 125 years ago. These remains include the survival of significant parts of the first 1754 gaol, including its Governor's residence, wrapped within the 1942 frontage police station building, long full-height lengths of the secure perimeter and internal separating walls of the nineteenth-century prison, and degraded fragments of two correctional structures (that is, buildings used for specific punishments). Although substantial harm was caused to the main gaol building in its conversion before the First World War into a Drill Hall (that is, a large space for the training of soldiers in marching) and later when one of its wings was demolished and other ancillary prison buildings around the site were cleared away, the continued secure institutional use of the entire site after its closure as a civil prison in 1884 has protected many elements that would otherwise have been particularly vulnerable to rapid loss. No doubt, the listing of two principal buildings in 1975 was an advantage in this respect, too. The statement of significance concluded that the extensive survival of disparate elements of the working eighteenth- and nineteenth-century gaol should be regarded as being of regional interest as a minimum, making it, as an assemblage, a non-designated heritage asset of medium significance. As the statement observed, in England, there has been a tendency not to designate ensembles of this sort, unless they have a cohesion and integrity that very few former historic gaol complexes are likely to achieve. That general lack of survival of integrity across this vulnerable asset type makes an objective assessment of the comparative significance of individual gaols all the more important; paradoxically, the secure and hence secretive nature of the asset type makes this all the more difficult to achieve.

Further issues of significance identified in the assessment process included the pivotal role and positive contribution of the 1942 frontage building as a focal point in the streetscape and in local views in each direction, and the archaeological potential of the site. In regard to the former, it is worth reflecting that the importance of the frontage building as a focal point and landmark is an element of value that could be vulnerable to being overlooked, due to the generally low regard held by the public for 1940s architecture. The statement of significance concluded that the site has high archaeological potential. The Historic Environment Record maintained by the upper tier local authority (Somerset County Council) shows that medieval remains relating to the town's defences and the extramural suburb have been found in the locality in the past. The site must have considerable potential to yield evidence about the prison and prison life in the eighteenth and nineteenth centuries, through finds of artefacts and below ground remains of buildings, and the interments of executed prisoners and possibly those of suicides. Moreover, the nineteenth-century scientific reports mentioned previously recorded discoveries of unusual palaeo-botanical and palaeontological interest in the excavated remains of a major buried forest of oak and other trees up to 60 feet (18.25 metres) long and the skull and bones of a woolly rhinoceros during construction of the wings of the main gaol building in 1843 and 1853. These deposits were reported as lying at a depth of 18 feet (5.5 metres) below ground level beneath the building and perhaps across some or all the wider site.

None of these conclusions means that the composite asset is incapable of redevelopment for a different or mixed use. Its survival is absolutely dependent upon that being possible. However, the assessment of significance sets a framework for that redevelopment, identifying critical constraints based on the relative significance of the asset's component elements and areas and its archaeological potential.

Case Study 4: Maintaining the Commonwealth War Graves

This second edition of this book has been written at the time of commemoration of the centenary of the start of the First World War (1914–1918). As a final case study, then, it is interesting and timely to consider how, 100 years on, the maintenance management of war cemeteries (specifically, those cared for by the Commonwealth War Graves Commission) has been influenced by their significance: the collation of the range of cultural values that they represent to society. The Commonwealth is one of the world's oldest political associations of states, with its roots running back to the former British Empire. The Commonwealth War Graves Commission was established in 1917 during the First World War, initially as the Imperial War Graves Commission. Its foundation was overwhelmingly the work and inspiration of one man, Sir Fabian Ware. The Commission's website (www.cwgc.org/about-us/history-of-cwgc.aspx) explains Ware's vision and the Commission's role thus:

> *Neither a soldier nor a politician, Ware was nevertheless well placed to respond to the public's reaction to the enormous losses in the war. At 45 he was too old to fight but he became the commander of a mobile unit of the British Red Cross. Saddened by the sheer number of casualties, he felt driven to find a way to ensure the final resting places of the dead would not be lost forever. His vision chimed with the times. Under his dynamic leadership, his unit began recording and caring for all the graves they could find. By 1915, their work was given official recognition by the War Office and incorporated into the British Army as the Graves Registration ...*
>
> *Ware was keen that the spirit of Imperial cooperation evident in the war was reflected in the work of his organisation ... The Commission's work began in earnest after the Armistice. Once land for cemeteries and memorials had been guaranteed, the enormous task of recording the details of the dead began. By 1918, some 587,000 graves had been identified and a further 559,000 casualties were registered as having no known grave.*

In 1914, H. G. Wells, the author and pacifist, put together a collection of his essays in a short book entitled, *The War That Will End War*, part observing, part prophesying:

> *This is already the vastest war in history. It is a war not of nations, but of mankind. It is a war to exorcise a world-madness and end an age ... For this is now a war for peace ... This, the greatest of all wars, is not just another war – it is the last war!*

The notion of the 'war to end war' was seized upon avidly by politicians, philosophers and ordinary people, becoming a constant theme – in every respect, a 'war cry'. As Joanna Scutts observes in her study, 'Battlefield cemeteries, pilgrimage and literature after the First World War' (Scutts, 2009):

> *From early in the war it was widely recognized that existing commemorative modes were not sufficient for this new kind of war; combatants and*

civilians alike reflected on its exceptionality and questioned how, where, when, and by whom it would be remembered.

The 'war to end war' trope was – and still continues to be – associated with the US President, Woodrow Wilson, although seemingly he only used it in a speech once. Reflecting changing mood and circumstances, the British Prime Minister, Lloyd George, played repeatedly with variations on the theme, saying, for example, in February 1917: 'There are rare epochs in the history of the world when in a few raging years the character, the destiny, of the whole race is determined for unknown ages. This is one', reputedly remarking before the end of the war in 1918: 'This war, like the next war, is a war to end war', and then on Armistice Day itself, in addressing Parliament: 'At eleven o'clock this morning came to an end the cruellest and most terrible War that has ever scourged mankind. I hope we may say that thus, this fateful morning, came to an end all wars.'

There seems little doubt that the famous opening lines of Rupert Brooke's 1914 poem, 'The Soldier':

If I should die, think only this of me:
That there's some corner of a foreign field
That is for ever England …

had an important, if in part subliminal, influence on the creation of Commonwealth War Cemeteries, especially those in France and Belgium. Scutts notes that its 'simple, stirring language … lodged deeply in the national psyche', catapulting it to cultural prominence immediately it was published, and she continues:

The poem's opening lines were precisely realized in the planning of the cemeteries [after the war had ended]: a fact widely noted in the press. British cemeteries in France and Belgium were created and walled off at the edges and 'corners' of former agricultural land – 'foreign fields' – and no matter how small these areas were, the foreign governments agreed to lease the land in perpetuity – were 'for ever [England]'.

In the months before the end of 'the Great War', and after a year's work and deliberation, the Director of the British Museum, Sir Frederic Kenyon, responded to his commission from the Imperial War Graves Commission with his report, *War Graves: How the Cemeteries Abroad Will Be Designed* (Kenyon, 1919). In it, he explained the Commission's rationale for the layout of these Commonwealth War Cemeteries:

Equality of Treatment

The Commission has already laid down one principle, which goes far towards determining the disposition of the cemeteries; the principle, namely, of equality of treatment; but since this report may be read by some who are not acquainted with the reasons which led the Commissioners to this conclusion, it may be as well to say a few words about it. As soon as the question was faced, it was felt that the provision of monuments could not be left to individual initiative. In a few cases, where money and good taste were not wanting, a satisfactory result would be obtained, in the sense that a fine individual monument would be erected. In the large majority of cases either no monument would be erected, or it would be poor in quality; and the total result would be one of inequality, haphazard and disorder. The cemetery would become a collection of individual memorials, a few good, but many bad, and with a total want of congruity and uniformity. The monuments of the more well-to-do would overshadow those of their poorer comrades; the whole sense of comradeship and of common service would be lost. The Commission, on the other hand, felt that where the sacrifice had been common, the memorial should be common also; and they desired that the cemeteries should be the symbol of a great Army and a united Empire.

It was therefore ordained that what was done for one should be done for all, and that all, whatever their military rank or position in civil life, should have equal treatment in their graves.

It is necessary to face the fact that this decision has given pain in some quarters, and pain which the Commissioners would have been glad to avoid. Not a few relatives have been looking forward to placing a memorial of their own choosing over the graves which mean so much to them; some have devoted much time and thought to making such a memorial beautiful and significant. Yet it is hoped that even these will realize that they are asked to join in an action of even higher significance. The sacrifice of the individual is a great idea and worthy of commemoration; but the community of sacrifice, the service of a common cause, the comradeship of arms which has brought together men of all ranks and grades—these are greater ideas, which should be commemorated in those cemeteries where they lie together, the representatives of their country in the lands in which they served. The place for the individual memorial is at home, where it will be constantly before the eyes of relatives and descendants, and will serve as an example and encouragement for the generations to come. A monument in France (and still more if further afield) can be seen but seldom; a monument in the parish church or churchyard is seen day by day and week by week, from generation to generation.

If any further argument is needed, I would say that the contrast now presented between the military and communal cemeteries, where they adjoin one another, provides it. The communal cemeteries are a jumbled mass of individual monuments of all sorts and sizes and of all variety of quality, packed much more closely than the monuments in an English churchyard; and the result is neither dignified nor inspiring. Side by side with these, the military cemeteries, whether French or English, with their orderly rows of crosses (the French ones bearing, in addition, a tricolour cocarde), have both dignity and inspiration. It is this impression which it is sought to perpetuate in the treatment now proposed for permanent adoption.

Here then was a formal espousal of the founding values of equality, permanence, dignity and inspiration that were felt to be of overriding importance (with equality in the vanguard) and which dictated so much of the carefully designed character of each one of many thousands of Commonwealth war cemeteries and in excess of one hundred memorials to the dead and missing of the First and Second World Wars.

Rudyard Kipling, who was employed as the literary advisor to the Imperial War Graves Commission from 1917 until his death in 1936, wrote in his pamphlet, *The Graves of the Fallen* (Kipling, 1919):

In a war where the full strength of nations was used without respect of persons, no difference could be made between the graves of officers or men. Yet some sort of central idea was needed that should symbolize our common sacrifice wherever our dead might be laid and it was realized, above all, that each cemetery and individual grave should be made as permanent as man's art could devise.

It is generally held that it was Kipling who was responsible for drafting King George V's speech, delivered when visiting war graves in France and Belgium in May 1922:

For the past few days I have been on a solemn pilgrimage in honour of a people who died for all free men …

Never before in history have a people thus dedicated and maintained individual memorials to their fallen, and in the course of my pilgrimage, I have many times asked myself whether there can be more potent advocates of peace upon earth through the years to come than this massed multitude of silent witnesses to the desolation of war. And I feel that we cannot but believe that the existence of these visible memorials will eventually serve to draw all peoples together in sanity and self-control, even as it has already set the relations between our Empire and our Allies on the deep-rooted bases of a common heroism and a common agony.

Standing beneath this Cross of Sacrifice, facing the great Stone of Remembrance and compassed by these sternly simple headstones, we remember, and must charge our children to remember, that as our dead were equal in sacrifice, so they are equal in honour, for the greatest and the least of them have proved that sacrifice and honour are no vain things, but truths by which the world lives.

These quotations all speak of the underlying founding objectives and values that were involved: equality, permanence, commemoration, education, valour and sacrifice, truth, and peace.

The solution that was found to the problem that previous modes of commemoration were not sufficient for the new kind of war was not without its
contradictions. Remembrance was focused on the importance of the individual:
'meticulously naming and recording every lost life', as Scutts has observed. Yet,
in highlighting notions of equality and commonality in service and death through
insistence on permanent uniformity, the importance of the individual was in one
sense subordinated (or sacrificed, to use Kenyon's term) to a greater good. An
article by journalist, John Lichfield, in *The Independent* newspaper in November
2013 reflected on a related contradiction:

> *The contrast between the blind slaughter which killed 10 million soldiers
> on all sides and the democratic respect for the humblest dead private is
> one of the great paradoxes of this most baffling of wars. Soldiers could
> be destroyed en masse, torn apart or liquidised by the new arsenal of
> high explosives, machine guns, poison gas, tanks, flame-throwers and war
> planes. But they were to be honoured individuals in death.*

The choices made by the Imperial War Graves Commission were, in consequence, the subject of extensive heated debate and, to many, deeply controversial.
That notwithstanding, they have proven to be enduring, creating ageless places
of remembrance with a powerful ability to evoke reflection and values. Scutts
emphasises that the Commission:

> *ensured the cemeteries' legibility as symbolic spaces both in themselves
> and as part of an international network of remembrance. By its contro-
> versial decisions to limit the scope for personal messages and to ban any
> individual monuments, the Commission imposed a coherent memorial
> narrative across the wide diversity of sites where the graves were located.
> Accordingly, despite local differences in horticulture and scale that lent
> the cemeteries a degree of individual character, the headstones and mon-
> uments were identical whether the cemetery was in Belgium or Bagh-
> dad. The uniformity of the cemeteries was meant to be thrown into relief
> by the diversity of the surrounding landscapes ... Each commemorative
> space was meant to recall the others, conjuring in the visitor's imagina-
> tion a web of remembrance connecting all the parts of the world that had
> been engulfed in the fighting. Furthermore, the sites would last forever:
> each headstone was a rectangular slab with a curved top, carved from
> British Portland stone, its shape and material being chosen to ensure the
> endurance of the cemetery for at least a thousand years. Permanence and
> uniformity were the two most important principles guiding the creation
> of the battlefield cemeteries: the effect of timelessness that is still striking
> today is not just a tribute to the labor and money devoted to their main-
> tenance by the Commission, but was a deliberate feature of their design.
> For the most part the stone appears as bright and stark now as it must
> have in the early 1920s.*

(a)

(b)

Figure 9.7 (a)–(c)   The inspirational Memorial and Commonwealth War Grave Cemetery at Cassino between Naples and Rome in Italy, designed by architect, Louis de Soissons, who was also the master planner of Welwyn Garden City.

(c)

Figure 9.7 *(Continued)*

The uniformity of these war cemeteries extended to uniformity for the cemeteries of both World Wars, which included the consistent use of common commemorative elements, such as the Cross of Sacrifice to Sir Reginald Blomfield's design and bearing Kipling's phrase 'Lest We Forget' and Sir Edwin Lutyens' iconic Stone of Remembrance, with its stepped stone base and Book of Ecclesiastes' inscription 'Their Name Liveth for Evermore' (Figures 9.7 (a) and (c)). Even in the inscriptions to these constant companions, there was inherent contradiction: 'Lest We Forget' placed in counterpoint to 'Their Name Liveth for Evermore'. Scutts refers to them as 'two poles of warning and reassurance', challenging cemetery visitors by their mutual ambivalence, inviting reconciliation.

So much about the war cemeteries seems to be pervaded by a sense of ambivalence. According to Kenyon's 1918 description of 'the general appearance of a British cemetery', the Stone of Remembrance was expressly intended as a great altar stone. So it is a tribute to Lutyens' deliberate ambiguity that it can be described by Scutts and other modern commentators as having 'no obvious religious or symbolic associations' or, as Julie Summers observes in her *British and Commonwealth War Cemeteries* (Summers, 2010), 'in its abstract form ... for those who wish it, the stone can be interpreted as an altar. For those who eschew specific religious associations, it stands simply as an object of remembrance.' Values are so often 'in the eye of the beholder' – viewers interpret according to their experience and personal belief systems.

Figure 9.8   The recently rebuilt entrance feature to the First World War Military Cemetery at Hebuterne in France's Pas de Calais.

Mirroring Scutts' final sentences quoted above, Lichfield's article in *The Independent* concludes:

> *the constant replacement of time-worn stones give [the Commonwealth War Cemeteries] a poignant, unsettling freshness absent from the German and French cemeteries. Something about the cemetery design compels the visitor to think of the dead, not as [Siegfried] Sassoon's "intolerably nameless names", but as husbands, friends, lovers, fathers, sons and brothers. Thus have the controversial choices made in 1919 been vindicated by time.*

But, of course, the constant replacement of time-worn stone is a matter of ongoing maintenance management: implementation of a policy shaped by end-of-Great War principles and significance. The Commission currently works to concurrent and coincident eight-year cycles of condition surveys and repair, reinstatement or renewal of defective fabric that such inspections reveal on memorials, commemorative features, cemetery walls and the like (Figure 9.8). The headstones and stone memorial panels inscribed with the names of the missing dead are maintained separately from this process, in principle being renewed as soon as any deficiency or degradation becomes apparent. As a result, these war cemeteries are unwaveringly maintained to a very high standard, well-nigh pristine and new – poignant and unsettling in their freshness, almost as though the war ended, if not yesterday, then no more than a handful of years ago. There is an argument that this, too, can and should be read as part of the cemeteries' essential ambivalence – say, 'They died long ago, but should we forget, this could still be our tomorrow.'

Without doubt, this, in ways, extreme, approach to maintenance management achieves the intended goal of retaining uniformity, while also subtly communicating that the dead have not been forgotten and that their individual names are still honoured and will live on in our memories. However, there are costs to such a policy: other heritage values may be harmed by iterative and all-pervasive renewal of the built fabric of the cemeteries, which, among other things, eradicates any sign of the patina of age that elsewhere is so often regarded as an important physical attribute of value. Moreover, from our current perspective, it also might be seen as representing an unsustainable management practice, that is wasteful of both natural and human resources.

There is an inherent assumption built into this – namely, that the war cemeteries are indeed heritage assets. By any reasonable definition, that must be the case. Patently, from all that has been said so far, they hold a meaning and value to society that transcend their function as simple places of burial. In truth, as assets, they are incredibly rich in cultural heritage values, although mapping those values comprehensively today is highly problematic, since they elicit such intense, diverse, even conflicting emotions within the visitor, and yet each visitor's experience is personal, being filtered, as has been observed already, through their own life-experiences and personal belief systems. This is one of those occasions where it is easier to plot the founding values of a century ago than it is to comprehend how those values or their relative potency have changed over time. The founding values of equality, permanence, remembrance, dignity and inspiration have already been explored. In the Prologue to his 2013 book, *Empires of the Dead*, biographer David Crane, talks of 1918 proposals being imbued with the values of the nation's 'long cultural traditions … its Christian roots, and … a human piety that is older even than those'. There were other underlying drivers that he suggests are less clear: 'Grief? Pride? Gratitude? Guilt? Atonement? Reparation? Political acumen? … Catharsis or [Horace's] "old lie" – "Dulce et Decorum est [pro patria mori]?".'

There can be no doubt that the way we value the war cemeteries has been modified over time by changing context and cultural perceptions. Although not directly writing about changing values (for her interest is cultural memory and literature, not significance), Scutts notes:

> In [the original] planning documents the cemeteries are talked of as enduring for a thousand years and were thus always understood as eventually changing their primary purpose from spaces for the grieving and recovery into sites that had to communicate with those who were not personally affected by the [wars], who would come as readers rather than mourners.

That is true. As visitors, we now read the immaculate 'as new' cemeteries, set in healed landscapes where the signs of war are no longer evident, and without the perspective of the bereaved or involved seeking resolution and comfort

(Scutts refers to the intersection of 'the healing of the landscape and the healing of individuals').

Until now, the Commission's approach to maintenance has remained constant, but, at the time of writing it is under review. Is perpetual renewal of fabric the only way to protect and project both founding and present-day values? Is this a case where a relative prioritisation of physical attributes of value might have a part to play, for instance, preserving the 'as new' standard for grave markers, memorial panels and perhaps elements of remembrance such as the Cross of Sacrifice and Stone of Remembrance in each cemetery, but allowing conservation principles to dictate the maintenance of shelter buildings, cemetery walls and so forth, so that the patina of age is also present? After all, a conservation-based approach to maintenance is not about allowing neglect, it is about appropriate care. There is an argument that the 'meaning' of the war cemeteries will be better read by today's visitors, if their age is also evident – should a 1918 or 1945 cemetery not reflect something of its time? The counterpoint between that evidence of age and the continued equality, uniformity and permanence of the headstones and principal elements of remembrance would in itself create a valuable ambiguity.

References

Crane, D. (2013) *Empires of the Dead*. London, HarperCollins.

Kenyon, Sir F. (1919) *War Graves: How the Cemeteries Abroad Will Be Designed*. London, HMSO.

Kipling, R. (1919) *The Graves of the Fallen*. London, HMSO.

Lichfield, J. (2013) The birth of the War Graves Commission – and the furious controversy it sparked. *The Independent*, 10 November.

Scutts, J. (2009) Battlefield cemeteries, pilgrimage and literature after The First World War: the burial of the dead. In *English Literature in Transition, 1880–1920* 52(4): 387–416.

Summers, J. (2010) *British and Commonwealth War Cemeteries*. Oxford, Shire Publications Ltd.

The Commonwealth War Graves Commission 'History of CWGC'. Available at: www.cwgc.org/about-us/history-of-cwgc.aspx

Wells, H. G. (1914) *The War That Will End War*. London, Frank and Cecil Palmer.

Index

aesthetic value   12, 20, 32, 58, 64, 65, 66, 67, 80, 102, 106, 114, 136, 219
age value   63, 108, 114, 231
amenity value   219
archaeological sites and monuments   9
archaeological value   9, 68
archaeology   8, 9, 11, 68, 73, 100, 135, 140, 153, 254
architectural value   67, 80, 108
archival evidence   *see* documentary evidence
artistic value   63, 70
asset types   6, 38, 45, 250
associational value   12, 66, 68, 71, 72, 73, 77, 80, 249, 252
authentic/authenticity   30, 52, 58, 59, 64, 86, 87, 106, 116, 188, 230, 231, 234

buffer zones   44
buried archaeology   6, 9, 11, 140
Burra Charter   2, 12, 49, 57, 61, 62, 65, 66, 68, 71, 88, 111, 114, 126, 127, 128, 188, 189, 223, 231, 233, 236, 237

care guidance   28, 156, 160
character   12, 24, 31, 100, 159, 180, 258, 261
    analysis of   100–104
characterisation   122, 156–160, 250, 253

Charter on the Built Vernacular Heritage   60
Charter for the Conservation of Places of Cultural Heritage Value   56
collective memory   51, 70
commemorative value   11, 12, 20, 64, 71, 72, 77, 80, 240, 252, 257, 261, 263, 264
communal value   66, 70   *see also* community values; social value
community values   65, 70, 104, 105, 106, 107, 111, 114, 127, 148   *see also* communal value; social value
    assessment of   104–107
comparative significance   109, 129, 167, 256   *see also* significance; relative significance
condition surveys   134, 140, 154, 192, 194, 197–214, 225, 264
conservation area appraisal   121, 122, 151–156, 157, 158, 243   *see also* historic area appraisal
conservation areas (historic areas)   24, 27, 28, 29, 31, 35, 37, 38, 40, 41, 44, 58, 59, 102, 121, 122, 149–157, 160, 173, 174, 179, 180, 181, 182, 183, 220, 236, 243, 248
conservation/management policies   5, 12, 45, 129, 130, 131, 138–143, 147, 148, 151, 156, 178, 179, 182, 203

Managing Built Heritage: The Role of Cultural Values and Significance, Second Edition.
Stephen Bond and Derek Worthing.
© 2016 Stephen Bond and Derek Worthing. Published 2016 by John Wiley & Sons, Ltd.